FRANCE

W9-BBE-662

MEDITERRANEAN

Philippeville
Bougie
Bizerte
Bône
Algiers
Tunis
aganem
Tell
Djurdjure
Kabylia
Sousse
an
Ouarsenis
Bibans
Constantine
dja
Aures
Sahel
Atlas
Sfax
Chott Djerid
Gabès
Saharan
Ain Sefra
Touggourt
Tripoli
Hassi Rmel
Ouargla
b-Béchar
Hassi Messaoud
LIBYA
GERIA
Edjelé
Trans-Sahara roads
NIGER

The United States and North Africa

MOROCCO, ALGERIA, AND TUNISIA

THE AMERICAN FOREIGN POLICY LIBRARY

CRANE BRINTON, EDITOR

THE
UNITED STATES
AND
North Africa

MOROCCO, ALGERIA, AND TUNISIA

Charles F. Gallagher

HARVARD UNIVERSITY PRESS
Cambridge, Massachusetts

TO WILTON AND VIRGINIA DILLON

Introduction

With this book the Harvard Foreign Policy Library makes its first venture into a continent of increasing importance to the United States and to world politics. It is true that Egypt figures largely in Ephraim Speiser's *United States and the Near East* (1947), now out of print. That country, however, is in little more than a formal geographic sense a part of Africa; in *human* geography Egypt is rather a part of what used to be called by Europeans and Americans, not without patronizing overtones, the Levant. The three countries of the Maghrib, Tunisia, Algeria, and Morocco, with which Mr. Gallagher is concerned in this book, though Muslim in faith since the Arab conquest of the late seventh century, and though in many ways thoroughly Arabized by that conquest, have never fully been, even when under Turkish suzerainty, a part of the old Levant. They are now in their new independence increasingly aware of their geographic identification with Africa, and in the United Nations often vote with other African nations. Yet historically they are essentially Western Mediterranean lands, long under Roman, and until yesterday under French, imperial control.

Mr. Gallagher in this excellent book quite rightly takes up much more space than is usual in a book in the Harvard Foreign Policy Library to explain the course of the complex prehistory and history of North Africa. It is a land often invaded, yet never wholly transformed. Mr. Gallagher has lived in the Maghrib and knows well both the land and the peoples. The history he so accurately presents is not so much political history as economic and social history, the kind that can make understandable to us a people very different indeed from most of those with whom we have had to deal in the past.

However, he does not neglect the immediate past and the present. He has been able to take into account the first troubled—indeed that term is too weak—the first catastrophic year of Algerian independence. In striking contrast to the virtuous superiority of most American newspaper writers toward the role of France in North Africa in the last decade, Mr. Gallagher holds the balance very fairly between the French and their Muslim subjects. He by no means glosses over the inhumanity with which many colons and some of the French military treated the Algerians during the long war for independence; and he makes plain the separateness, almost the *apartheid,* of the European and the Muslim communities under French rule. But he also shows clearly how much the French occupation has meant in all three countries, how far it has put them all onto the road of modernity. He does not minimize the grave difficulties now facing the independent lands of North Africa, but this is not a complaining, not a bitter, book, and it closes on a note of soberly eloquent optimism and sympathy. Americans, who in spite of what happened on the shores of Tripoli in our infancy as a nation, and in spite of our invasion of North Africa in the last war, have really had very little concern with the Maghribi lands. We are bound to have much more concern in the future. Mr. Gallagher's book will help us to make that concern more effective.

CRANE BRINTON

PREFACE

Late in 1959 the editors of the American Foreign Policy Library, Professors Crane Brinton and Lincoln Gordon, suggested that I undertake the task of adding North Africa to the long and distinguished list of volumes that have already appeared in this series. I accepted with a hesitancy stemming from my realization of the many gaps in my knowledge of the area, and with the reservation that the book not be completed until the Algerian revolution then in full swing had ended, and all three countries of the Maghrib were independent.

This came to pass in the summer of 1962, and now that the passions of revolt and some of the pains of decolonization have subsided for all concerned, we are able to look at North Africa in a more subdued and reflective frame of mind and begin studying it as a whole almost for the first time. The new North Africa has been born out of the old—the emphasis on the historical background in this book makes clear my convictions on that score—but it is also strikingly new in many respects, and serious American study of this Western wing of the Arab World has likewise only started in the past few years. One of my main hopes is that this volume will draw an accurate picture of the society of these countries and their relationships to the rest of the world at a moment in history which I think most suitable for pausing to survey the North African scene. My other principal hope is that this work will help further the progress of North African studies which are springing up at several American institutions, and will stimulate greater interest in the area among those interested in foreign affairs and the public at large.

This book is the result of more than ten years' residence and study in North Africa. During most of that period I have been associated with the American Universities Field Staff, and it is to this organization, in particular to its director, Teg C. Grondahl, and its former director, Phillips Talbot, that above all I owe thanks for the chance to work as freely and uninterruptedly as I have. Part of the period, almost a decade ago, was spent in field research under grants from the Ford Foundation, to whom I am also grateful. It is impossible to list all those scholars, journalists, and government officials—not to mention the thousands of ordinary citizens—in the countries concerned to whom I have become indebted over this span of time.

Tangier, Morocco   Charles F. Gallagher
May 1, 1963

A NOTE ON TRANSCRIPTION

The transcription of Arabic, or almost any Oriental language, into the Latin alphabet raises numerous problems and is often the cause of scholarly polemics. In a work of this kind designed for a broad public, where the complex diacritical marks often used to transliterate Arabic had to be dispensed with, the guideline used was that of the convenience of the reader, intelligibility, and as great an internal consistency as possible.

Because North Africa was for so long under French control and influence, special conditions existed which were not applicable to other parts of the Arab world and which affect the transcription of many names. French was the official language of Algeria until last year and is still overwhelmingly the working tongue; geographical conventions regulated the spelling of place names; and the bulk of all literature in Western languages has been in French. This has meant giving preference to French spellings of ordinary place names with two exceptions: those that have a recognized English form (such as Fez, Marrakesh, Algiers, etc.), and those in the former Spanish parts of Morocco where the Spanish orthography is retained (Tetuán, rather than French Tétouan or Arabic Tsittawin). The names of living or modern individuals are transcribed wherever possible as they have indicated them (and some North Africans are quite insistent on this point); otherwise as they commonly appear in the press and current publications. It is because of this that we find Mohammed Dib, whereas the traditionally correct form of Muhammad has been kept for the Prophet, and Muslim pre-

ferred to Moslem. Historical terms are transliterated in a modified form which suppresses the final consonant of the *ta
marbuta*, uses the diphthongs *ai* and *ei* in place of *ay* or *ey*
(except as finals), keeps the *q*, where Arabic uses it, instead of
k, retains *'ain* as a consonant marked with the ' but eliminates
the *hamza*. The plurals of Arabic words, as well as a few
Turkish ones, are indicated by a hyphenated -s added to the
singular, for few readers could be expected to know that
shurafa (or *shorfa* in the Maghribi dialect) is the plural of
sharif. The only exception to this is the use of the plural form
'ulama, inasmuch as this term is now widely found in political
literature in Western languages. In a few cases where accepted
English forms exist they have been used, for example, Koran
and Koranic, in place of what must seem to many the un-
pronounceable Quran and Quranic. The worst feature of this
transcription is that it was the haphazard choice of the author,
although it seeks to be consistent; its best quality, I hope, is
that it tries not to mislead or confuse the reader unnecessarily.

C. F. G.

CONTENTS

The United States and North Africa

MOROCCO, ALGERIA, AND TUNISIA

I. The Land and the People

THE LAND

To the north of the Sahara Desert and west of the Gulf of Sirte on the Mediterranean an irregularly shaped quadrilateral rises from the African continent. This lofty, isolated region, studded with mountain chains and high plateaus, forms a compact geographical entity. Shut off on three sides by the seas and an unwelcoming coastline, and on the fourth by a formidable barrier of mountain and barren desert, it is an island on the land. Its history, as far back as it is known, has been marked by great cultural unity and a high degree of ethnic homogeneity. Today as well, although it is divided into the independent countries of Morocco, Algeria, and Tunisia, with a geographical appendage in the coastal strip of Tripolitania in Western Libya, the similarities of the whole eclipse the divergences of its parts.

It is a land without a true name. It seems never to have given itself one and from the time it is first noted in foreign chronicles its nomenclature is that bestowed by the outsiders who came to its shores. By them it has been called a variety of names, none of which describes it in a fully satisfactory way. To the ancient Greeks all the regions north of the Sahara inhabited by white Africans were Libya, as opposed to Ethiopia, the land of the blacks. The Romans in their turn bequeathed us several names. They took from a Punic root the term "Afri" and applied it from the time of their wars with Carthage to their adversaries and their mercenaries. Later on, "Africa" became the region around Carthage, substantially northern and central Tunisia, and finally was extended to the whole continent. Another term perpetuated by Rome, which was general at first and subsequently localized, as was the case with Libya, is Mauritania. The land of the Mauri, or "Moors," was the term originally applied to roughly the western half of North Africa, all that part of Algeria west of Algiers and most of Morocco. Today it is the name given to a country south of Morocco which marks a transition, in human and geographical terms, from white to black Africa.

In the seventh century the invading Arabs arrived from the East and with the sharp eye of nomadic observers saw the area for what it was, an island. Appropriately they named it "Jazirat al Maghrib," the Island of the West, just as they had always called their own peninsula the "Jazirat al 'Arab," the Arab Island. So today in Arabic the word "Maghrib" is used in a generic sense to denote the three countries of Morocco, Algeria, and Tunisia, but from a modern, political standpoint—and particularly in terms of self-identification—it now rarely refers to Libya, even though a segment of that country shares partially in the common geographical and historical heritage of the others. The term is useful but confusing because it applies also specifically to the Kingdom of Morocco (Al Mamlakat al Maghribiya), and partly for this reason it is customary in spoken Arabic in the Middle East to refer to the region as the "Maghrib" and the country as "Marrakush."

Because the speech of the inhabitants of North Africa was unintelligible to them, the Greeks lumped them among the barbarians (barbaroi), and the Romans and the Arabs finally consecrated this as the name of the indigenous population, the Berbers (vulg. Ar: beraber). When European contact with the region was intensified in the Middle Ages the names "Barbary" and "Berbery" became common, especially in association with the pirate operations carried on by the coastal city-states from the sixteenth to the nineteenth centuries.

With the coming of the French in 1830 and the installation of colonial rule in the three countries for a century and a third, the romantic overtones of the Barbary Coast were transferred to Western literature, and after a short vogue of "Africa Minor" (coined by analogy with Asia Minor) the term "North Africa" came into favor, first in French, then in English and finally among the inhabitants themselves. If we use it today, it must be with the qualification that it does not include the entire littoral, and while Egypt may be put conveniently but illogically in the Middle East, it leaves Libya shorn of its geographical rights in a kind of limbo which corresponds in fact to the ambivalent position in which it finds itself in the Arab World, belonging to neither the eastern nor western wing of it.

The lack of a suitable name for a region which nature has sharply delimited is only one of the many paradoxes to be found in North Africa. Although it is isolated like an island, it stretches out bridges to the north and east as if to invite enticingly the penetration which its rugged terrain in fact makes so difficult. The one from Spain is the closest, but offers the least appealing hinterland; the passage between the tip of Tunisia and Sicily, across the narrows separating the Western and Eastern Mediterranean, invited the first European invasion in classical times; and the eastern land bridge, a narrow corridor leading into southeast Tunisia from Tripolitania, traverses some four hundred miles of wasteland along the Gulf of Sirte, where the Sahara comes right down to the sea.

Just as anomalous is the fact that North Africa is placed on or near what has been the center of our Western world stage for two thousand years, but it has itself almost never been an active participant in history. Its isolation has persisted as it were in the very midst of interaction; it has preferred to be the object rather than the subject, and after those brief flurries during which it has been stirred into movement, it has constantly turned in upon itself for a period of aloof and taciturn withdrawal. Moreover, within its boundaries so well-defined from the outside, a certain formlessness exists. The region has no natural focus, and no geographical center. The long mountain chains running from West to East form lateral axes that stretch the long sides of the quadrilateral, and numerous smaller ranges cut off and compartment regions in a way which has at most times impeded internal unity. And although internal renewal has always in the past come from the most rugged and inhospitable regions of steppe or high mountain, the great cities of today, to which the population flocks in steadily increasing numbers, are all coastal ports facing outward to the sea.

As an object of history, North Africa has come under three great outside influences. The substratum is certainly African; there is a feeling of Africanness that comes out in the most basic aspects of life: the sound of folk music, the sudden sight of a brush-hut village, the loneliness of the landscape, the earliest art, and in religion many of the clandestine survivals of pagan practices. Upon this permeable matrix, which will probably never be fully understood by scholars, have been impressed in successive waves the higher cultures of Asia and Europe. From the East came early invasions in the Neolithic period which brought language and a higher technology, and in the historic period the contacts with the Phoenician traders which ended with the establishment of Carthage, a mercantile city-empire which was the first amalgam of a North African and Oriental state. Then came the Roman era, which lasted nearly eight hundred years in some parts of the area and might well have been considered definitive by an observer studying the scene halfway through that period. That the Roman era turned out to have left relatively so little imprint culturally is a good warning against the certainty that Arab civilization, which has been dominant since the conquest of North Africa late in the seventh century, is the definitive pattern for this area. During the past century it has met and seemingly repulsed a political challenge for hegemony instituted by Latin Europe, with France in the vanguard, Spain and Italy following—a kind of neo-Roman affirmation of the integrity of the Western Mediterranean. But there are elements at work in all the North African countries today which make it impossible to say with surety that in other, nonpolitical ways European influence has not actually gained ground in most recent years at the expense of Arab culture.

Thus North Africa is today, as before, still an object undergoing the assault of external forces beseeching and besieging it. It makes up, as the Maghrib, the western wing of a revivified Arab world now neatly balanced between its African and Asian parts. It receives the major part of its intellectual and technical sustenance from Europe, to which the practical demands of modern life closely bind it. And, whether in an effort to attenuate the pressure from these sources, or as part of the search for its elusive inner personality, it has lately, and increasingly, felt itself to be a part of Africa and a leading element in the continental struggle for a new place in the sun. Eclectically passive, taking something from all but giving nothing, North Africa is, now as always, a cul-de-sac into which much has flowed but from which little has emerged. Its physical ramparts of rock and sand have often in the past been a protection, but even more usefully defensive in the long run has been the sponge-like capacity of absorptive indifference which Berber society has practiced for three millenia. To many foreign conquerors North Africa has surrendered its lands and riches, but with none has it fully shared its spirit.

This is not harsh criticism alone. There are several areas of the world of which it can be fairly said that, at least till now, more has come in than gone out: Southeast Asia, Black Africa, and much of Latin America come to mind. North Africa is, like all of these, a civilization of synthesis, but what needs stressing at the same time, when it appears that so much of what has gone into the mixture is of pure external inspiration, is that almost unnoticeable resistance of the inner self which alchemizes the different ingredients into a new and unique compound.

If an arbitrary line is drawn from just below Agadir at the southwest corner of Morocco to the Mediterranean shore at 12°E longitude, what is generally called "useful North Africa" will have been encompassed. This is the inhabited, productive 450,000 odd square miles of the area, which excludes large parts of the Sahara under Algerian political control and contested by its neighbors Morocco and Tunisia. The top of the quadrilateral thus formed, running along the Mediterranean coast from Tangier to Bizerte, extends for some 900 miles. But it is the depth of the Maghrib which is the important point in all respects. In the 350 to 400 miles that lie between the two imaginary lines on our map we proceed from 37°N latitude to 28°N and we have made the transition from a subtropical, Mediterranean region to a rocky, steppe-desert pocked with huge sand dune patches of complete aridity.

The southern boundaries of North Africa depend on the perspective from which the area is being viewed. The Sahara extends to the south of all three countries for a good thousand miles and there are some geographers who choose to include it as part of North Africa. This is not general practice, however, and there are good reasons for looking on the desert as a separate phenomenon, although the political pressures of the day would not permit many North Africans to agree with this. The boundaries of Algeria, as presently constituted, take up vast portions of the Sahara, and the integrity of these artificially drawn frontiers was a cardinal point of the revolution. Morocco, for its part, claims large areas in the western half of the desert, including all of the present state of Mauritania, parts of southwest Algeria, and the Spanish Sahara, down as far as the Senegal River.

Historically as well as geographically, the desert has had a deep influence on the regions north of it. Moroccan claims stem from southerly penetrations in the sixteenth and seventeenth centuries and scattered residual allegiance paid thereafter by certain tribes. On several occasions groups have come out of the Sahara to conquer North Africa proper and change its destiny, and there has always been a sense of the "weight" of the desert hanging over the countries of the region, as if by its mere emptiness it were a positive force. Perhaps a useful analogy is to look upon North Africa as a stage on which all the action takes place, while the Sahara represents the backstage from which, from time to time, new players appear. Just as no play is put on behind the scenes, so the Sahara has not had a coherent or continuous historical development but has only provided on occasion the raw materials for neighboring areas.

The transition from Mediterranean verdure to the rigors of the desert is nowhere identical throughout the area, but in general north-south patterns of coastal valleys and plains, followed by mountains, high steppes, more mountains, and finally desert, tend to reduplicate themselves vertically. The outstanding geographical element is the long and mostly continuous chain of mountains, the Atlas, which forms a horizontal backbone running across the entire length of the three countries from southwest Morocco to northeast Tunisia. Depending on its height and thickness, it more or less successfully cuts off the desert to the south from more fertile regions north of it. The Atlas is more uplifted at its western end in Morocco, where the highest peak reaches 13,600 feet, and the solid mass of the High and Middle Atlas forms a sturdy protective barrier for the Atlantic plains of that country. In Algeria, the greatest elevation does not exceed 7,600 feet, and as the mountains dwindle down toward the east nothing in Tunisia raises its head above 5,200 feet. The Atlas is not a simple mountain range. Three strands of it run together in Morocco, and the Rif Mountains in the northwestern part of the country, geologically a continuation of the Cordillera Boetica of Southern Spain, come down almost to join the Atlas east of Fez in the Taza Gap. In Algeria there are nearly parallel ranges in the Saharan Atlas, the Quarsenis range, and the coastal peaks, and in eastern Algeria the pattern breaks down into a jumble of interlaced chains running from the coast down to the gates of the desert north of Biskra.

North Africa is a high country almost everywhere. Even in Tunisia the average elevation is about 1,000 feet, while in Morocco it comes to 2,600 feet and in Algeria 3,000 feet. Much of this is in the form of great empty intermontane plateaus dotted with lakes that are salt because of insufficient drainage for their waters, the whole recalling the more unfavored parts of the American Great Basin in Nevada or Utah. But in other parts, as if in revenge, the relief is intricately tormented and level land hardly existent. Such are the Rif in Morocco, and Kabylia in Algeria. In both these regions jagged mountains rise almost directly from the sea to heights of 6,000 and 7,000 feet. The valleys are little more than narrow gorges without adequate intercommunication, fed by short, swift streams which tumble into the sea. A good part of the Mediterranean coast between Tangier and Bizerte is thus enclosed, so that in effect North Africa is bounded by a double barrier on both sides: to the south there is not only the desert obstacle but the insulating mountain chains which flank it, and to the north the sea is often buttressed by a mountain wall for a shore line.

This geographical inaccessibility is a key to the understanding of much in North Africa. Until the twentieth century, when the artificial port of Casablanca was built at great expense, the harsh Atlantic coast of Morocco had no safe anchorage and winter storms often lasting two to three weeks made trade risky and unprofitable. The estuaries of rivers like the Bou Regreg at Rabat and the Loukkos at Larache were useful primarily to buccaneers who profited from their knowledge of the tides and sand bars to sally forth and retreat to safety.

The few good harbors along the Algerian coast, like Algiers, Bougie, Philippeville, and Bone, had miniscule hinterlands which limited commercial and agricultural possibilities. Only along the eastern shore of Tunisia, in the Sahel from Tunis to Sfax, did there exist that combination of good ports and flat or rolling fertile back country which tempted merchants and conquerors. The first of these stimulated a fruitful intercourse which has made the Tunisian population of the Sahel the most truly "Mediterranean" and open culture group in the area, and the second were responsible for all the major invasions of the Maghrib—Phoenician, Roman, and Arab—until the techniques of modern Europe overcame in the past century the natural obstacles which had long held attackers at bay.

In a country of such size and diversity one cannot expect a uniform climate. The romantic view of the region has stressed the spring-like lushness of the coastal plain and the bright, transparent skies of the desert winter. The reality in both cases is more bitter. The climate of the strip along the coast is essentially Mediterranean, with warm, dry summers, hotter in the east than in the west, where the cool Canaries current reduces temperatures along Moroccan shores, and mild, rainy winters. Thus, July averages are 72°F for Tangier, 76° for Algiers and 79° for Tunis; in winter the reverse is generally true: January means are 50.5° in Tunis and 53.5° in Tangier. But as soon as one moves inland even a score of miles, the temperature goes up rapidly in summer and down in winter. The valleys between the coastal and interior mountains often have the worst of the bargain in both temperature and humidity. But since so much of the area is high table land or mountain, the rigors of the climate are increased in winter without a comparable compensation in summer, owing to the prevalence of southeasterly and southerly winds from the Sahara.

More than temperature, rainfall is the key factor in the life of the country, however. North Africa has been described as a cold country with a hot sun; that is exact, but it is also a subarid area with a considerable amount of rainfall at the wrong time and place. Most of the Atlantic plains of Morocco and the northern part of that country receive sufficient precipitation, and as much as 60 inches have been measured in the Jbala and Western Rif Mountains. Likewise, central and eastern Algeria are well watered, but the value of the rainfall in most regions there is mitigated because the land is either too high or too rough. One good index is the 16-inch rain line, outside of which nonirrigated cultivation is hazardous. Beginning at Safi on the Moroccan coast, it includes the western plains of the country and the High and Middle Atlas, disappears into the sea in Western Algeria (because rain-bearing clouds coming from Spain have not enough time in the short passage across the Mediterranean to recharge themselves), follows the Algerian coast at a distance inland of less than 100 miles until it picks up strength as the Mediterranean widens, and then dips down to include the Aures Mountains, before following the Atlas dorsal into the sea just south of Cape Bon in Tunisia.

Even here a word of caution is necessary, for the irregularity of the annual rainfall increases in proportion to the aridity. Thus, while the better watered regions of Morocco and Algeria can count, with some assurance, on an adequate amount of rain, as one approaches the Sahara precipitation may vary from year to year by five to ten times, and the idea of a norm is useless. Also, much of the rainfall is concentrated in a few winter months when it falls bunched together often in violent cloudbursts on land which has been baked to impermeability by six to nine months of hot, dry sun. Accordingly, it runs off wasted or does more damage in flash floods than it does good to agriculture. Thus, running the gamut from a maritime to a continental climate, and with rainfall ranging from seventy inches or more in the Collo Peninsula and the Babors of Algeria to less than four at Tozeur in southwest Tunisia, North Africa shows in its climate that same tendency to extremes that characterizes it elsewhere.

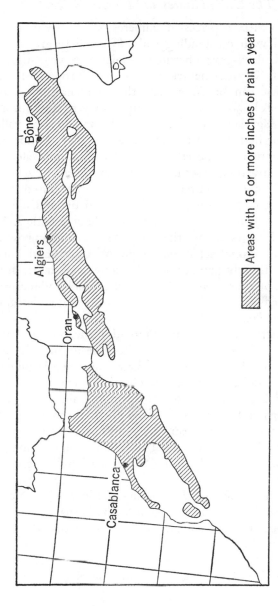

Areas with 16 or more inches of rain a year

North Africa—16-inch rainfall line

To add to these caprices of climate, North Africa has not been blessed with outstanding soils. Here there are no rich, well-drained, dark-gray chernozem soils that have made the grasslands of North America and Eastern Europe so fruitful. The best that can be found are the rendzina-type humus-carbonate soils in areas corresponding closely to the Moroccan plains, the Algerian and Tunisian Tell, and coastal valleys. These are far better than tropical soils but they do not come up to the best temperate earths; they are shallow and calcareous and under cultivation, as some of these have been for very long periods, their humus content tends to decrease rapidly. The rest of the best agricultural area is covered by podzolic soils with much leaching of nutrients and considerable acidity. As to the other soil types found, there is always something wrong: they are either too saline, in the steppes of Algeria and Tunisia, or skeletal with only patches of soil among rock debris in central Tunisia, or encrusted with limestone, which reduces fertility by impeding root development, in the high plateaus of eastern Morocco.

On this earth has been superimposed a cover which everywhere near the coast is fully Mediterranean: maquis forest, cork, oaks, and higher up a Mediterranean scrub mountain forest. The hillsides of much of coastal North Africa could pass at a quick glance for those of Spain or California. But this area is limited and it soon gives way to the barrenness of the plains steppe or high plateau, the home of esparto grass. At higher altitudes are found green oaks and Aleppo pines, and above 5,000 feet, especially in the Moroccan Middle Atlas, large stands of cedars.

North Africa is one of the regions of the world which has most suffered from man tampering with the natural environment. Archeology and paleontology confirm that the Sahara was once very different from the desert it is now; it was far less dry and North Africa proper was better watered and had a fuller vegetation. Later the testimony of classical writers is available as proof that Tunisia was a principal source of grain for imperial Rome, and the olive groves of Africa Proconsularis were famous in the ancient world. Early Arab authors give descriptions of the region around Kairouan, in central Tunisia, which the modern visitor finds difficult to credit from the evidence before his eyes. It is true that a gradual drying up process has been taking place, apparently as part of a long cycle, but this has been much abetted by human intervention. The question of which caused which—whether nature or man is primarily responsible—is something like the chicken and the egg at this point, but that man shared in the responsibility is the important thing.

A precarious balance had always existed between the sedentaries of the more favored coastal regions and pastoral groups condemned to nomadize farther inland. In general, when order prevailed under a powerful organized state, the pressure was from the center outward, whereas when there was a breakdown in the establishment, the tendency was for the nomad to close in on the more effete, settled areas and set up his own looser hegemony, to the detriment of what had been built up in preceding times by the practicers of agriculture. The growing desiccation of the Sahara certainly was one factor in nomadic pressure inward upon sedentary life, and the introduction of the camel around the beginning of the Christian era, made those groups who had been forced out onto the steppes and the fringes of the Sahara by Roman policy in the High Empire more mobile and dangerous. Meanwhile, the introduction of colonies, the growth of the population under Roman rule, the extension of agriculture, and the exploitation of North Africa as a source of primary materials, of which high quality thuja wood was one, all combined to contribute to deforesting the countryside. Then during the decline and fall of Roman power in North Africa, from the third to the fifth centuries A.D., the countryside was devastated by the incursions of nomadic and seminomadic Berber tribes returning from the

confines to which they had been forced by the Roman occupation.

A further serious blow came in the Middle Ages in the form of a large-scale invasion of the region by nomadic Arab tribes from across the Libyan desert. The writers of the period immediately following, notably Ibn Khaldun, contemplate with horror the destruction they wreaked on the land, and while verbal excess is common in Arab writings, they seem to have had a cumulatively grave effect. Like locusts, it is said, they ravaged the country, cut down trees, destroyed waterworks and wells, and moved on to further depredations, leaving only ruin in their wake. Large sections of the still fertile areas of central Tunisia, the Algerian Tell, and the wooded Atlantic plains of Morocco were seriously deforested by these tribes as they moved westward.

Not all the forfeits of history can be laid at the door of the nomads, however. A general negligence has been the hallmark of most of the inhabitants, and destructive practices are attested to constantly by direct observation in the past century. One example is that of the mountaineers, who lazily obtain wood without going to the trouble of cutting down trees; instead they light a ring of fire at the base of the object desired, often coincidentally and prodigally wasting great stands of trees nearby. Another example is that of shepherds who at times try to increase the size of their pasturage by burning off scrub and forest land which is not of immediate use to them. Even today a casual visitor to the modern cities of North Africa will be aware of the depredations of goats and sheep in them, particularly harmful to the young plants and trees which can easily be reached by these animals. The ambiguous role of the European colon can also not be overlooked. The rapid extension of agriculture, especially in Algeria, in the nineteenth and twentieth centuries pushed back the natural cover. At the same time the native population, which began to expand suddenly under new conditions of health and security, was forced to cultivate marginal lands in hill and mountain areas which were subject to ever-growing problems of erosion. Even the benefits which European colonization brought thus had their bitter dregs.

All has not been completely black, however, in the past century. What man has destroyed in North Africa he has begun to remake in part. The official French policy of setting up forest domains, even though they were sometimes opened up for private sale, established the foundations for an intelligent reforestation program; and the settlers themselves were not exclusively destructive, for they were busy draining swampy areas, reclaiming wasted land, reactivating the soil, and fixing it by planting old and new varieties of trees and plants. The famous olive groves around Sfax had disappeared by the nineteenth century but were slowly reconstituted and extended out onto the barren steppe. Two alien species were extensively planted, the barbary fig, in reality a cactus originating in Mexico, and the eucalyptus from Australia, so that today North Africa must look strikingly unlike what it did a few centuries ago. The colonial authorities made sincere efforts in the fields of forestry, flood control, irrigation, and the stopping of excessive erosion—to the extent that it might be said they cared more for the land in North Africa than they were concerned with the indigenous human there. Moreover, the example has happily been taken up by the independent countries. One of the most hopeful portents of the day is the way in which they are attacking the problem, especially in Tunisia, where widespread reforestation and hydraulic improvement projects in the past few years have begun to make noticeable changes in the face of the countryside.

THE PEOPLE

It needs stressing that North Africa is, above everything else, the land of the Berbers. This is because the outside world tends to look on the inhabitants indiscriminately as Arabs, something in which it is encouraged by the modern, political orientation of the North African countries and their leaders. Thus it is politic today in Tunisia, Algeria, and Morocco to refer to "Arab North Africa (Al Maghrib al 'Arabi)" and it is on the whole a tenet of the vibrant, new nationalism that the so-called "Berber issue" be ignored or underplayed. But despite the political passions of the times, and regardless of the complete Islamization and the thorough cultural Arabization of the region, when we come down to ethnic cases North Africa can only be described as being overwhelmingly inhabited by peoples whom anthropologists and historians, for want of a better term, have called Berbers.

But once having made this categorical statement, we come up against problems of definition and explanation. First, we must note that the term Berber is today used primarily a means of linguistic identification—"Berberophone" would be more exact—to separate the some five to six million North Africans, out of a total of more than twenty-five million, who speak Berber. Some of these use it exclusively, and others are bilingual; in the second case, Berber will be the language of the home, the fields, and the women, and Arabic the tongue of contact with the outside world, of commerce, and of men.

Berber linguistic unity is that of a group of closely related dialects of a language forming part of the Hamitic family. This tongue, which might well be called Libiac, once apparently covered all North Africa west of Egypt, but its range is now limited to more specific, isolated, smaller areas, mostly in the more inaccessible mountains of the area. Thus today Berber dialects are found as far east as the Oasis of Siwa in western Egypt, in the Jebel Nafusa of Tripolitania, among the Tuareg in the remote mountains of the central Sahara, all of these islets surrounded by non-Berber speakers. In Tunisia, because of its geographical accessibility, Berber has been just about completely lost, but to the west in the mountain country of Algeria and Morocco we find the most solid clumps: in the Aures and

Kabyle mountains in Algeria, and in the Rif and throughout most of the Middle and High Atlas in Morocco. The percentage of Berberophones in Algeria has been estimated at from 20 to 25 per cent, and as high as 40 per cent in Morocco, although these figures do not necessarily take into account the operating Arabo-Berber bilingualism which is high among the men. As a language which is spoken but not written, Berber in the North African countries has come under the twin assault of civilization and Arabism for more than a thousand years. It has slowly given ground, and the sections in which it is found today are typical refuge areas; in the most recent past, despite a French attempt for a time to resuscitate it to the detriment of Arabic for political reasons, it has continued to recede bit by bit and the current Arabist educational policies of the North African states put it at a further disadvantage. But it still has reserved hours in the state broadcasting systems in Morocco and Algeria, and there are large areas of both countries where, if government officials who speak only Arabic are sent out from the capital, they cannot communicate with the people.

Language is of course a prima facie argument that anyone who speaks Berber is a Berber and strongly indicates that he has preserved along with his speech an amalgam of indigenous culture which can be considered representatively Berber and which has survived with surprisingly little change throughout North Africa for several thousand years. The main material elements in this continuum are that it is primarily a pastoral culture, in which sheep and goatherding predominate, supplemented by the cultivation where possible of cereals, and in the mountains by orchardry. The gradual pushing back of Berberophones to the refuge areas mentioned above has tended to favor sedentary as against nomadic activities. A collective mode of life is common, with the sharing of crops and their storage in a joint, usually fortified granary. Woodworking and pottery-making are practiced and first-rate weaving is found. Jewelry is extensively worn by the women, and art and architecture show a strong bias toward geometrical abstraction but without the involutions and arabesques typical of Middle Eastern artifacts. (It would take an expert in many cases to tell North African Berber pieces from Navaho blankets and Pueblo pottery of the American southwest.) Socially, the culture has been marked by an extended, agnatic family system in which inheritance passes through the eldest surviving male of the group; no individual property holdings; a localized, egalitarian authority centered in an assembly of elders; extreme fractionalization of groups into small segments, which have been called "cantonal republics" by some writers, relying on temporary defensive alliances and counteralliances (the liff system) for protection, and extending these in times of trouble to achieve an ephemeral unity; and an unwritten, customary law of great antiquity and stability. It would not be excessive to say that in many parts of the rural Maghrib, Berber society as it exists today hardly differs from that observed by the Romans, save for the introduction of Islam; and even that powerful force underwent significant alterations as it was adapted in the area over the course of several centuries.

There is no such thing as an ethnically homogeneous Berber race, however. Berbers exhibit a diversity of types about whom prudent anthropologists are unwilling to make few more generalizations than that they are basically white, usually with brown hair and eyes, but having a percentage of blondism—reddish or blondish hair with blue or green eye coloration—significantly higher than that found in Southern Europe. Two particularly common types are signaled: one is the small-statured, longheaded, round-faced type which predominates in mountain regions like Kabylia and the Rif; another is a tall, elongated, longheaded and longfaced specimen of which the Tuareg of the Hoggar are an excellent example. The first type may well be older, and it is often considered apparented to the early Mediterranean populations of southern Europe; certainly it is usually impossible to tell a Berber of this sort from a

Spanish or Sardinian peasant if both are divested of super-ficially identifying cultural accessories. The second type recalls one predominant Hamitic-linked type often found in northeast Africa, and it gives ground for suspecting that it may have been this later, intruder stock which brought in to the earlier group of food-gatherers, toward the end of the neolithic period —perhaps 3000 B.C. at a round estimate—the domestic ani-mals, cereals, and techniques described previously, in addition to the language.

There are other groups which do not correspond to these two main types, such as the short, roundheaded Djerbans and Mzabites, and there has clearly been much mixing over a long period of time in North Africa, with both inbreeding and out-breeding. The Shelha of the Moroccan High Atlas, for example, often present a series of traits usually called Mongoloid: yel-low-brown skin coloring, mongoloid eye fold, flat (non-negroid) nose, which bring up the question of possible crossing with very early negroid elements probably present in the Mediterranean in prehistoric times. These are not to be con-fused with the later admixtures of true Negro elements brought in as slaves in recent centuries, who are found extensively in the cities but almost never in the countryside.

Apart from these practical difficulties of classification and description, Berbers present some rather unique psychological problems. By and large they are an elusive and non-self-identi-fying society to a degree almost unmatched elsewhere. Just as the region as a whole had no internally given name, so the Berbers themselves exist unaware that they are thus called. Their consciousness of themselves, generally limited to their tribe or the mountain region in which they dwell, did not con-ceive of the link beyond. So they have no fixed name, although many style themselves *imazighen* "the men," in the manner of many primitives; and while one may hear Kabyles or Rifians using these terms (both originally Arabic words) to refer to themselves, identification by birthplace or tribe is more common. The Berbers, situated at the western end of the Arab world, have sometimes been compared to the Kurds in the northeastern corner, but no self-conscious Berber separatism or nationalism exists as is the case with the Kurds. Still it is impossible to deny that some feelings of apartness exist among Berber groupings and recently efforts have been made by at least one political party in Morocco to capitalize on them. It is perhaps not accidental, too, that the only serious internal troubles in that country since independence have been uprisings in the two principal Berber areas, the Rif and Middle Atlas; while in Algeria the struggle for power within the leadership of the revolution, both before and after independence, was at least partly connected with the role played by the more than two million Kabyles and the large contingent of them which had emigrated to France.

Berber elusiveness is marked in another way in the rest of the population of North Africa. There are about twenty million persons who speak Arabic and who have been to varying degrees "arabized" over the centuries since the conquest beginning in the mid-seventh century. All the evidence points to the fact that all immigration, from whatever sources, in the historical period has had little mathematical chance of making much change in the basic ethnic make-up of North Africa. But the coming of the Arabs and Islam did affect the Berbers culturally, and in accepting Islam they took up many facets of Arab civilization, in particular the language, which were intertwined with it. As their localisms had given in to the Roman Empire, they could not resist the universal Arabo-Islamic state, but this time in a seemingly fuller way they surrendered and assimilated themselves to the Arabs, down to the extremes of compiling complete genealogies tracing their ancestry back to a forefather from a noted Arab family or tribe. Today a qualified anthropometrist may himself be quite convinced that his subject, a North African who may be, say, an Arab-speaking resident of Meknès, with family attestations going back to pre-Islamic Arabia, is a fine specimen of a certain Berber type, but it will usually be a difficult and perhaps even dangerous undertaking to convince his interlocutor of this.

In sum, the Berbers seem to have oscillated, through all the history of their relations with outsiders, between putting up a violent, yet somehow romantically hopeless, resistance and, that finally failing, succumbing completely to the invader. But this collapse of resistance, and we have seen it occur on three quite separate occasions—with the Romans, the Arabs, and the French—is complex. It carries with it a kind of passive indifference; it is an assimilativeness, but not a true assimilation, which is in the end a means of continuing the struggle. It is not surprising that a favorite Berber tale, one repeated in the twentieth century during the French conquest of Morocco after having first been told in respect of the Arab conquest, is that of a chief who has ferociously fought the foreigner enjoining his descendents on his deathbed to make peace with the enemy and thus preserve their people. Further, once the Berbers have accepted outside penetration they have always worn the foreign mantle with a deep impassiveness, ready to discard it with astonishing speed and thoroughness. Such was their behavior as regards Christianity, which they took up with fervor and in many of its variant forms, like Arianism and Donatism, only to throw it over for Islam, where they repeated the history of extremes of zeal, heresies, and backsliding for several centuries. They have been compared in tenacity to the French Canadians and, with perhaps more justice, to the Basques. There are many differences, but in one way they resemble both; they are enracinated in their land, almost unconsciously a part of it, as enduring as their environment, despite the cultural trappings of any particular millenium. Coon puts it succinctly in speaking of the five waves (Phoenician, Roman, Arab, French, and neo-Arab Nationalist) which have washed over the Berbers throughout their long history, when he concludes ". . . They can adjust themselves to the fifth wave as readily as they have to the fourth, while retaining their essential rocklike quality of being and remaining Berbers no matter how much water splashes over them, from either direction." One suspects they will continue to be a part of the scene for a long time to come.

Aside from this indigenous pool of Berbers and Arabized Berbers, the most important contribution to the peopling of North Africa has been made by the Arabs. They arrived beginning in the mid-seventh century, and over a period of several centuries they managed to transform Berbery into a part of the Arabo-Islamic world in much the same way that Latin America was later brought into the Christian-Mediterranean frame of civilization. The question that interests us here, however, is how many Arabs and what kind actually came to North Africa, what effect they had on the racial composition of the area, and what percentage of the whole they now make up. No figures are certain, but some approximation can be made.

The Arabs came in two principal waves, one right at the beginning of the conquest, the other dating from the mid-eleventh century, and in decreasing numbers spanning the following several hundred years. The first arrivals have been estimated at not more than 150,000; this group was made up of the invading armies, cavaliers, tribesmen, and all the baggage of a foreign occupation. To them must be added a certain number of women, children, and hangers-on, but not in a heavy proportion; the disparity between the sexes in numbers, always present in a country of immigrants, should be kept in mind in the North African case. Through intermarriage with local women the invading group began to be diluted very early in many cases, but because of the Arab insistence on tracing genealogy through the male line alone, theoretical purity was usually maintained. The second wave involved several full-scale tribal immigrations which began with the Beni Hilal and the Solaim, who had been dispossessed of their territory in Egypt and driven westward across the Libyan Desert. They moved into Ifriqiya, what is modern Tunisia, from about 1050 on, and then gradually inched their way across North Africa. They were invited to Morocco by a government which failed to foresee the profound changes they would work on rural life; they ensconced themselves in parts of the plains and steppes, became special corps in the service of local rulers or served as garrisons in towns, and received territory and power for their services. During the whole period of tribal immigration, at a generous estimate, perhaps three hundred thousand individuals entered North Africa.

In between these incursions separated by some four centuries the Maghrib, like any new country of promise and adventure, received a steady trickle of individual immigrants from the centers of Arab life elsewhere. Some of these came as refugees; whenever there was a change of fortune in Baghdad or Cairo a few of the unlucky political losers dissatisfied with the new regime would turn up. Many of these came with prestigious names and religious affiliations; the success of 'Abderrahman I in reestablishing Umayyad fortunes in Spain after they collapsed in Syria was matched by that of Idris I, a descendant of 'Ali, the son-in-law of the prophet Muhammad, whose noble origins enabled him to unite factious Berber tribes under his rule and found the first national dynasty in Morocco. These immigrants were moving from city to city, rather than from country to country, within the elastic bounds of the House of Islam which did not conceive of fully separate states and national boundaries or sentiments. Thus, Fez was founded at the beginning of the ninth century by the Idrissites, but was peopled in large measure by urban refugees from Cordova and individuals from Kairouan, itself the first city established by the Arabs when they arrived in Tunisia. These were people of quality: intellectuals, religious savants, merchants, and craftsmen, and the exclusiveness of their interurban migrations tended from the very beginning to keep town life quite separate from that of the unsophisticated countryside nearby.

In Ifriqiya, where there was naturally more contact with the centers of the Middle East, this movement back and forth of a governing class and a select aristocracy was more pronounced than in Algeria or Morocco, which were cut off from an early date. Later on, after about 1000 A.D., the movement of religious figures became more important: Sufists propagating new mystic doctrines, wandering preachers, Marabouts and holy men, and always among them the *sharif*-s, descendants of Muhammad. The caravan trade routes across the Maghrib to the East not only exchanged goods but, especially through the institution of the pilgrimage to the holy sites in Arabia, became a lifeline which permitted a steady spiritual renovation of Arabism and Islam in this "Western Island."

As with the Berbers, language is a useful key to the Arabization of North Africa for the type of Arabic spoken indicates when and by whom any given area was influenced. Urban dialects are found in the long-established traditional cities like Tunis, Fez, Salé, Tlemcen, and such, but in the countryside they appear only in the villages and towns of eastern Tunisia with its ancient tradition of settled civilization, in Little Kabylia in Algeria, and the Jbala region of northern Morocco (both of the latter important passageway regions likely to be influenced early.) Everywhere else in North Africa the Arabic used is the bedouin variety brought in by the second wave of nomadic tribes, and this underlines the extent to which the countryside was still almost completely Berber in language through the eleventh century.

If we take the total of the two principal Arab groups and add half that number again as a fair estimate of the individual arrivals plus group stragglers that came to the Maghrib, we can arrive at a maximum figure of about 700,000 dispersed in a population which was very probably in the neighborhood of six to seven million at the time when the Almohads were ruling an orderly and prosperous state at the end of the twelfth century. But it should be recalled that they were scattered over a considerable period of time and space and that intermarriage was practiced. So it is hard to admit, even on the most generous basis, that Arab blood (without even going into the question of how truly "Arab" were the elements coming from a Middle East which had itself long been a racially mixed area) could have formed as much as ten per cent of the population of the Maghrib at any time in its history, and the odds are that it makes up much less than that.

The lasting results of the Arabs' entry into North African life, of course, far exceed their numerical importance. The urban newcomers were an elite group carrying the torch of learning and religion, and they established centers of civilization and foyers of Islamic culture. The nomads, on the other hand, contributed much to the degradation of the land and the widespread collapse of sedentary rural life. Coming on the scene with the elan of conquerors, speaking the purest and best form of the holy tongue, powerful and mobile, they attracted to themselves and their ways of life part of the peasantry. The latter sought protection from them, tried to speak their language, tended to assimilate themselves to them, and in the end at times took the name of the Arab fraction or tribe with whom they dealt, in order to be considered one of theirs. Probably this social destruction was as important as the material havoc wreaked by the nomads. It had grave consequences, one of them being that, unlike Europe, the peasantry had no chance to develop and become a source of sustenance and renewal for the cities; Fez and Florence in the fifteenth century were Mediterranean cities cut out of the same cloth, as anyone who reads the description of Leo Africanus will feel, but the primitive rural structure of Morocco could not replenish the metropolis to the extent that the Tuscan countryside did for the city of Dante. Urban civilization had always had a hard existence in North Africa, except for coastal Tunisia perhaps, but by the

time this transformation of rural life had been effected, that
is to say from the end of the fourteenth century, it was in
effect besieged in a hostile land.

The third major group that has helped shape modern North
Africa is the European component, but it has this peculiarity
that it has not in any way altered the racial composition of the
indigenous population. It now seems certain that, like the
Romans and the Vandals in the past, the European of today
will leave no ethnic mark in North Africa. They came, lived
an alien life, brought with them their own social, economic,
and cultural patterns, and were themselves remarkably unaffected by their environment and all other inhabitants of the
area. But in a relatively short period of a century and a quarter
they have made changes in the native society, by precept,
example, and coercion, of such profound extent that this society will never be the same.

The pattern of European settlement makes North Africa
almost unique among those parts of the world which came
under the domination of one of the colonial powers. For no
other temperate area, save perhaps South Africa under quite
different circumstances, ever received such a large contingent
of Europeans intending to settle permanently in the midst of an
already existent native population of considerable number. The
Europeans reproduced on the southern shores of the Mediterranean as much as they could the conditions of life in their
homelands in France, Spain, and Italy. The tragedy in the end
has been that North Africa was so near the original home and
so like it that the settlers came to believe that the facsimile
civilization they had installed was the proper and eternal order
of things, whereas it turned out that the area was just different
enough so that Latin civilization per se, for the second time,
did not take.

At highwater mark just before Tunisia and Morocco became
independent in 1956, the European population of the Maghrib
(including the places of sovereignty (Ceuta and Melilla) which

Spain still holds to be integral parts of the Spanish state, but to which Morocco has claims) came to just under 2,000,000, about eight per cent of the total population. At the end of 1962 it had been reduced to about 700,000, or less than three per cent, of whom nearly 300,000 are in Morocco, 200,000 in Algeria (where figures are uncertain because of the sudden and massive departure of so many Europeans), fewer than 100,000 in Tunisia, and slightly more than 100,000 in the Spanish enclaves.

The pattern of colonization was different in each of the three countries. In Algeria it began early and was officially fostered. Veterans of the army of Africa were encouraged to stay and were given land, emigrants were lured to North Africa in lieu of other destinations which had been promised them, humble vintners fleeing the phylloxera blight in France and silkworm raisers dispirited by the crises of the industry, and robber barons in the best nineteenth century tradition of unrestrained capitalism combined to produce a population which embraced all classes from great landed estate owners and businessmen to butchers, bakers, and dock workers. Most of the French immigrants came from the Mediterranean parts of France: Corsica, Provence, and the Languedoc, with a sprinkling of Alsatians after 1870. But western Algeria was principally settled by the Spanish, many of whom came to work as farm hands when the plains of Oranie were put under the plow. Although here as elsewhere in the Maghrib the European population was mostly urban, only in Algeria was there any true rural element, including a good number of small holders as well as large, and often absentee, landowners. (In the 1950's European farmers who represented 2 per cent of the entire rural population held more than a third of all the cultivated land in Algeria and produced 60 per cent of the total crop by value.) The relative antiquity of the Europeans of Algeria is also noteworthy. More than half a million were in the country by 1890 and after 1911 increase was mostly natural without benefit of further immigration. The feeling that they formed a fully self-contained community which was in the majority in the largest cities and the sentiment among many of those who were third- or fourth-generation immigrants that they had no other home help explain the bitterness of the Europeans during the last stages of the Algerian revolution when it became clear that power was going to be transferred to the Muslim majority.

In Tunisia there had been a number of resident Europeans dating from before the occupation by French forces in 1881. Most of them were Italians, with some Maltese, Greeks, and Levantines. Italians outnumbered the French in the protectorate for a good while; as late as 1911 there were 88,000 of them to only 46,000 French nationals, and touchy relations between the two segments of the Europeans community overshadowed those with the Muslim Tunisians until World War I. Gradually, however, the situation changed in both Algeria and Tunisia as the result of French naturalization laws under which the descendants of European foreigners born in those countries automatically became French citizens upon attaining their majority unless they specifically claimed their original nationality. The French in Tunisia came from those same southern regions of France which had previously supplied the bulk of the emigrants to Algeria, and from Algeria itself; but the presence in Tunisia of a more mixed Mediterranean population, to which the Tunisians themselves were closer because of their own variety, meant that on the whole there was always less cultural antagonism there than in the other parts of North Africa.

The colonization of Morocco was a much later affair. There were a few Europeans in the country, mostly in the port town of Tangier, before France and Spain decided to assert control in the first decade of this century. But no large-scale settlement could be made until the end of World War I and it was not really until the late 1920's that a sizable number was established in the country. During the great depression and the years immediately following, the inflow continued on a reduced scale, but the period of heaviest immigration was just after World War II, when Morocco was viewed from a ravaged Europe as a hopeful new land in the sun. The Europeans in Morocco differ from their compatriots in Algeria and Tunisia, therefore, in being younger on the whole and richer (per capita income among those in the French zone of Morocco was higher than that in metropolitan France and double that of the Europeans in Algeria). They were also less stratified by class; there are, broadly speaking, no poor French in Morocco. Furthermore, problems of nationality did not arise because with the partition of Morocco into zones of control, the Spanish, of whom there were more than 100,000, stayed mostly in their own zone or in the international city of Tangier. Finally, if one judges rightly, there was a sense of raw adventure and ambition among many of these latecoming Europeans, unlike the peasant tenacity of the earlier arrivals in the other Maghrib states. Having come last on the scene, they were more aware of the national entity which was Morocco, and the smell of a different era was already in the African air for many of those who disembarked in the late 1940's. Thus they were, even if only slightly, better able to face the prospect of political change, whereas their compatriots in Tunisia and most of all in Algeria were ill prepared to have the world they had painfully constructed for several generations collapse under them.

It is perhaps too early to make a definitive balance sheet of European colonization, but some impressions stand out sharply. The presence of such a large number made inevitable, like an ill wind, the modernization of the basic infrastructure and a Europeanization of countless small lifeways which make North Africa a colonial case very unlike those in which the native population was exposed only to a handful of foreign administrators. In particular it sharpened differences between North Africa and the Middle East. Algiers, Oran, Casablanca, and to some extent Tunis became large European cities in which it was impossible for North Africans to live without coming into extensive contact with a new mode of life. Like Pandora's box, the Europeans brought both good and evil almost hopelessly mixed at random in the wake of the economic and social disturbance they caused. The effort now being made by the newly independent countries to decide on the acceptance or rejection of separate items and values proffered is the story of North Africa today.

There are still other groups which have made significant contributions to the human scene in North Africa, among them the Spanish Muslims, the Jews, the Turks, and the Negroes.

The Muslims of Spain had even less Arab blood than did North Africans; they were overwhelmingly those Spaniards who had been converted to Islam during the long period in which the peninsula was divided religiously. From the earliest centuries of Muslim rule in Spain, there was a lively interchange of goods and people between Cordova, one of the great capitals of the world at the time, and the still rustic Maghrib. Later, for two and a half centuries ending in 1340, Morocco was actively intervening in Spanish affairs and the human contact was even closer, culminating in the period when Fez gradually took up the banner of Hispano-Mauresque civilization which was abandoned by the dying mountain kingdom of Granada. The greatest single wave of immigration from Spain to North Africa came after the Christian reconquest ended in 1492. For a century, scattered numbers of individuals and families crossed over to live with their coreligionaries. Finally, the expulsion of the remaining Muslims in Spain, the Moriscos, was decreed in 1609, and very large contingents came to swell the population of several Maghribi cities. Rabat and Tetuán in Morocco, Tlemcen in Algeria, and Tunis and its surroundings all received sizable quantities of refugees, whose total number must have been at least several hundred thousand. These were people of skills and culture, townsmen and talented artisans and garden farmers whose migration was a loss to Spanish life and a genuine gain for North Africa. They gave a new impetus to city life where they settled, became eager and daring pirates to assuage the hatred they bore their oppressors, and especially in Tunisia they grafted themselves on to the already existing village life and played an important role in maintaining the stable and prosperous environs of the capital. Even today, wherever they are found, they mark urban life with a cachet expressed in the quality of their houses and the variations they show in food, language, and household customs.

The Jews of North Africa, who numbered more than 400,-000 in 1950, seem to have come from several sources. Some certainly came to the area after the destruction of Jerusalem in 79 A.D., and they appear to have made converts among the Berbers even before the Arabs brought Islam. Many of these Judaized Berbers are found today in remote mountain regions like the Moroccan High Atlas, quite often ethnically identical to their Muslim covillagers. Most of the urban Jews, however, and more than half of all in the Maghrib, fled from persecution in Spain in 1492 and the years following. They have been active since then in banking, business, and many crafts. Treated as a protégé (*dhimmi*) under Muslim law, the lot of the individual Jew was sometimes difficult and always subject to the caprice of the authority at hand, but on the whole it is fair to say that treatment in the world of Islam was as good or better than that which Europe meted out at most times. The Jews had full citizenship nowhere in North Africa until the French naturalized those in Algeria en bloc in 1870. Today there is theoretical equality in all three countries but the vestigial taint of being considered second-class nationals and the new problems which have arisen from the Arab-Israeli conflict have caused many to leave. All but 20,000 of the 130,000 Jewish community in Algeria departed by the end of 1962, nearly half of the more than 200,000 in Morocco have gone, and the exodus from Tunisia, where probably greater opportunities for true integration existed than elsewhere, was stepped up when the Bizerte crisis in 1961 gave a heightened religious and pan-Arab tone to Tunisian nationalism. Most of the Jews who left have gone to France, at least temporarily; as a general rule the wealthier and more Europeanized Jews have chosen to go to France, and the poorer Jews and those from rural regions have emigrated to Israel.

During the sixteenth and seventeenth centuries when Algeria and Tunisia were regencies dependent on the Ottoman Empire a number of Turks was added to the racial composite of those states. The administrative class and their hangers-on came out from Constantinople, a militia corps was recruited from Anatolian peasants, and Turkish garrisons were stationed in the principal towns. A special class of *kulughli*-s, the descendants of Turks who had married local women, played an important role in local political life. The Turkish element tended to lead a separate existence, especially in the Algiers regency, and in some quarters of cities like Tlemcen their descendants can still be identified today. In more cosmopolitan Tunisia, fusion was easier and most of the Ottomans have been incorporated into the national body.

The seemingly very old Negroid contribution to North African stock has been mentioned before. But the dark skins that are from time to time seen in the area today have nothing to do with that. They come from the Negroes brought in more recently, particularly from the sixteenth to the nineteenth century, as slaves. In Morocco they were used extensively in the royal household and still form an elite bodyguard for the ruler. (Both men and women were introduced for the special Black Guard in the seventeenth century and marriage allowed only within the group so that continuity was assured.) In Algeria certain Saharan tribes paid their annual tribute to Algiers by sending shipments of slaves, some of whom were sent on to Constantinople and the east. Everywhere the use of negro concubines was common among the urban bourgeoisie, and almost any townsman with a little money and a large household kept slaves. For these reasons, skin color in the cities of North Africa is more varied in all shades of light and dark than in the countryside where the people were almost completely untouched by the admixture. Moreover, darkness of skin is not a social impediment or even an indication of status, for the darker individual may be either the descendant of humble freed slaves or the offspring of some of the best families.

In taking a kaleidoscopic view of North African life, compartmentalization is certainly one key to understanding. We have seen how it is geographically fragmented in ways which do not complement each other, and that there are important linguistic and cultural divisions. These disharmonies are reflected in a socioeconomic way, too, in the principal lifeways which the area supports. There are at least six distinct rural patterns that should be mentioned.

The first of these is the true nomad of the desert, south of the anti-Atlas and the Saharan Atlas, who served—until the advent of the truck and airplane began to squeeze him out— as the porter plying between the oases and the outside world, trading dates for grain, tobacco, and sugar, selling protection to travelers, and pasturing camels and sheep. In summer the nomads must often go several hundred kilometers to the north in search of less parched lands, and on this score, too, modern life is undoing them; the increasing mechanization of agriculture has deprived them of much of the money they used to earn by helping to bring in harvests near their summer grazing regions. The rapid extension of cultivation throughout North Africa has also reduced nomadic freedom of movement (especially in Algeria a battery of decrees interdicted large areas to them at certain times) and sharpened hostile feelings between them and the advancing farmers. A second classic type is the seminomad of the steppe-desert, usually located in a slightly better environment than the nomad and found largely through the plateaus of Algeria north of the Saharan Atlas and in central Tunisia. The seminomad is often perched on the precarious line where settled agriculture is barely possible in good years, but stock raising is surer most of the time. So his life lacks the functional regularity of the nomad, and he must decide each autumn whether the rains are going to be sufficient to permit the sowing of a crop, or whether he should head for other regions (for the winter in the high plateaus can be bitter). His livelihood is indeed precarious, for his flocks can be wiped out by extreme cold or extreme drought, and a dry spring may ruin a crop that looked promising at the beginning of a rainy autumn.

A third pattern is that of the mountain transhumant; those in the Moroccan Middle Atlas are a good example. They bring their livestock down to the sheltering plains in winter and ascend to Alpine-like meadows in summer, ofter sowing an interim crop between transhumances, and operating within a narrow radius with transit rights strictly bargained for between neighbors. Some of those that live in tents come close to a seminomadic pattern; others that have houses of permanent construction approach a sedentary way of life. Sedentary Berberophone mountaineers cover all the Rif and most of the High Atlas in Morocco, and there are more than two million of them in the mountains of Kabylia in central Algeria. These are both farmers and orchard-keepers who have terraced gardens out of ungrateful soil on the slopes of steep mountains and grow olives, figs, almonds, and fruits. Overpopulation in a small area is the curse here and it has led Rifians traditionally to emigrate for seasonal labor, notably to the European farms of western Algeria; also, it has caused nearly 400,000 Kabyles to cross the Mediterranean to work in France.

Almost unclassifiable is a large bloc of tribes and loosely organized groups found in the coastal plains and the meseta of Morocco south and east of Casablanca and in many parts of eastern Algeria. They might be lumped together in a fifth rural pattern whose exponents are in the process of fixing themselves on the land but are not completely settled. Many of them practice both pastoral activities and agriculture, and some have given themselves over to farming to the extent of living in a fixed site near a source of water; however, they entrust their herds to paid workers who graze them elsewhere. Finally, in a sixth important type, we find the only true village life in North Africa. This occurs in the old, settled areas of northeast Tunisia, in the Cape Bon region, and along the Sahel of the eastern shore. Here, in villages which have well-constructed, whitewashed clay and stone houses with blue-painted doors and elaborate iron grillwork decorating the windows, is the highest degree of rural sophistication in the Maghrib. The wheel, used in Roman times but forgotten elsewhere, survived here in the form of the two-wheeled Sicilian cart, and the villages contain a small but regular market place (not an itinerant weekly market which is common in other regions) with shops, a mosque and perhaps a communal hot bath, and an industrious and peaceable population capable of making and repairing things, the whole surrounded by well-tended gardens and farms. That this is the only occasion in the Maghrib where the competence of the specialized city reached out to be in contact with rural vitality has not been without effect on the whole gamut of social and political development in modern Tunisia.

North African urban life includes almost as many disparate patterns. First of all come the traditional cities of Islamic civilization: Fez and Tunis head the list, then Rabat-Salé, Tetuan, and Tlemcen have the best qualifications. They are old, urbane, and have a proud bourgeoisie which has kept alive the best tradition of eastern Arabo-Islamic culture mixed with a special flavor of Muslim Spain that entitles them to be legitimately called "Moorish" cities. Quite unlike them are the heteroclite port towns of the coast: Algiers, Tangier, Oran, Bougie, and (in another aspect of its personality) Tunis. Like their counterparts everywhere in the Mediterranean, they seldom reflected their own civilization at its best; many of them were cut off from the country behind them and were stations in limbo from which to deal with or prey on the outside world. Different from both these types is the strategic regional center, founded for reasons of economic or political advantage. Such are Marrakesh in Morocco, established by the Almoravids in the eleventh century to command the passes of the High Atlas leading to the Sahara and a natural caravansary for the whole south of the country, and Constantine, endowed with strong natural defenses and favorably placed to control all eastern Algeria. And in the past century completely new towns have been built by European colonials. Most of them, like Casablanca and Kénitra, Bone and Philippeville, faced the sea and were meant to speed the raw materials of the Maghrib to new European markets, but some smaller ones (Sidi bel Abbès, Setif, and Fort National in Algeria, Petitjean and Khouribga in Morocco) were established for reasons of security or to exploit natural resources used by the modern economy.

But even the individual city, taken by itself, has seldom been an integrated, functioning unit. Fez is composed of three separate agglomerations, each a considerable distance from the others. The traditional, commercial city or medina (Fez el Bali) was founded around 800; in the thirteenth century the new, imperial town of Fez Jdid, also walled, was constructed to house the sultan and his court, attendant officials, and garrisons, with the *mellah*, or Jewish quarter, attached; and in the twentieth century under French rule the New Town (Ville Nouvelle) was built a half-mile away to provide for the European administration and settlers. In a city like Casablanca, almost completely a creation of this century, although there is no official segregation of any kind, in practice a strict separation has been enforced by economic causes. Under the protectorate the Europeans lived in their own sections; the Jews and a part of the older Muslim population divided the cramped and unhygienic Old Medina between them; newer Muslim arrivals clustered in the sprawling, lower-class New Medina; and the latest comers, fresh from the country and forming the lowest rung of the urban proletariat, lodged in slum towns called *bidonvilles*, which surrounded the metropolis, as they do all the large cities of North Africa, like a ring of reproach. To say that there was nothing in common between the luxury apartment houses and villas of the European town and the *bidonville* hovels made of mud, flattened jerry-cans, and corrugated iron is a profound understatement; they were two cities which merely happened to share the same name.

In the end the dominant impression that emerges from a study of the raw material from which North Africa has been shaped is that nothing seems to fit; something is askew everywhere. Much of the country is too hot, or it is alternatively too cold at high altitudes; too dry in many parts, or too wet at the wrong times and where it does little good. Certain regions are heavily overpopulated, but others are great desolate wastes. Upon an ancient land with a well-defined indigenous culture and a long-standing traditional civilization has been imposed the vast edifice of modern European life, with the result that at least two—and it could be argued three—separate societies have been living side by side in separate economies for the past fifty to one hundred years. Its original lack of internal unity on the human level has been aggravated by the European intrusion and the heavy internal migration to the cities in recent years. The hostility between sedentary and nomad, which was prevalent from the earliest times, is matched by antagonisms between mountaineer and plainsman, and city and country have traditionally held each other in fear and contempt. With Muslims, Europeans, and Jews dwelling unto themselves in towns scattered across an arid landscape, with the city pent within its walls and having a minimal effect on the world around it, and with the countryside often rent by disputant groups exulting in their splendid anarchy, what has been transmitted to the present generation which must shape the future of

North Africa is a jigsaw of isolated and disjointed groupings whose only common bonds, for the great majority, are the old faith of Islam and the new appetite for the nationalisms of the day. The tasks of the leaders of all three independent states today are many, but the main one is that of putting the pieces together to make modern nations of their lands and citizens of their inhabitants.

II. The Past

THE PUNIC AND ROMAN LEGACIES

North Africa has long been close to the center of the stage of history. Its past dates back three thousand years, which makes it as venerable chronologically as ancient Greece and second only to the Middle East whence came the spark that first brought historical attention to it. This was the establishment, around 1100 B.C., of the first factories and trading posts founded in the Western Mediterranean by seafaring Phoenician merchants. Here was one of the earliest known cases of mercantile empire-building, and it set a pattern for North Africa which was from then on to be the meeting ground of Asian and European currents contesting its soil. Beginning in northeast Tunisia, where Utica and Hippo (now Bizerte) were founded, a chain of settlements—meant for trading rather than colonization—stretched along the coast of North Africa to the Straits of Gibraltar and even beyond to Gades (Cadiz), Tingis (Tangier) and Lixus (Larache).

One of these many stations, probably established shortly before 800 B.C., was Carthage—Qart Hadasht, the "new town" —whose beginnings were as humble as those of its neighbors but which was destined to play a capital role in Mediterranean and, indeed, world history. The site, commanding the passage between the two parts of the Mediterranean, was propitious and Carthage was also favored by the capacities of its business aristocracy, originally emigrants from Tyre in Phoenicia. Until the sixth century it remained a Tyrian colony but it had already begun to colonize on its own, starting in the Balearics. As the Levantine homeland felt the effects of the troubled times in Western Asia, Carthage prospered and expanded and so came into contact with the Greeks, who were also interested in the western Mediterranean. The center of conflict early in the fifth century lay in Sicily, whose western end was held by the Carthaginians while the rest of the island contained Greek settlements. A severe defeat in 480 temporarily set Carthage back in its quest for control of the seas, but it had some more permanent effects on Africa.

It was during this century that Carthage, turning inland for the first time, devoted itself to carving out a modest hinterland as a base for its far-flung maritime exploits. A good part of what is today Tunisia was fully occupied and given over to agriculture; under a Carthaginian oligarchy large estates were competently farmed, the vine and olive were introduced, and the punification of the region introduced to the primitive Berber culture which had preceded it the notion of a stable, although harsh government. Most of all, this part of Berbery was given a head start in the race of history which it has never lost in respect to its neighbors; the homogeneous entity which was sketched out would never wholly lose its identity, and it has become modern Tunisia. But as agriculture was spread and the nomads pushed back to the west and south, the beginnings were laid of a nomadic-sedentary opposition which was constantly to plague North Africa.

With the growth of Roman power in Italy and Sicily in the third century B.C., the weakness of the Carthaginian position as a tyrannical overlord ruling over a distant group of vassals and relying for its armed strength on mercenaries and coercive alliance became clear. The Syracusans under Agathocles terrorized the countryside in 310–308 B.C. after making a surprise landing on the African coast near the capital, and Rome proved a more formidable and determined foe. In the protracted Punic Wars, Rome could count on the loyalty of much of the Italian countryside while Carthage, despite brilliant exploits by Hannibal and other military leaders, failed because it was betrayed in its crucial hour. When the city was finally destroyed in 146 B.C., after a particularly bitter siege, it went to its death unloved and unmourned by those who had been under its yoke.

The Carthaginian heritage in North Africa, however, was far from unimportant. Despite a creeping Hellenization of the metropolis toward the end, it was essentially an oriental state and many of its customs struck root in the area. The long tunic, the skull cap, and the voluminous cloak were Carthaginian dress and persist today; the language, brought from the Levant, was a close cousin of the Arabic that would follow much later—it probably did much to prepare the group for it —and was thus distantly related to the Hamitic tongue spoken by the Berbers. Intermarriage with Numidian nobles from the Berber principalities and confederations nearby helped spread Punic language and culture far beyond the formal boundaries of the city-state. Because of Carthage, most of Tunisia and a part of eastern Algeria were integrated for the first time in the classical Mediterranean world and brought out of the shadows of prehistory.

The Punic era in Berbery came to an end after eight centuries had passed, and the Hellenistic order which followed it lasted about the same length of time. The Romans at first occupied only a small portion of the Tunisian peninsula, not going much farther south than what is today Sfax, and for a long time Punic influence did not diminish, but was rather spread to Berber regions which it had only partially penetrated before, just as much later under French rule Arabic made headway in Berber-speaking regions where it had met with no previous success. But from the reign of Augustus for nearly three centuries orderly Latin life flourished in the easternmost provinces of Africa Proconsularis and Byzacena (extending approximately from Bone to Tripoli). Roman Africa became one of the principal granaries of Italy, Roman towns came into being, fused with or alongside of Punic ones, army veterans and Italian farmers were brought in, and the olive groves, vineyards, oil-pressing factories, and aqueducts and roads all attested to the prosperity of the region. Under the Pax Romana there was security and the lot of the peasant on imperial lands or great private estates was, at the beginning at least, no worse than it had been under the Republic or the Carthaginians. Looking only at these heartland provinces at any time in the first century A.D., one would have concluded that Latin civilization had come to stay.

But to the west, in Numidia (Algeria) and Mauritania (Morocco) the situation was quite different. Punic influence had been much less and independent Berber states of varying size, power, and cohesion, existed. Some of them, like the Numidia of Masinissa, had been active allies of Rome against Carthage, and after 146 B.C. Rome treated them as vassals to be given certain pompous honors, to be let alone but watched from a distance, and to be encouraged to fight each other if any one of them began to grow too strong. This came to pass when the grandnephew of Masinissa, Jugurtha, an outstanding and ambitious chieftain, tried to extend his hegemony to his eastern neighbors; he was finally subdued with the help of a rival prince, Bocchus of Mauritania, who received the western third of Numidia in reward. Jugurtha died in Roman hands in 104 B.C., and is considered by some Algerians of this generation as the first authentic nationalist hero of their country.

Although Caesar made slight changes in the actual frontier by creating the province of Africa Nova out of a part of Numidia, for nearly two hundred years Rome felt little need to annex the rest of Berbery. The step was finally taken by Caligula in 40 A.D., after he had murdered the last vassal ruler of Mauritania, and all North Africa was divided into Roman provinces. West of Algiers, however, there was only a very limited occupation stretching parallel to the coast in a narrow corridor which came out to the Atlantic at Sala (modern Rabat) in Morocco. The mountain regions of Morocco and Algeria were explored occasionally, and cantoned off by the *limes* system of fortified towns and frontier settlements, or by constructing in places a true Chinese wall-type defense, the *fossatum*. Outside the *limes* and the *fossatum*, on the steppes and in the mountains, Berber life went on unchanged and unlatinized, but even inside the cities of Mauritania were few and isolated compared to the flourishing urban life in the Africas and Byzacena, where the population was, although still very largely of Berber-Punic stock as it had been in earlier times, as Romanized in custom as anything outside of Italy.

The golden age of Rome in North Africa lasted until the middle of the third century when here, as elsewhere, external and internal pressures began to converge on the empire. The number of revolts increased sharply after 250 and the Romans withdrew from all Morocco (save the enclave of Mauritania Tingitana, the region around Tangier, which was attached to Spain) after 284, at which date inscriptions and coinage cease in the capital city of Volubilis. Africa did not suffer the depredations which other parts of the empire underwent in the third century, but the Berbers were clearly stirring and ready to take advantage of the contraction of imperial frontiers which was taking place everywhere. Social problems seem to have gradually been exacerbated, and perhaps because of that, or perhaps owing to the Punic preconditioning in matters of religion, with its emphasis on sacrifice, immolation, and emotional ceremonies, we find the remarkable growth of Christianity.

It is certainly safe to say that North Africa was one of the most heavily Christian parts of the world in the third and fourth centuries. The number of martyrs and saints, beginning with Tertullian and Cyprian and culminating with Augustine, is long and distinguished; equally notable is the fervor with which the Christians of Africa accepted martyrdom and death during the persecutions, even though their bishops had not nearly so proud a record during the inquisition of Diocletian at the beginning of the fourth century. To explain the passion that Christianity aroused is not easy, all the more so in view of the way it was later abandoned, but it may well have sprung from a combination of social and psychological factors. On the one hand it represented hope for the rural proletariat which was being increasingly ground down on the large estates, and at the same time it offered itself as a means of opposing the imperial power, and thus foreign domination, to those who still considered themselves Africans. If Christianity was more anti-Roman in a political sense in Berbery than elsewhere it says a good deal about the failure of Latin civilization to take permanent hold there.

The Donatist heresy, which swept through North Africa in the fourth century and nearly won the day, exemplifies many of the peculiarities of North African Christianity. It was not originally a heresy of dogma in any sense, merely a quarrel between bishops, but as it developed it took on interesting local colorations. While it would be going too far to label it a social or nationalist movement, it had these overtones. It made little headway among the educated and the upper classes, and it therefore tended to be anti-Latin; the sense of its being native to North Africa certainly stimulated its adherents; it went to extremes in seeking and welcoming martyrdom, and its literature betrays the emotional stigmata of violent abuse, indifference to reason, and the smug self-righteousness of the social revolutionary. Its tenet that suicide was the equivalent of martyrdom clearly calls up Punic antecedents, and the over-all preoccupation with schism which highlights the period seems to recreate in the domain of religion the political penchants of North African Berbers at all times; the passionate interest shown in the East for doctrinal quarrels was absent here, and in fact we see one of the constants of the North

African personality, that comes out later in Islam in the guise of the veneration of saints, in the tendency to personalize issues and deal with individuals and concrete acts instead of abstract ideas.

In the end most North African Christians returned to the fold. But Donatism was only extirpated by the Vandal invasion beginning in 429 and a parallel heresy, Arianism, which the Vandals brought with them. This incursion can be summarized simply. The invaders had an easy task as they went through the area from west to east; there was almost no resistance from the peasants and the many of Latinized townspeople in the east fled to the relative safety of Italy. But the Vandals, for all their efficient conquest, made less impression on North Africa than any other group which came to its shores.

The Vandals were eliminated in their turn by the Byzantine reconquest in 534 which brought a version of Latin civilization back to the shores of Tunisia for a century in a last, feeble renaissance, but which flickered out with the arrival of the first Arab raiders from the East in 647. They thus remained in Berbery for a century as conquerors at the beginning but as an isolated and unassimilable group in the end. It would appear that by the fifth century Africa was already slipping out of the grasp of the neo-Latin world; the kind of fusion that northern Barbarians could work out with the remnants of Roman life in Gaul and Visigothic Spain was not possible here. Africa was too foreign, and it would be another synthesis of barbarism and civilization which mattered here: the meeting of the Berbers and the oriental civilization of the Arabs, itself in part a legacy of Hellenism transmitted through Damascus and Alexandria.

ISLAM AND THE ARABS

Only fifteen years after the death of Muhammad in 632 the Arab armies made their first reconnaissance raid into the eastern marches of the Maghrib. Impelled by the flame of the new faith of Islam they had already conquered large areas of the Middle East and overrun parts of two great empires, the Byzantine and Sassanian. In 640 they had occupied Egypt and from there they struck out across the Western Desert to arrive at the outskirts of Ifriqiya. The Byzantine forces in the provinces of Africa offered not much more resistance than they had in their first contacts with the Arabs in Asia. Kairouan on the steppes of central Tunisia was founded in 670 as the first permanent Islamic settlement in North Africa and soon afterward 'Uqba ibn Nafi' scouted farther west and perhaps even reached the Atlantic coast of Morocco. But he was ambushed and killed on his return in 683 in southern Algeria and the Arab conquest was set back by the unexpectedly stubborn resistance put up by the Berbers, who retook Kairouan at one point and expelled the invaders from all the territory west of Tripolitania.

In the second and better prepared wave of the conquest, Carthage was taken in 698 and finally the whole of the Maghrib was brought under Arab rule by 710. But this was not done without overcoming further bitter opposition from, among others, a semilegendary female chieftain whose forces in the Aurès Mountains held up the westward advance for some time. As the Arabs gained the upper hand their ranks were swelled by the Berbers converted to Islam and these formed the bulk of the force which crossed the Straits of Gibraltar and invaded Spain. The peninsula was reduced in a campaign lasting less than a decade, and for a time after that intermittent Arab-Berber forays penetrated north of the Pyrenees until a sharp defeat near Poitiers halted them.

Two seeming contradictions have been noted about the conquest of North Africa. Compared to the speed with which the Arabs destroyed great states in the East and the Visigothic Kingdom in Spain, it took a long time—more than half a century—to complete this conquest. But, once resistance had been overcome, Berbery turned its back on its past and attached itself to the religion and civilization of the Orient. Resistance was spotty in the Maghrib; the heavily Latinized areas seem to have given way without much opposition and the Berbers, certainly one of the most robust peoples the Arabs had yet fought, resisted doggedly at certain times and places but were incapable of organizing their defense on a consistent basis. As to the second, the psychological weapons of the Arabs were probably as important as their excellent mobile tactics. They were close to the Berbers in a way of life based on movement, plunder, and pastoral nomadism; close enough to be understood in a way that the Romans never had been, but superior in details of power and because they brought the prestige of a new form of higher religion about which they must have been able to communicate their ardor—which contrasted with the sterile ecclesiasticism of the Byzantines. The Berbers, as we have seen, had been remarkably susceptible to religious conversion on a simple level, and Islam must have appeared to many of them who were sometime Christians as merely a variant of the faith and thus appealed to their tendency to heresy. Moreover, the new arrivals surely smelt of victory, and if to the affinities already existing is added the pull to go along with a winner, to join together under the sign of divine approval and sack Spain, or whatever else was at hand, the speedy conversion can be better imagined.

But life after the conquest was not to be for the Berbers a simple change of masters with booty for all. Early in the eighth century the Umayyad caliphate established a government in Kairouan for all North Africa and Spain. Taxes were heavy, for the material goals of the conquest had not been forgotten in the midst of spiritual zeal, the new overlords were often arrogant—neither Arabs nor Berbers have ever been noted for their tractability—and, here as in the Orient, the conquerors set themselves apart in a clique which refused to admit the newly converted to the equality guaranteed by Islam. It was not surprising therefore that Berber revolts should soon break

out, or that they be placed under the sign of kharijism, a
politico-religious movement originating in the Orient which
stressed the equality of all Muslims and taught that the only
hierarchy among them was that of the intensity of their faith
and the rectitude of their conduct. Beginning in the western
Maghrib in 742, the insurrection reached Kairouan by 776
and threatened Arab control of the entire area. To save something from the wreckage, the 'Abbasid rulers in Bagdad sent
reinforcements and, in a crucial decision, recognized Ifriqiya
as a semi-independent vassal. Thus, from the end of the eighth
century there was never again direct Arab rule in the Maghrib
by the Eastern caliphate. The Aghlabid state in Tunisia was
autonomous, and Algeria and Morocco splintered off and went
their own ways without further interference.

During the ninth and tenth centuries those ways were to
form small, unstable, anarchic Berber states based upon Islam
or one of its heretical manifestations, within which urban life
nourished by immigrants from the Orient and Spain was slowly
born in a few key cities. In Morocco, a shi'a* refugee called
Idris, a direct descendant of 'Ali, the son-in-law of Muhammad.
founded the city of Fez and his family held most of northern
Morocco for the next century, during which time they did
effective work for the propagation of Islam by combating
kharijism, extending religion into the countryside, and, from
the purely local viewpoint, first established in Morocco a
government of sharif-s, descendants of Muhammad, who with
their hereditary spiritual and temporal power have left an
indelible mark on the country.

At this time Algeria was dominated by the kharijite state
of Tihert, founded by a group of Persian immigrants, the
Rostemides. Like the Idrissite state in Morocco, the Rostemide
principality was built on the support given by a native popu-

---

* The shi'a, or partisans, were another politico-religious formation which
claimed that the leadership of the Islamic community devolved through
Ali and was hereditary rather than elective.

lation to a foreign prince or religious figure in the name of Islamic principle, even when that principle, kharijite egalitarianism, might seem to clash with the reality of an Iranian-born dynasty. In other parts of the Maghrib, more remote areas were left on their own to arrive at some form of Islamicization, and many were the peculiar cults which sprang up. The Barghwata of the Atlantic plains of Morocco are a good example: their ten prayers a day, instead of the usual five; their dietary laws forbidding the consumption of chicken; their reserving Thursday rather than Friday as the day of public prayer, and so on, illustrate a primitive confusion of the practice and the meaning of religion, just as the fertility and rainfall rites practiced in northern Morocco by the followers of Hamim, show the difficulties Islam met in areas with a long-settled peasantry— where today the solar (Julian) calendar of the Romans and Berberized Latin words for field, plow, and such are still used.

After its period of kharijism, Algeria was also host to a *shi'a* dynasty. In this case it was the Berbers of Little Kabylia who were the support of a movement which, in a bizarre odyssey, overthrew the Aghlabids in Tunisia, established itself in power there for sixty years, and then departed en masse for Egypt, which they conquered and made the seat of their government, with manifold consequences for the whole Middle East.

In sum, what emerges of lasting importance in the confused history of the three centuries following the conquest is the slow assimilation of Islam by the masses of the Maghrib who were trying to adapt this or that tendency of the religion to the solution of local problems. The formal leadership was almost always external, the causes and slogans were Islamic, but the real issue was the social organization of Berbery and the development of a Maghribi personality.

The eleventh century was marked by two important events. One, the invasion of Arab nomads, has already been mentioned. The other was the establishment of the first of three indigenous empires which, during the next four hundred years, gave classic dimensions to Maghribi history, and started at least two of the three countries of North Africa off on the road to forming something like their modern character. The Almoravid empire was the work of nomads from the western Sahara and Mauritania, Berber-speaking and veiled, just like their Tuareg kinsmen of the Hoggar today. Already Muslims of a dubious sort, they were stirred to a greater conformity and strictness by the preachings of a jurist who had returned from the pilgrimage. He imposed on them for a time a monastic life which gave them their name: *al murabitin,* the people of the *"ribat,"* or fortified monastery. They were driven to break out of the desert by several factors: the growing dryness of the Sahara, the blocking of passes to the north by hostile peoples, and the diversion of caravan routes. Their new-found puritanism also served to convince them that they should bring the truth to heretics like the Barghwata, who were still active in Morocco. In the mid-eleventh century they invaded and conquered Morocco, founded their capital at Marrakesh in 1062, and a generation later were called on by the princes of the city-states of Andalusia, who had inherited the splinters of the Caliphate of Cordova when it fell, to save them from the menacing Christian *reconquista.* The Saharans, ferocious and uncompromising, dressed in simple woolen garments and subsisting on meat, barley, and camels' milk, soon turned out to be more fearsome and alien than the Christians, who were bound to the Muslim Spanish by every tie save religion. The appeal was bitterly regretted when the principalities lost their independence and the brightest century of Muslim Spain was brought to a dismal end: its leaders killed or exiled to Morocco, its books burnt on Almoravid bonfires, and intellectual speculation reduced to a strict orthodoxy.

Eventually the charm and culture of Andalusia conquered its conquerors, so that the barbarian was pacified in two generations and disappeared in three. But the role of the Almoravids was paramount. They were the first dynasty to unify Morocco, and at one time their rule extended as far as Algiers. They forged a physical link between the Maghrib and Muslim Spain which lasted two hundred and fifty years and brought immense benefits to the former and prolonged the life of the latter. Some of the greatest monuments of the Maghrib, the Great Mosque in Tlemcen and much of the Qarawiyin in Fez, are the product of this initial flowering of the joint Hispano-Mauresque civilization. And, on the religious plane, they eliminated heresy for good and installed a strict orthodoxy of the rather severe Malikite school (named after an eighth century *imam* of Medina, Malik ibn Anas), from which North Africa never subsequently deviated.

Their successors, the Almohads (1147–1269), broadened this base, but were very different. With them we sit up and take notice because it is clear that here is something profound and original in the Maghrib, certainly the high point so far of Berber history. The Almohads (*Al muwahhidin*, the "Unitarians," so-called because they insisted strictly upon no association of any kind with the concept of God) were sedentary Berber mountaineers of the High Atlas who, like the Almoravids, were ignited by a religious teacher who had studied in the Orient, itself then engaged in a struggle between the formal edifice constructed by orthodox theologians and a more personal or mystic view of God. Ibn Tumart, the spiritual founder of the Almohad empire, inveighed against the dissoluteness of the times, and condemned wine, music, and the customs of the Almoravids in general. It is true that the latter had lost a good deal of their original zealotry, and one of the most constant patterns in North African history was repeating itself: reform followed by indolence and decadence, in turn succeeded by a new wave of puritanism. Moreover, it might be noted that the Almohad tribes of the High Atlas had the added incentive of looking literally down on nearby Marrakesh from their fastnesses and comparing the lascivious indulgence of the one-time desert nomads, for whom they had no love, with their own pious poverty. The Almoravids seemed ripe for taking, but it required a goodly time to overrun Morocco: from 1130 to 1147. Then, in 1152, they undertook the conquest of all the Maghrib which was completed eight years later. In Spain, the Almohads inherited much of the territory held by the Almoravids and, although Christian pressure was being stepped up, the Moroccans gained at Alarcos in 1195 the last major Muslim success in the long struggle for the peninsula.

From almost every aspect the Almohad state contributed something of lasting importance to the Maghrib. Politically it unified North Africa under a single home rule from Agadir to Tripoli for the only time in its history. There was an aura of genuine power about the Almohads, and when 'Abdelmumin took the title of caliph he was truly the equal of any other ruler in Islam or Christendom. The empire was the culmination of Berber political capabilities and the administration was marked by local habits such as the egalitarian councils which, arising from Berber custom, became a fixture of the state. A cadastral survey was made and uniform taxes applied to all productive lands. A tribal hierarchy was set up, under the provisions of which some were enlisted in the armies fighting in Spain, others were assigned to police the homeland, and, in a fatal move, invader Hilalian tribes were invited from Ifriqiya to the central and western Maghrib and given land and garrison functions. There was security under the Almohads, and it was one of those rare eras when an uprotected individual could journey from end to end of the Maghrib in safety. In Andalusia they were present at the decisive moments of the reconquest and although they could not stem the tide in the end, their victory at Alarcos was helpful in postponing the inevitable. After the Muslim defeat at Las Navas de Tolosa in 1212, all the Guadalquivir Valley including Cordova and Seville fell into enemy hands, leaving only the besieged mountain kingdom of Granada to survive on sufferance for two hundred more years.

In religion they continued the orthodoxy of their predecessors; their unitarianism with its vituperation of the "polytheists" did not remove them from the domain of the *sunna*. They also tolerated the first outcropping of Moroccan mystics, the Sufists who, like their predecessors in Spain and the East, were trying to soften the rigors of official Islam with a more humanistic understanding. But at the same time, with them we see a new tone of xenophobia and intolerance creep into the Maghrib, in the forced conversion of Jews, illegal by Koranic standards, and the requirement that they wear distinctive clothing. Under Almohad rule literature and philosophy did well; Ibn Tofail and Ibn Rushd (Averroes) worked successfully if not always happily at the court of Abu Ya'qub Yusuf. But it is in the arts above all else that the Almohads left their imprint. They were great builders and their work, unlike that of the Andalusian contractors of the Almoravids, was indigenous, genuine, and of classic simplicity. Each of their three capitals—Marrakesh, Rabat, and Seville—was endowed with a great mosque and minarets, two of which are the outstanding structures of the age: the Kutubiya in Marrakesh and the Giralda in Seville, and the monumental gates of Rabat testify that the Almohads understood their place in history. So, too, do later generations, for it was not without meaning that Muhammed V of Morocco, on the first Friday after his return to the country from exile in 1955, held services in the ruins of the Hassan Tower in Rabat, the third of the minarets which sum up the rude sense of power and grandeur which the Almohads conveyed as their legacy to modern Morocco.

Thanks to the Almohads, at the end of the thirteenth century Morocco was an accomplished fact, established roughly within the limits of its present frontiers. The Beni Merin, or Merinids, who followed them, made their own contribution to the enriching of this entity by the brilliant urban life which they patronized. The Almoravids had brought the harshness of the desert, the Almohads had offered the peasant sturdiness of the mountain, and to this the Merinids added the civility of the city. The Merinids mean Fez, and Fez in the fourteenth century was the equal of any town in the world. A concentrated burst of building lavished on its mosques and markets, schools, hospices, elegant private houses, and courtyard gardens, and within its walls dwelt a population of refinement and taste, living the best life afforded by western Islam.

In Spain the Merinids had continued the hopeless defense of Muslim Spain which was shrinking with each century, but relations between the two parties had changed. Morocco was no longer the aggressive intruder; Fez was the sister city of Granada and citizens passed back and forth without hindrance. At home, the Merinid state made sporadic efforts to dominate the rest of the Maghrib but it could not equal the Almohads, although Algeria was ravaged several times and Merinid armies reached the edge of Hafsid Tunisia on one occasion. Merinid governmental organization was simpler and less efficient than that of the Almohads, but they were not completely to blame. The western Maghrib was no longer the simple Berber stronghold of yore; the introduction of Arab tribes had already begun to have its effects in the impoverishment of the plains and a steady withdrawal of sedentary life to less exposed regions. From around 1400 the whole area began to exhibit an imbalance between population and natural resource areas: peasant and village life were confined mainly to the less productive mountain sectors and the fertile plains were left sparsely inhabited and given to the careless mercy of the nomad. At the end of the Merinid epoch also, the city and country were splitting from each other and the ossification of the former had started. Fez at the time contained everything that it had when, withered and half forgotten, it was opened to the outside world at the beginning of the twentieth century. A Moroccan proverb says, "After the Beni Merin there was nothing," and, while this is a simplification of history, a long period of formative vigor certainly came to an end with them and with the first approach of a resurgent Europe when the Portuguese occupied Ceuta in 1415.

During much of the same time that Morocco was being

hammered out of these diverse elements, the future of Tunisia was being shaped by a branch of the Almohad dynasty founded by one of their lieutenants. These were the Hafsids who were installed in Tunis during the brief period of North African unity at the beginning of the thirteenth century. Tunisia had suffered first and most heavily from the Hilalian invasions and it was caught in a cross fire between the nomads on one side and the attacks from Normans and Italians by sea on another. Thus it welcomed the Almohads who soon granted a large degree of autonomy to their governors in Tunis. Later the Hafsids became independent in fact and constituted a dynasty of their own which ruled Tunisia for nearly three centuries.

The Hafsids have the air of being the first really national dynasty in Tunisia, and their reign is a period when the country becomes recognizable as the forerunner of Tunisia today. They reconstituted the national territory, and a shade more, from Constantine to Tripoli. The first trickle of refugees appeared from Muslim Spain, adding much to the diversified culture of Tunisia, and Jews arrived from the Balearics and Catalonia. A cosmopolitan atmosphere in the capital was fed by the mingling of traders from all corners of the Mediterranean and the typically Tunisian village life blossomed along the coast. The country was oriented toward the sea and the society open. It made no great or original contribution to Mediterranean thought or art—although Ibn Khaldun, perhaps the greatest intellectual of the Arab Middle Ages, was born and lived some time there—but it was a cultivated, tolerant, multiracial society of mercantile burghers in the capital and hard-working peasants in the clusters of villages in the Sahel. The worst problem of Hafsid Tunisia was how to maintain a balance between the two threats that hung over its prosperity: one from the restless interior, the other from the maritime states across the sea. The nomads were occasionally used as auxiliary troops to discipline and pacify the countryside, but usually they were more of a nuisance than a help and their existence in more than half the country was a constant source of insecurity. At the end of the Hafsid rule, the external menace proved greater and Tunisia was caught up in the sixteenth century in the battles of Christian Europe and the Ottoman Empire. But the solid sense of self which the country had developed under the Hafsids, enabled it to withstand the Turkish occupation and treat it in the end as an embellishment to be assimilated into the national patrimony, quite unlike what happened in Algeria.

By 1500 things had changed greatly. The reconquest of Spain was complete and the situation was reversed. The Maghrib was no longer in a position to intervene in the peninsula; on the contrary, it was the Iberian powers who were now on the march and the beginnings of modern history in North Africa were ushered in by their expansionist assaults on the coastal cities of the region. Because the attackers and the responses were different, the history of Morocco and that of Algeria and Tunisia now diverged for several hundred years, but for all three countries the results were far-reaching.

The Portuguese had tried to get a foothold in Morocco as early as 1415. For a century and a half afterward they continued their attacks, at the beginning in the north where they were unable to keep anything more than a few ports. Later in the south they had more success, indirectly controlled large amounts of territory, and even threatened the city of Marrakesh. Morocco had internal difficulties and a succession of weak governments was powerless to oppose the Portuguese thrusts. But, beginning late in the fifteenth century, resistance crystallized around religious leaders, Marabouts, who went about the country calling on the people to defend their religion and their homes. The principal purpose of the complex maraboutic movement in Morocco (and to a lesser extent elsewhere in North Africa) was to make Islam accessible to the masses and the countryside, and it had started as a reaction to the moribund schools of theology patronized by the learned in the cities. It functioned, however, especially in its heyday from about 1450 to 1650, as a vast rural revivalist cause: simple, emotional, popular, and uniting faith with the new stirrings of patriotic sentiment in a country under fire from the infidel. After the Marabouts had sparked resistance, the burden passed later to two families of *sharif*-s, whose descent from Muhammad made them likely candidates for a religio-national renaissance. The first of these, the Sa'adi *sharif*-s, who had emigrated a short time before from Arabia (but whose credentials, unlike those of their successors, are somewhat doubtful), gained power in the mid-sixteenth century. They ended the most serious Portuguese invasion threat in 1578 and restored Moroccan self-esteem if not territorial integrity; they also prevented the Turks in Algeria from adding Morocco to their conquests and thus preserved the country as the only Arab area fully outside the Ottoman sphere of influence. Since then, Morocco has been constantly ruled by a sharifian family—the present family of 'Alawi *sharif*-s has been on the throne for three hundred years. The Berber tendency toward anthropomorphism which appeared in early Christianity in North Africa seems to have reappeared here in the adoration of Marabouts as saints and the veneration of the *sharif*-s which is still strong today among many humble country folk. The depth of this feeling is unusual by normal Islamic standards but its importance in modern political developments in Morocco can hardly be overemphasized.

Although busy fending off Christian attacks from the north, Sa'adi Morocco found time to engage in a bit of imperialism on its own in black Africa. Toward the end of the sixteenth century its armies crossed the Sahara to the Niger and Timbuctoo; they conquered much of the Sudan and held it for most of the next century. The goal then was gold but the re sults today are the substantial numbers of blacks introduced into the country as slaves and soldiers, and Moroccan claims to parts of the Algerian Sahara and all of independent Mauritania. Meanwhile, after its victory at the Battle of Three Kings in 1578, Morocco was able to hold its own vis-à-vis the European threat. Trade with Europe, particularly England and the Netherlands as Protestant enemies of Spain, was active, and Morocco was a factor in the power struggle between Elizabethan England and Philip II, as well as between Spain and the Ottoman Empire. The Moriscos, dispossessed from Spain, brought with them a passion for revenge and a knowledge of boat handling; the pirates of Salé and Tetuán were as much a scourge as their more famous counterparts in Algiers and farther east.

Over a period of time, however, Morocco felt the effects of being shut off from the outside world by the barrier of the Turkish occupation of Algeria and the resolutely hostile Iberian Peninsula in the north. From the end of the seventeenth century, after a last effort had cleared most foreign enclaves from its shores (except Mazagan, Ceuta, and Melilla), stagnation set in and a taciturn isolation was the dominant note of the age. There were the constant skirmishes with Spain, which had now replaced Portugal as the difficult neighbor, but it, too, was in decline and the tides of history were flowing elsewhere. Contact with the Arab Orient, itself vegetating under Turkish rule, was reduced to a handful of travelers. For nearly two centuries no new ideas or pressures impinged on Morocco until it was roused from its torpor by the French move into Algeria. Then the inevitable conflicts began between a modern European power which wanted to establish a fixed frontier and see it respected—except when it coveted more territory—and a traditional religious state which gave shelter and aid to Muslims in Algeria fighting the Christian invaders. They ended in a short war in 1844, marked by the shelling of some coastal cities and a border adjustment. Imperceptibly and inexorably, after 1830 Morocco found itself drawn into the whirlpool of European colonial history, and by 1860 it was engaged in a full-scale war with Spain of a kind it did not understand.

In the other two states of the Maghrib, the Spanish were the protagonists. They had occupied Mers el Kebir, Oran, Bougie, and Tripoli by 1510 and made other ports pay tribute. The city of Algiers turned then to some freebooting Turkish sailors for help in ousting the Christians from a fortress they had installed on a small island just off the harbor. A pair of brothers, the Barbarossas, as they are known to history, answered the appeal, installed themselves as masters of Algiers, and soon tried to take the whole area as far west as Tlemcen. The elder, 'Aruj, died and the enterprise seemed in danger of failing, whereupon the younger brother, Khaireddin, offered to become a vassal of the Ottoman state. For seventy years until 1587, Algiers was ruled in the name of the sultan by his agents, the *beylerbey*-s; after that date separate regencies were created for Algiers, Tunis, and Tripoli.

Of the three, Algiers was the most complex and ephemeral, and the one which soon seized the imagination of Europe as a fearsome and vicious enemy. Some of this reputation was undeserved, for the piracy of the seventeenth century was little more or less than undeclared war as waged between most European states at the time. Western sources tend to be biased and see only the horrors of the slave markets in the city, or conversely exaggerate the power of the corsairs in the customary romantic prose of the day. Plunder and the sale of Christian captives were certainly profitable, but they were not the only occupations; commerce flourished, especially during the halcyon age of the city in the seventeenth century. After that, there was a steady decline in the fortunes of Algiers for two reasons: the growing supremacy of European arms at sea from the mid-eighteenth century and the fact that Algiers had no roots in its own country, from which it was spiritually and physically cut off; its walls and forts were as well prepared to defend it from attack by land or sea.

Turkish rule never took in the country. Garrisons were stationed in the towns but in many places the Turks had no authority or power and were content simply to draw a salary and let a local administration take its course; in other cases the militia had to fight its way across country to reach its post. And outside the towns anarchy and internecine warfare prevailed more often than not. In Algiers itself the rulers were seldom secure; at one point rivalries between the janissaries and the sea captains led the authorities in desperation to consider using Kabyle mountaineers as their defense force. In the late seventeenth century the power of the militia was weakened and the corsairs succeeded in putting one of their own men in power as *dey,* an office elective in theory but around which intrigue and assassination ceaselessly revolved.

But the history of the city-state of Algiers, while colorful and fascinating, is not the history of Algeria at the time, and what went on in the capital (if the word can be used) had almost no effect on the relatively changeless course of life in many of the smaller towns and, especially, in the Arabo-Berber countryside. The main connection between Algiers and the country really lies in the eventual retaliation taken by Europe, through the agency of France. Whether justified or not, and there is a whole school which holds that piracy—which was well in the grave by 1830—was only a pretext for a colonial adventure, the existence and reputation of Algiers, established firmly in the European mind as a sordid city deserving destruction, did bring about a chain of events which led to the end of traditional life in the central Maghrib, and eventually all North Africa, even for the isolated nomad out on the steppes who had never heard of pirate ships or *dey*-s or insulted French consuls.

In Tunis, which also was placed under Ottoman stewardship after the Turks had beaten off a Spanish attempt to hold the coast, the design was similar but the end product different. In part this is imputable to the more docile Tunisian temperament which never took to so aggressive a policy as that practiced by Algiers, and in part to the homogeneity of the country and its solid traditions, which meant that the capital was not so isolated from its surroundings and that there was a sizable body of literate notables who could not be ignored by the Turkish governing group. Thus, when an officer of the garrison seized power and a hereditary dynasty was proclaimed in 1705 by Husain Bey, it was expressly sanctioned by an assembly of the local elite, and the process of Tunisifying the foreign power holders was under way. The Husainid Regency showed from then on reasonable internal stability and in foreign policy it tried to steer a middle course which would allow it to stay independent of Constantinople without becoming a victim of European states stronger than itself. Commercial agreements and treaties were negotiated with the powers and respectability obtained. Significantly, in 1819 Tunis carefully heeded the demand of the Congress of Aix-la-Chapelle that it outlaw piracy. Algiers did not, and its defiant attitude had more than a little to do with its demise. In the end it was this spirit which doomed Algiers in the fullest sense. History can move quickly and ruthlessly at times, and it had long since passed the corsair city-states by. Algiers was an anachronism after the Napoleonic Wars—the bombardment of the city by Exmouth and his squadron in 1816 was a portent of the future —but, ostrich-like, it refused to see what was happening in the Mediterranean and how different the nineteenth century was going to be.

THE COLONIAL PERIOD

Few subjects in politics or history have aroused such passion as the conquest and colonization of Algeria. For more than a century it was hailed and defended by a whole official school of French historians and literary figures as a generous and disinterested work of civilization. Largely in reaction to such claims, an antithetical viewpoint was presented by two sources. One was that of Arab nationalist writers, beginning in Algeria itself with Tewfiq al Madani in 1932, who justified the blossoming nationalist feelings by all means, including an over-glorification of the past and an indictment of the colonial period as responsible for all ills. The other was that of the anti-official school of writers in Western languages, many of whose adherents were of the French left; their focus lay in the doctrinaire belief that only certain aspects of Western socioeconomic patterns, such as the collusion of monopoly capital and military imperialism, were the cause of the unhappy state of colonial areas. In between, there has been a handful of moderate analyses of the social problems of Algeria by sincere observers who have proved in deed as well as word their devotion to objectivity and the quest for a solution of a complex question.

Gradually political passion is cooling into historical detachment but it is still early; we cannot begin to foresee, for example, what the over-all results of a hundred and thirty years of European presence will finally be or whether the material development of Algeria will outweigh in the end the social breakdown and the cumulative national losses of the revolution. At best, certain guesses can be made. But, in looking back, if there is some validity in most approaches to recent history in this country, it is also true that most writings have shown an excessive amount of prejudice and pride (if only because they have been written overwhelmingly by French and Algerians, who only rarely have been able to divorce themselves from the temptations of cultural nationalism, however unconscious). It is not necessary to romanticize one era or culture in order to denigrate another by comparison. The Regency of Algiers had many seamy sides, and the conquest was often sordid and, on occasion, of ghastly brutality. Likewise, the revolution that broke out in 1954 as a long-term but direct consequence was a blood-soaked affair and the attempted repression of it often merciless. The chain of horror and hate may seem endless in Algeria, but if there is any place in history to remind ourselves that we are all sinners, this is it.

The first question about the conquest is: Why did it take place at all. The answer to that is not so simple as that offered to French children in the *Nouvelle histoire de France* (Bernard and Redon):

In Algiers there ruled a barely independent Turkish chief called the dey. His name was Hussein and he had an irritable character. One day during a discussion he struck the consul of France on the arm with a fan. An expedition against Algiers became necessary . . .

There were other threads, too: the debt owed by France since the time of the Directory which it refused to pay without further concessions from the Regency; French claims to a privileged bastion on the coast in eastern Algeria; and the need for a shaky regime, which was to be overthrown anyway a few months after the conquest, to find a stirring and patriotic external diversion. Revenge for the past effrontery of Algiers, a vague desire for prestige, and ill-defined sentiments stirred by the post-Napoleonic imperialism also played their part. This was the first step in a great revival of French colonial ventures after the eighteenth century collapse in Canada and India, and the conquest of Algeria led eventually to the depths of black Africa, the Valley of Mexico with Maximilian, and the shores of the Pacific. Actually the Algerian affair is a suggestion of the blindness of history, for the economic and strategic motivations, which fully existed in the later cases of Tunisia and Morocco, were almost nil, and there is little evidence to show premeditation for a thorough-going annexation of all Algeria. Not only blindness but madness, for ultimately this was an event which makes one suspect that the theory of the psychotic drive of Western civilization, driven by internal forces of constructive-destructive energy—from the empire-building of Rome, through religious and colonial wars and racial intolerance to nuclear threats—has some basis.

The expedition to Algiers was as successful as the conquest of the country was difficult. The troops left Toulon with fanfare and enthusiasm on May 25, 1830; they landed June 14 and on July 5 the capital surrendered. But it took forty more years before the whole of Algeria was in hand. The French were surprised by the ease of their initial victory and did not know what to do after it. They had come with no long-range plans, they had no knowledge of the country, and it was several years before they decided to stay in force. Even then a policy of limited occupation of coastal enclaves was adopted, and treaties were signed guaranteeing the autonomy of other areas. The Treaty of Tafna in 1837 limited French holdings to Oran, Mostaganem, Arzew, and Algiers with the Mitidja plain around it. This policy changed under pressure from the first settlers, who demanded more security, and the reaction of the Arabo-Berber countryside as it saw with prescience that this was not going to be a temporary occupation and that, unlike the fortresses and footholds of the Europeans in the Middle Ages, here was a new and deadly threat to their liberty, land, and religion.

Recognition of this was signaled in the raid on the Mitidja settlements in 1839 by a young nationalist, 'Abdelqader, who came from a marabout family in western Algeria and had rallied tribal resistance around Islam, the one sure pillar which united everyone in the land. His struggle was daring but hopeless when the full weight of French power, supplemented by new, mobile tactics, was brought to bear. Much of the conquest of Algeria can be best understood in terms of settler-Indian conflict in the American west: there is the same story of treaties made and broken, the frontier pushed continually back; outposts built to protect the homesteaders; friendlies and hostiles, and sporadic surprise raids of frustration and vengeance by the natives as they are gradually tracked down and cornered. As 'Abdelqader went inexorably to defeat, the battle was continued by religious brotherhoods like the Darqawa, but after enormous bloodshed all resistance was broken by 1847, except in the mountains of Kabylia. There a stubborn opposition was overcome by scorched earth raids on livestock, crops, and villages, against which a sedentary population was less able to defend itself. Kabylia was officially considered under control by 1857, but there were revolts in 1864 and, after a serious famine, a general uprising in 1871. When that was put down, the entire country lay prostrate and the Muslim population, estimated at about three million in 1830 and officially listed in the census of 1861 as 2,732,000, had been reduced to 2,125,000. Algeria was pacified but its population had been drawn and literally quartered.

As the Algerians lost their freedom they also lost their land. At first colonization was sporadic, and a hectic speculation was the keynote of the first years; some tracts were sold long before they were conquered. But by 1833 habus land (religious property given in unbreakable permanent trust) had been confiscated and some private holdings to which no valid title could be shown were taken. In that first decade many of the officers of the Army of Africa installed themselves in pleasant estates in the Mitidja and with the arrival of General Bugeaud in 1841 official colonization got under way. The 1840's were decisive: army veterans were offered land; in 1843 the first vineyard was founded at Staoueli and the principal crop of the new Algeria began to be cultivated. *Arrêtés* in 1844 and 1846 created state domains from lands whose proprietors could not justify previous title, and the theory of the cantonment of the tribes in selected areas was developed. An ordinance in 1845 prescribed confiscation in case of "hostility to the French presence." (This was used after 1871 against the Kabyles.) The two principal kinds of land holdings under Muslim law are *mulk*, or private holdings, and *'arsh* lands, which are undivided communal or tribal property. In 1845 a first law dividing communally held lands was promulgated, to be consecrated in the Senatus-Consultus of 1863, when tribes were divided into *douar-s* (villages) and property personalized, thus destroying chiefly authority and tribal cohesion and, most importantly, facilitating the sale of land by individuals. Meanwhile, propaganda for official colonization was begun; settlers were offered from four to twelve hectares, with free transportation, seed, and livestock, and the army was used to build roads and found villages. In 1846, 46,000 arrived and 25,000 left, for it was a hard country, and so by 1851 measures had become liberalized: there was no longer need for prospective settlers to justify minimum resources, the natural products of Algeria were allowed entry into France without duty, and colonization by private enterprise was given all encouragement. There were also the deportations of criminals and the shipment of some orphans to the colony, and in 1851 152,300 Europeans were resident.

Under the Second Empire the pattern changed somewhat. By one of those truly French paradoxes, this empire was more understanding toward Muslim Algeria than the republics which preceded and followed it. Napoleon III saw the Arabs primarily as noble warriors in his service, the country as an "Arab kingdom," and himself as their emperor-chief. By temperament, he looked down on the colons and they feared him and his predilection for the natives. This paternalism did not prevent the government from confiscating 200,000 hectares of forest and 60,000 hectares of tribal lands, in favor of private companies which made loans to the state. But Napoleon's policy was vacillating and unproductive, for he tried to believe to the end that there was no incompatibility between continuing colonization and the welfare of his Arab protégés.

When the Second Empire came apart in the Franco-Prussian war, Algiers exulted. In the new era the colons ejected its representatives and 1870 became the year that sealed their triumph. They got political rights and Algeria was given the form it would keep with minor modifications until the revolution. The country was divided into three departments, the whole presided over by a governor-general, and the prefects in each department were assisted by a general council whose members were elected only by local French citizens. After 1871 land came into European hands at a faster pace; in the decade from 1871–1880 some 400,000 hectares were acquired. The phylloxera blight in France brought vintners and wine growing was greatly extended. The tendency was toward ever greater concentration, absentee ownership, and commercial exploitation. By 1900 nearly 2,000,000 hectares were privately owned by Europeans, and in 1940 this reached more than 3,000,000 hectares, representing about 23 per cent of the arable area and almost 4 per cent of all land actually farmed.

From the beginning the political and personal status of Algerian Muslims caused problems. For a while the Arab tribes were allowed to govern themselves, with chiefs selected and approved by officers of the *Bureaux Arabes*. These often held the reins with a light and humane touch; many were or became specialists in the language and culture and they were the forerunners of the system introduced later in Morocco, in which country they were known as the Affaires Idigènes officers. But in Algeria there was constant and heavy pressure by the settlers to remove the tribes from military control, extend the territory under civil authority, and put the natives under administrators who would be more susceptible to settler influence. During the first decades there was open talk of terror as an instrument of policy and, indeed, it was practiced on a large scale. Then in 1848 Algeria was declared part of France in the first move toward assimilation, and departments were constituted. The Senatus-Consultus of 1865 made Algerians legally French subjects, but not citizens unless they renounced their religious status, that is, the Koranic law to which they adhered. Jews, on the other hand, were made full French citizens in 1870 by decree. Perhaps the most effective device for governing the Muslim population was the *Code de l'Indigénat*, which was in effect from 1881 to 1944, with some modifications in 1914 and after. Among the twenty-one infractions listed in the revised code of 1890 are found such crimes as: speaking against France and the government; delay in paying taxes; keeping stray animals more than twenty-four hours; giving shelter to any stranger without permission; leaving the commune without notice; neglecting to have a travel permit visaed wherever one stops for more than twenty-four hours; the gathering without permission of more than twenty persons on certain festive occasions; opening any educational or religious institution without permission; and the unauthorized exercise of the profession of elementary teaching. The Indigénat provided for punishments which were applicable only to Muslims, among them collective fines, confiscation, and administrative internment, and summary judgments made by the administrative officers of the mixed commune in which the infraction was committed were without appeal.

After 1871 the doctrine of the Third Republic was a return to the theme of the assimilation of Algeria, but not all Algerians. For some time the administration was directly attached to relevant ministries at home, but there were disadvantages in this from the viewpoint of efficiency, and while the system assuaged the fears of the Europeans in one sense, it did not meet their requirements for sufficient local control in others. The upshot was the reorganization of Algeria, over several years, beginning in 1896, into a unique territory in which the settlers finally had their cake and ate it. The three departments of the north, from which the military territories in the Sahara were excluded, were under a governor-general appointed from Paris and assisted by directors who were in fact his ministers. This ensemble dealt with all matters except education and justice, which were directly attached to the home ministries, and the governor-general had broad powers to legislate by decree and to apply or withhold metropolitan legislation by administrative decision. Algeria had its own budget, prepared by the administration and voted by the Financial Delegations, a tripartite assembly in which the Europeans had a two-thirds majority. With their ability to withhold consent for the budget, the settlers had the key to power. In the departmental organization, the prefects and their assistants were attached to the Ministry of the Interior in Paris, but were at the same time responsible to the governor-general as the supreme authority in the country. Local subdivisions consisted of several hundred full communes, equivalent to their namesakes in France, wherever Europeans were numerous enough; elsewhere mixed communes were set up which were agglomerations of Muslims, with a sprinkling of Europeans in most cases, under a French administrator possessing the almost unlimited power of the Indigénat and assisted by appointed Muslim functionaries.

In practice this administration worked somewhat differently. The powers of the governor-general were limited by the complexities of the bureaucracy, largely staffed at medium echelons by local Europeans. A weak governor-general might not fully control his own subordinates. Moreover, the settlers had important connections in Paris, both in the business world and in Parliament, where they had representation. High officials were rotated with fairly fixed tours of duty and if they displeased the settler power group or resisted their demands they could be bypassed, boycotted, and harassed into a transfer. So the Algerian administrative machine became gradually a closed corporation, with its own prerogatives, its own hidden workings, and its methods for resisting pressure. The efficiency of this machine could be seen as late as 1961–1962 when the government in Paris was unable *in extremis* to insure that its orders would be carried out by the civil service in Algeria.

Tunisia went unscathed in 1830; the Bey even sent a propitious note of congratulations to the new occupants of Algeria. But it could not maintain its independence indefinitely once French power was camped on its western frontier, and its weakness excited the ambitions of several European powers. However, when its turn came in 1881, the respite of half a century proved to have been useful, for it did not suffer the same fate of utter annihilation which had befallen Algiers. The world had become subtler during this period, and Tunisia had changed, too. International politics was forced to pay lip service to ideas of civilization and progress and to the claim of the West that its mission was to foster these goals among the benighted. Moreover, Tunisia had been generally recognized as a functioning state earlier in the century, and it was impossible at this late date to deny it that quality. In the meantime, it had made remarkable efforts to modernize itself in the Western image. Under Ahmed Bey (1837–1855) slavery was abolished and most religious restrictions removed from non-Muslims; foresightedly but without success the sovereign began to form a regular army, tried to establish a polytechnic institute and officers' schools, and to build a fleet and make a new naval port for it near Tunis. His successor granted an embryonic constitution, a covenant under which Tunisia was governed for seven years beginning in 1857 but which was suspended partly owing to the pressure of foreign consuls. The new ruler took further steps toward Europeanization: roads, sewers, waterworks, and a telegraph service were created, and foreigners were granted property rights. Many of these measures were laudable and even necessary, but most were unpopular with the masses because they were upsetting, they were of benefit to foreigners primarily, and they were costly. Taxes had to be raised, there were revolts, and the increases were canceled. Then loans had to be floated from abroad to pay for the improvements and when 12 per cent interest payments could not be kept paid up, the creditor nations in the West, who demanded modernization as one of the proofs that a country had a level of civilization sufficient to be allowed to exist as an independent member of the family of nations, were given an opportunity to foreclose. Unsound finances were a good part of the Tunisian dilemma in the 1870's; last ditch efforts at fiscal reform were made by an outstanding minister, but at the Congress of Berlin France was given a free hand in Tunisia by England and Germany; it was eager to forestall suspected Italian designs on the country. It did not take long to arrange a border incident—in this case the incursion of some Khoumir tribes from northwest Tunisia into Algeria—in retaliation for which French troops quickly penetrated and occupied the country, establishing a protectorate which lasted for seventy-five years.

Under the terms of the Treaty of Kassar Said, Tunisia agreed to a "voluntary" and "temporary" limitation of its external sovereignty, the period to be indefinite. France assumed this sovereignty in the person of its chief official in the country, the Resident-General, who became Foreign Minister of the Bey. Two years later, in 1883, the abandonment of sovereignty was completed by another treaty by which Tunisian internal authority was put under French supervision and control, and the Bey agreed to accept French suggestions for whatever reforms might be considered desirable or necessary in the functioning of the state.

Through this supple formula, which was subsequently applied and perfected in Morocco, two parallel administrations existed in Tunisia all during the protectorate period, although the Tunisian one was reduced at most times to a shadow life: at the beginning there were only two ministers on the Tunisian side. Newly established government departments known as "*directions*" came into being, staffable in theory by French or Tunisian nationals, but run on European lines by Europeans and, after a large settler group was present in the country, largely for Europeans. The idea of parallelism and supervision (*contrôle*) was carried out at the level of local administration as well. The traditional local executive, the *qaid*, was retained but his activities were overseen and checked on by civil supervisors (*contrôleurs civils*) from 1884. At first the controleurs limited themselves to observation, comment, and approval, but, in the image of the bureaus in Tunis they gradually usurped the prestige of the Tunisian officials—having, as they did, control of the police and the power to use troops if necessary—and finally their functions. The *qaid*-s had been originally appointed by the Bey but later on they were reorganized and put into the civil service with a salary. The same process took place with the tribal *shaikh*-s, who had never been government officials but were representatives of their tribes to the administration. They were made civil servants in 1905, appointed by the *qaid* with the approval of the controleur, and with this move effective French authority was extended to the tribes over the head of the Bey or any intervening Tunisian officials.

But, as can be seen from this most summary description, the concept and functioning of the protectorate were utterly different from the spirit of the conquest of Algeria. In other ways, too, Tunisia reflects the change which had come over the spirit of colonialism at this later date. It can be argued from a distant vantage point that the parallel administrative system of the protectorate laid the groundwork for an efficient, modern state (and modern Tunisia gets high marks on this score compared to many of its fellows) and that the European-organized administration would be, and indeed was finally, infiltrated by Tunisians beginning in the 1920's, while the Algerian system offered not even a ray of ultimate hope to the native population right up to the time of the 1954 revolution, which was made inevitable by desperation.

Colonization patterns differed in Tunisia, too. Even before 1881 there were Europeans resident and the sale of land to large companies had begun; thus the Société Marseillaise took over the great Enfida estate (60,000 hectares), and 150,000 hectares were held by four large companies. Commercial colonization, which was also making headway in Algeria at that time, was impersonally stern but the emotional tone which European settlement took on right from the beginning in Tunisia was one of no-nonsense business which was the contrary of the personal and savage nature of early Algerian days.

Of course, the fact that there was only slight armed resistance to the occupation in Tunisia also contributed to this difference. In innovations such as the immatriculation beginning in 1885 of land under a system modeled on the Australian Torrens Act, the factor of emulation was important: slowly, Tunisians saw the value of having their holdings inscribed on the register. Likewise, *habus* lands, which had been confiscated in Algeria, were respected, but a way to put them into productive use was found through the device of renting them in perpetuity, the so-called *enzel* right; and after 1905 the sale of the *enzel* right itself was authorized. All this is not to understate the disruption of rural life caused in Tunisia by colonization. By 1913, 550,000 hectares of the best land, about one-sixth of the cultivated surface, were in European hands and the pauperization of many Tunisian rural groups was well under way.

The European elements proved to be nearly as much of a political problem in Tunisia as they had been in Algeria. By 1921, forty years after the establishment of the protectorate, they numbered 156,000 in a population just over 2,000,000, nearly 8 per cent of the total. For a long time the French and Italian components of this group did not blend, but gradually the encouragement of French immigration and the effect of the naturalization laws redressed an imbalance which had at the start much distressed Paris. As the community grew, it became conscious of its economic supremacy and its opportunities for applying political pressure. Some of the settlers had come from Algeria and were used to more ruthless methods of dealing with the natives, others from the metropole insisted on the rights they had known at home. Here they failed, for they never did get full rights as Frenchmen although they had official representatives in Paris (not to speak of even more powerful private lobbyists), and they never won the long battle they waged for cosovereignty with Tunisian nationals in Tunisia. But they were given a series of sops, such as participation in municipal councils and the elected advisory Grand

Council which gave advice on local financial and economic questions, something which violated the letter of the protectorate and rankled Tunisian nationalist feelings. But whereas in Algeria the Europeans had been able to suppress any possibility of Muslim evolution, the colons in Tunisia could hinder the emancipation movement and at the end harass the French authorities when they were sincerely promoting reforms, but no more. Yet they remained at all times a threat to the unity of the country and one of the main factors in the early development of a strong, counterbalancing Tunisian nationalism.

The turn of Morocco came next, but it was a long and complicated undertaking to subdue this difficult country. The Moroccan problem was one of the constants of international affairs toward the end of the nineteenth century; this had much to do with staving off annexation for a long time, for the Sharifian Empire was able to play off one power against another and avoid a showdown. The process had begun after the war with Spain in 1860, when the Spanish occupied the city of Tetuán and refused to evacuate unless paid a heavy indemnity which they knew Morocco could not afford. But Great Britain, because of its preferential trading position in the country and its strategic interest in the Straits of Gibraltar, was unwilling to see Spanish power established in the north of Morocco and bailed the Sultan out with a loan. All through the rest of the nineteenth century, in fact, Britain was useful to Morocco as a ploy against France, and after those two countries were reconciled in 1904, Germany served the same function.

One of the principal issues of the Moroccan question was the status of the subjects of the powers in that country and of Moroccan nationals, called protegés, who were assimilated and granted the rights of subjects, including exemption from local laws and taxes, by the nation which offered them protection. Beginning in 1856, treaties had been signed with various powers, and in order to adjudicate differences in treatment a conference was summoned in Madrid in 1880, attended by the leading states of Europe and the United States. Its importance lay less in the decisions it took than in the fact that this was the first full internationalization of the Moroccan problem. Until 1894 the country remained in fairly good shape under the rule of a strong sultan, Mulay Hassan, who maintained internal order and, thanks to a flourishing export trade, kept Moroccan finances sound. On his death, however, he was succeeded by a young and weak ruler, and within a few years the state was in difficulties. Internal troubles broke out, with tribal revolts in the northeast and a more picturesque banditism in the northwest, where the foreign powers were angered by occasional kidnapings of their nationals or protegés. (The seizure of an American of Greek origin, resident in Tangier, brought down on the head of one brigand the wrath of Theodore Roosevelt but eventually gained him a handsome ransom and a governmental post.) All this kept the Moroccan government in a state of embarrassment and apology, and its troubles were compounded by the prodigality of the sultan. He was the victim of traveling salesmen who sold him useless baubles, one of them a miniature railway made of gold on which he could ride between his palaces in Fez, and he was addicted to lavish displays of fireworks on the occasion of his numerous sumptuous entertainments. The state rushed headlong into bankruptcy, the more easily because some of the loans contracted abroad had a 40 per cent servicing commission deducted by creditor banks.

Now that France controlled two-thirds of the Maghrib, its intentions were clear and it devoted its efforts in the first decade of the twentieth century to preparing the final action. Agreements with Italy traded a free hand in Morocco for a release in Tripolitania, and the accord with England in 1904 removed a more serious obstacle. Later in that year a secret agreement was concluded with Spain to partition Morocco into zones of influence. New loans were sought by the sinking

Moroccan treasury and an international consortium began to organize the ports. The last stumbling block for France was imperial Germany; on a visit to Morocco in 1905 the emperor had spoken pointedly about German wishes of seeing Moroccan independence respected. This led to a cabinet crisis in France and, to settle the problem definitively, a second international conference was called at Algeciras in 1906. The Act of Algeciras, to which the United States as well as the European powers subscribed, reaffirmed the independence and integrity of the sultan's domains, established an open-door economic policy, and intervened on a multinational basis in the sharifian administration; the Banque d'État du Maroc was set up by creditor institutions to supervise Moroccan finances and insure the repayment of loans, and police and customs were to be reorganized under international direction. One crucial provision was that allowing foreigners to buy property without the authorization by the Moroccan government that had previously been required.

The Algeciras Conference, which had only vaguely recognized a paramount French concern in Morocco, represented a setback for Paris, but French ambitions were hardy and other means of attaining them were found. The press in France carried on all through the period a campaign of intoxication about the instability and anarchy in Morocco, French parliamentary figures—and foremost among them those from Algeria—described annexation as a sacred duty and the fitting culmination of the mission to civilize North Africa, semipublic committees were formed to promote the idea, members of the government planned openly how best to accomplish the conquest without repercussion in the European concert, military journals plotted the campaigns, and French nationals in the region eagerly awaited and tried to hasten the day. Incidents in Casablanca during the construction of the port caused French marines to be landed in 1907, while troops from Algeria occupied Oujda and fanned out into the eastern regions. The sultan was labeled a coward by Moroccan opinion and his brother, Mulay Hafid, proclaimed in Marrakesh, thus giving France an excuse to protect the "legal" sovereign. After nearly a year of skirmishing, the new ruler was recognized by the European powers, but meanwhile French forces had been inching their way inland and in 1911 the Spanish joined in and occupied some ports in the north. A final agreement with Germany exchanged territory in central Africa for liberty of action in Morocco for France. But Moroccan popular frustration had been growing each year and their hostility was directed largely against those whom the people felt had sold themselves to the foreigners. So, Mulay Hafid, who had been selected in 1908 for his intransigeance toward the French encroachment, was now attacked for his weakness. In 1910 Fez was threatened by tribal uprisings and the sultan called on French troops to rescue him. There was eventually a price to be paid for salvation: he signed the Treaty of Fez, on March 30, 1912, instituting a French Protectorate over Morocco for the next forty-five years.

Morocco was not conquered by the stroke of a pen, however. It took twenty-two years, just half the time the Protectorate was fated to endure, before the last opposition in the anti-Atlas mountains was overcome. In this way Morocco is unique among the countries of North Africa; there are men alive today who still remember from their childhood the pre-French days of independence, and many more mountaineers in their fifties who as young men in the 1920's were fighting to keep their freedom. By the beginning of World War I in 1914 only the plains and the communications axis to Algeria had been occupied; this line was held with minimum forces until after the Armistice. The Berber mountain regions of the Rif and the Middle Atlas were unusually difficult to subdue. The war in the Rif against the "Republic" of 'Abdelkrim lasted five years, during which the Spanish suffered one disastrous defeat and numerous small reverses. In the end only joint operations by both powers, using heavy artillery and aviation, ended the unequal struggle in 1926, although some isolated actions went on until the following spring. The Middle Atlas was "pacified in the name of the Sultan," as the official phrase went, only in 1930–1931. And, Morocco alone of the three Maghrib states had what could be called continuity of resistance, for as the flames of the traditional tribal battles died down the new nationalist movements came into being in the cities, manned by a new generation with a different outlook but with the same over-all objective of freedom.

The Treaty of Fez installed a regime which was modeled on the Protectorate in Tunisia, but it more thoroughly abolished Moroccan sovereignty in one swoop. France undertook to safeguard "the religious condition and the prestige" of the sultan and to "lend constant support" to his person and throne. The initiative for any measures necessitated by the new regime would come from the French government which was solely responsible for all reforms, for national defense, foreign affairs, and economic and financial questions. As in Tunisia, the French presence was represented by a resident-general, and some of the most famous French military names occupied the post. The note of the Protectorate was struck by the first resident, Marshal Lyautey, a brilliant and unorthodox man, who saw, especially in his later years, some of the errors into which the protectorate regime was falling, and who looked sympathetically but paternalistically on Moroccans as a species of noble savages to be preserved in a romantic archaism. This image of the good Moroccan—valiant, simple, and loyal (to the sultan and France)—lasted through World War II, in which the corps of *goums* from the Middle Atlas under Marshal Juin made a name for itself in the Italian campaign. The image had no counterpart in Algeria or Tunisia (which the French never admired as they did Morocco), but it did echo the sentiments of men like Lawrence and Glubb in the Middle East, and in both cases the antithesis was the unpleasant, vociferous, city intellectual and nationalist agitator. And although it was recognized that Morocco was truly a nation, with institutions and traditions behind it, this emphasis encouraged the retention of medieval social structures and helped confirm the great feudal families, like the Glaoua of Telouet in the High Atlas, in their almost unlimited powers, and, in a move which was perhaps not an unmitigated evil, insisted that the European towns be strictly separated from the native medinas, quarters and dwellings of which were at times classified as historic monuments and whose maintenance and repair could only be effected through a maze of bureaucratic paperwork.

An originality of Protectorate Morocco lay in the existence of two other administrative zones besides that which France managed. The northern tenth of the country and a small barren plot in the far southwest were put under Spanish protection in an agreement made in 1912 between France and Spain, which put Spain in the position of subletting a part of Moroccan territory. The formal organization of the Spanish Protectorate closely resembled that of the French. There was a High Commissioner, a mixture of direct and indirect administration, and a service of *interventores*, who corresponded to the *contrôleurs* in the French zone. Actual conditions were very different, for the northern zone reflected the poverty and greater inefficiency of the Spanish and was never developed as the French part was. At most times it was held under a stricter military occupation, partly for reasons of Spanish politics, which used Africa as a training ground for troops and a convenient camp in which to keep them out of the homeland. Politically, Spanish Morocco played a very important role in Spanish history at the time of the 1936–1939 revolution (see under Hispano-Moroccan relations below) and the zone was also a pawn in Spanish foreign policy, notably during the 1952–1955 period when it was pro-Arab and bitterly anti-French. It was then that Spain, by refusing to recognize the disposition of the legitimate sultan and permitting Moroccan nationalists to operate semiopenly with its blessing, sought to make itself a bridge between the Arab world and the European community by which it had been ostracized. These negative features of Spanish rule were partly counterbalanced by the greater human sympathy prevailing in the north, which stemmed from the mixing of poor Spaniards and Moroccans and the similarity of most of their customs; sometimes it seemed that only religion separated them. There was no de facto segregation as in French Morocco, both peoples lived side by side in the same quarters, and the spectacle of a mixed crowd taking the evening air in a *paseo* around the municipal bandstand in the cities of northern Morocco was something unthinkable in the French-built settler towns a score of miles away.

The third administrative entity in Morocco was the small Tangier enclave which was provided for in the Treaty of Fez in order to insure that no power would hold this strategic position alone. The regime, delayed by World War I, was formally established in 1923 by France, Spain, and Great Britain, and in 1928 Italy and Portugal joined. After World War II, during which Spain had been tempted by the likelihood of an Axis victory to occupy Tangier by force, the administrative arrangements were changed again. Spain was forced to withdraw and the United States and the Soviet Union joined a nine-power Committee of Control, although the latter never actually participated. The political life of Tangier was of secondary importance to Morocco, although it served as a limited haven for nationalists on occasion, provided they were discreet. After World War II its principal focus was on economic ties to Europe, which it served as a free money zone with extensive banking facilities, and it reached maximum prosperity during the period of the Korean War, when it sheltered European flight capital.

The French Protectorate had strong and weak residents, but real power was always found in the hands of the secretary-general of the Protectorate, the perfect administrator through

whose hands all legislation and *dahir*-s originated by the eager
neo-Sharifian administrations had to pass before going to the
sultan for his token approval. Three important directorships
completed the area of maximum authority: Interior (originally
Political Affairs) which controlled the security forces and was
in close liaison with the palace, ever vigilant lest any initiative
escape from the cloistered throne to the country; Finances,
with close ties to the colonial interests and the right of final
approval of all papers; and Public Works, whose resources
were a potent means of persuasion. Behind these "gray
eminences" in the garden city the Protectorate had built for
itself, stood the vast, interlocking network of holding companies and their financial and commercial enterprises for whom
the Protectorate was turning Morocco into a promised land.
The Banque de Paris et des Pays-Bas headed the list; it was
the parent of the Banque d'État du Maroc which controlled
currency circulation and credit and held the tobacco monopoly. Alongside came the Compagnie Marocaine with large land
holdings and the Port of Casablanca, a child of Schneider-
Creusot; the Mas group with its large-circulation French
dailies in Casablanca; the Compagnie des Transports Marocains,
a creation of the Banque de Paris, which grew into the all-
powerful Omnium Nord-Africain in 1934, and handled transport, commerce and mining activities; the great shipping lines,
C.G.T. ("transat") and Compagnie de Navigation Paquet, and
others who had bought into these holdings—the Hersent and
Walter groups, and the Banque Rothschild. Presiding over this
hierarchy, at the most honored level, were the presidents of
the Chamber of Commerce and Industry of Casablanca and
the Chamber of Agriculture. Woe betide the hapless incoming
European who offended one of these autocrats; Morocco was
distinctly not the land of the small colon. Nor was it a scene of
land grabs to the same degree as Algeria or Tunisia. At the end
of the Protectorate, slightly over 1,000,000 hectares were in
settler hands in the French zone (Spanish settlement on the

land was minimal). This represented about 6 per cent of the cultivable area and 8 per cent (600,000 hectares out of 7,500,-000) of land actually under cultivation. As might be expected, concentration of holdings was even more extreme here than in the other countries of the Maghrib: of 6,000 European farms, some 900 were larger than 300 hectares and these accounted for 56 per cent of all holdings of Europeans.

If Algeria expressed the rudimentary rapaciousness of European colonialism of the mid-nineteenth century variety and Tunisia was a transition between the pioneer settler coming from the poor regions of southern France, Italy, or Algeria and a growing commercial colonization, Morocco was the perfection of carefully planned large-scale exploitation by state-supported private interests. This is not to minimize the role played by the large commercial interests in Algeria as the country developed, but theirs was not the sign under which the conquest was carried forth, and the existence of this dominant ethic of efficient management in Morocco helps explain why the native society was left comparatively untouched except when it was needed as a labor force or for military purposes. Morocco was conceived of as an enterprise installed by and for the profit of the European minority and what was unnecessary to this end could be kept and retouched as a colorful museum.

The year 1930 is a convenient date to pause and take stock of what had happened to North Africa in the European era. It was the year of the Centenary of the conquest of Algeria and has been called the "false apogee" of the colonial period. It came when the old-style resistance in Morocco was coming to an end and in all three countries a Pax Gallica ruled which reminded one of the calm of North Africa at the high point of Roman rule in the first century A.D., a reminder that could be strengthened by witnessing a torchlight retreat ceremony of the French legions, consciously modeled on another epoch. The Centenary was celebrated with pomp and great expenditure and the same year the Eucharistic Congress was held in Carthage, now a bougainvillea-covered suburb of Tunis. Eldest daughter of the church, France had implanted the statue of Cardinal Lavigerie facing the gates of the medina of Tunis, bearing in his upraised hand the sign of the civilization and belief of a latter-day Rome, if not in active proselytization then with a total disregard for the offense that was given by these displays of the completely assumed superiority of the conqueror. On the surface, the country was calm, and much changed from what it had been decades before. Roads and railroads, ports and cities had blossomed, the countryside had been brought to life again, the land invigorated and given new cover. Modern hygiene and security were among the benefits introduced, and to the passing observer or the tourist who went to Biskra in the footsteps of Gide, an unruffled prosperity and Cartesian order reigned in the midst of exotic mystery and color; by some miracle Versailles had been built in the Garden of Allah.

But 1930 had another side, too. The calm was the exhaustion of a society which had struggled long but vainly and was taking a breath between rounds. Colonization had brought in a new world of a capitalist economy oriented toward the exterior; this had taken over the functions of the traditional economy and society, bettered them and shamed them, or discarded them as inferior if not useless. The psychological defeat of the Maghrib was as important as its material and social disarray. While elite minorities claimed at one extreme that salvation was to be found only through acceptance and assimilation of the new European order, at the other extreme it was held that a return to the purest wellsprings of Islam and Arabism was the proper course. Meanwhile, the bulk of native society shrank into a defensive apathy which underscored the humiliation and uncertainty they felt. Europeans and North Africans lived, not together and certainly not in any symbiosis, nor were they separated as enemies. Rather they opaquely cohabited the same area and passed through each other without recognition. Each was anchored in his own world, but while that of the European was satisfied and unquestioning, the Muslim was haltingly but with growing confidence beginning to rearrange the fragments of his disrupted culture into a new mold which was held together by the social cement of nationalism.

THE NATIONALIST STRUGGLE

North African nationalism has grown out of mixed soil. It began as a direct reaction to European colonialism, and it has been most decisively influenced at all times in its ideology, terminology, and structural organization by European political thought, particularly that of the French left. But it has many ties with, and forms one wing of, the great national revival which has been afoot in the Arab world since the early nineteenth century. Once again we see North Africa in a typical dilemma, torn between European and Asian influence, as it pursues a renaissance of its Arab soul but uses the logic and techniques of modern Europe for the task.

The Arab Middle East itself had been awakened by the hand of Europe during the Napoleonic invasion of Egypt in 1798, and much of the nineteenth century history of that region is its search for a way to accommodate Arab-Muslim tradition with the modern West. Typically this took the form of a literary and linguistic (and hence essentially religious) revival at the start, changed slowly into an intellectual and scientific questioning, and then moved on to a political plane around 1900. The Arab renaissance in the Middle East is still largely in that phase today, but its current trends no longer directly concern North Africa or us. However, when the Maghrib was first affected by nationalism, it got some of the backwash from the Orient, and a continuing influence can be discerned, although strictly speaking it has always been more lateral than vertical. The same themes of Islamic orthodoxy, the return to the "purity" of the past, the emphasis on the glories of yesteryear, the assiduous construction of a theory of Arabism, have all been taken up in the Maghrib, but often with local variation. On the other hand, the penetration of European thought and culture has been and still is much deeper than anything experienced in the Middle East. While all the principal North African statesmen have been to the Orient at some time in their careers, and some have been deeply impressed by aspects of accomplishments there, a greater number of leaders and a large majority of the younger generation which is just now stepping into important positions in the society have been formed either in France or by Frenchmen under a French system—most of all in Tunisia, a little less so in Algeria, and least in Morocco. For this reason there is almost always a schism in Maghribi nationalism—between those of the East and the West, between secularism and religiosity, between the modernist, reformist, and traditionalist views of Islam—which is of critical importance. It is, furthermore, a struggle now going on daily within almost every thinking individual in the area, and one whose outcome is not at all predictable. In essence, in the rest of this book we will be dealing with nationalism in one form or another—in social structure and change, religion, government and political life, or foreign relations. In that sense the title of this chapter is misleading, for nationalism is, as a distinguished Arab writer, now foreign minister of Jordan, wrote, "the principal movement through which the Arab peoples are trying to reconstruct the foundations of their life after centuries of suspended animation." Nothing could be more all-encompassing than that.

Tunisia was the first of the three Maghribi countries to turn to modern nationalism. The Tunisians had been more exposed to both Arab and European influences in the mid-nineteenth century, as a body of Tunisians had been abroad, in Constantinople and a few in Paris, and it had the experience of its own short-lived but remembered renaissance of the 1850's. For almost a generation after the establishment of the Protectorate in 1881 it was somnolent, but the first efforts to regroup its forces came then in the form of Islamic renewal. A famous Egyptian scholar, Muhammad 'Abduh, propounded the idea of national reform on his first visit in 1884, and although it reached a limited audience it led to the formation of a private school in 1895, the Khalduniya, designed to teach Tunisians something about the rest of the Muslim-Arab world. Another more secular stream issued from the Sadiqi College, founded in 1875 as one of the last reforms of the preprotectorate period, which produced in 1905 the Young Tunisian Movement, a grouping of alumni of the institution (who form a majority of the government officials in Tunisia today). Despite differences in approach, both these groups were important educative forces, and it is perhaps best to look on this whole period at the turn of the century as one of learning. A number of young Tunisians were getting a European-type education in public and private schools, the traditional Koranic schools were being dusted off, literary and cultural life quickened, and the first newspapers were published.

As the Young Tunisians moved toward political action, their first goal was reform: they wanted the right to manage their own affairs and they sought posts of responsibility in the government, but the principle of the protectorate was not questioned. The Evolutionist Party formed by them was made up of lawyers and journalists, civil servants and intellectuals, the best elements of the bourgeoisie of Tunis, versed in French as well as Arabic, and most of them with a modern education. The first popular groundswell in support of nationalism came in 1911 when riots broke out over the forced registration of a cemetery which was religious property, but the real cause of which was the tension between the Tunisians and the growing European settler population. On the whole, however, nationalism at this time was not a mass movement, it had no specific doctrine to make a widespread appeal, and there was no real tie of interest between the elite and the people.

The next surge came after World War I. Tunisia, like many colonized countries, had been stirred by Wilsonian principles. Moreover, the example of the Arab movement in the Middle East, whose success of the moment made a more emotional impression than its final failure in 1920, was present. The nationalists formed a new party, the Liberal Constitutional Party, and taking their name from the Arabic word for "constitution" (Dastur) they got to be known as Destourians.

The period of Destour nationalist activity, from 1920–1934, can be better understood if the character of the party is clear. Destourian supporters were largely middle-class urbanites, but the bulk of the bourgeoisie in traditional (or semitraditional, as Tunisia was then) Arab societies is quite unlike the middle-class, venturesome entrepreneur type who was active in the great movements of postreformation European history. The Maghribi bourgeois tended to be a conservative, property-conscious, family-oriented, and deeply religious man who disdained physical activity and excess labor, and who avoided long-term commercial and banking commitments (which were left to the Jewish minority), preferring the simple buying and selling of the market place. (Islam with its prohibition on usury has always favored the direct and immediate transaction of quid pro quo.) If he had risen a few generations back from the country peasantry or the artisan lower-middle classes, his aim was to hold on to what he had and to see his sons established with houses and land, posts in the administration, or as religious teachers and learned men. This ideal of the traditional bourgeois was already somewhat changing in the twenties in Tunis, but not fast enough for some of the younger generation. Moreover, the Destour itself was aging and the elan of the prewar period was not now sustained; most of the Young Tunisians were middle-aged, and their demands for

equality and jobs had been satisfied. It was this split between
generations which finally led to the birth of the neo-Destour.
But first the Destour spent a decade in failure. The Protectorate
was able to compromise with it on minor reforms and it was
happy to be offered posts in the Grand Conseil or the other
bodies set up in the reforms of 1922. Protectorate policy, during the residency of Lucien Saint, was unscrupulous and successful. Mixing rewards with firmness, it successfully divided
the nationalist movement and reduced it to impotence for a
decade, and when the Destour tried to shake off its lethargy
around 1930 the differences of opinion between the new generation and the old leaders had grown too wide to be bridged.
After much disputation, a majority group of younger activist
broke away at a special party congress held in March, 1934,
and founded the neo-Destour Party.

The neo-Destour had been animated from the beginning by
a remarkable young Tunisian lawyer, Habib Bourguiba, who
was thirty-one when it was formed, and who eventually led
the party and the country to independence, turned Tunisia
into a republic, became the "father of his country," and is
generally regarded as the foremost Tunisian of modern times,
if not the outstanding statesman in North Africa. Bourguiba
was representative of neo-Destour leadership in his background
and training: he came from a modest family in the Sahelian
town of Monastir, was a lawyer and a writer as well as a
vibrant orator. He argued cases and contributed to the Destour
journal before founding in 1932 his own organ, *L'Action
Tunisienne*. Compared to the old school, neo-Destour nationalism was quite secular, although it used religion as a political
weapon on occasions, and it had new overtones of economic
concern, stemming from the world depression of the period
and the party's broader base of representation in the country.
For it had broken with the bourgeoisie of Tunis and turned
for support to the masses throughout the country. Bourguiba
and other leaders had been arrested soon after the neo-Destour

was founded, but when released in 1936 he barnstormed Tunisia, addressing the people in the local dialect and recruiting membership from workers, the lower middle class, and peasants. Party organization spread throughout the country, from the Executive Committee, through local committees to some 400 sections which enrolled 100,000 members (this in a country of around two million). The neo-Destour made history in several ways at this time. Through its mass appeal to varied groups it helped blunt the sharpness of social stratification, it taught a rudimentary democracy to cell members through the discussion sessions on national political and economic issues, and it cut the ground out from the extreme left by its capture of the working class.

The advent of the Popular Front in France in 1936 provided a respite during which this organization work was carried forward, but as France moved closer to World War II its policy in all the North African countries grew more rigid. A nationalist general strike in 1937 had irked the authorities and continuing civil disobedience led in April 1938, to the arrest of party leaders. This was answered by more riots and bloodshed which led to the proclamation of a state of siege. Bourguiba was held for trial, but his case was never judged. The war intervened and until 1943 Tunisian nationalism, at his express wish, did nothing to embarrass the French war effort. Nevertheless, on his return to Tunisia, Bourguiba narrowly escaped arrest on unsubstantiated charges of having collaborated with the Axis powers. Some popular sympathy accrued to the Beylical family at this time, too, as Moncef Bey took the daring step of constituting a ministry with Destourian sympathizers without residential approval, an act which brought about his forced abdication and exile in France, where he died in 1947. Just as the war was about to end, all the Tunisian parties (neo-Destour and Old Destour remnants plus some independent intellectual groupings) joined in a demand for internal self-goverment, and the neo-Destour in 1946 called for full independence. Bourguiba left the country to plead the Tunisian cause abroad and spent some time in the Middle East, a move of dubious value but one which convinced him that Tunisia's future must take a different and more positive course than that followed by the independent Arab countries in the Orient.

The period from 1947 to 1951 was marked by a relative détente in the nationalist struggle. A new resident brought reforms, and those of 1947 gave a considerable measure of authority to Tunisians at a time when young functionaries were moving up into middle-echelon positions of responsibility in the government. This relatively long apprenticeship which the Tunisians had in governing themselves is without doubt a major factor in the efficiency of the administration today. After Bourguiba returned to Tunisia in 1949, negotiations were held with a specially constituted Tunisian ministry looking toward full autonomy by stages, but the obstacle which could not be overcome was the nationalist demand for a Tunisian parliament elected by universal suffrage. The neo-Destour, foreseeing the breakdown of the talks, withdrew its approval of them, and thus put itself in a better posture for the ultimate conversations in 1954–1955.

The collapse of negotiations led to the first real bloodshed of the Protectorate. A harsh wave of repression hit political leaders, who were arrested and in some cases deported. Groups of guerillas, the *fellagha*-s, sprang up in the countryside and by the spring of 1954 they were tying down nearly 70,000 French troops. This was doubly important because France now had to face resistance in more than one Maghrib state. In Morocco, urban terrorism had broken out after the deposition of the sultan, Muhammad ben Youssef, in August 1953, —and, as a further sign of the way in which North African politics was now becoming interlocked, the Moroccan struggle had been touched off by a strike in Casablanca in late 1952 protesting the assassination of a Tunisian labor leader, reputedly killed by European settler terrorists. The recourse to violence by the colonists, common in both Morocco and Tunisia in the early 1950's, and to be repeated on a much larger scale in Algeria later, was a last-ditch effort to save their position when it was clear that an accommodation was envisaged by metropolitan France. For a time it was successful in persuading opinion at home that concessions would lead to disorder and bloodshed, but in the long run it hastened the end by alienating the metropole and thus giving the French government a moral cover for decisions which it planned all along to make on the basis of political sense or necessity.

Early in 1954 France had its hands full. Aside from the war in Indochina, which was bleeding it white, it had reached a political impasse in Tunisia, where elections were boycotted and physical security in the country was slowly breaking down. The Tunisian question had already been discussed at the United Nations with growing sympathy for the nationalist cause on each occasion; now the troubles in Morocco threatened further repercussions. At this time Mendès-France assumed the premiership and concluded in July an agreement to end hostilities in Indochina. He then decided to break the deadlock in Tunisia with a bold stroke. At the end of the month he flew to Carthage without advance notice and offered full internal autonomy to Tunisia. The proposal was accepted and negotiations were begun in September. The final convention was signed the next June, and Bourguiba, freed from house arrest in France after having approved the talks, returned home to a delirious welcome as the "Supreme Warrior."

The period between autonomy (June 1955) and independence (March 1956) was short but it brought the internal difficulties in the neo-Destour into the open. Bourguiba had accepted the autonomy agreement as a worthwhile step along the road to independence, in line with his belief in gradualism (later to be called Bourguibism) as the basis of Destourian political philosophy. But opposition to this principle came from a wing of the party led by the Secretary-general, Salah ben Youssef, who had gone to Cairo during the period of repression. In a national congress in the fall of 1955 the neo-Destour upheld Bourguiba and ousted Ben Youssef but stressed that its aim was unconditional independence.

This was reached sooner than expected, in large part owing to the surprisingly rapid resolution of the Moroccan crisis. When an agreement was reached with that country by France in November 1955, which called for "independence within interdependence" Tunisians were upset that a country which had begun its nationalist struggle much later than they, and which they felt was less prepared for freedom, should precede them to it. Accordingly, they put pressure on France for a quick revision of the autonomy agreement, but only partially succeeded, for Morocco officially became independent on March 2, 1956, and the Franco-Tunisian accord was reached on March 20. As in the Moroccan case, the protocol of agreement solemnly recognized Tunisian independence, but left the details of interdependence for further negotiation.

Algerian nationalism came into being next in chronological order and it had from the beginning a very different coloration. It is probably not too much of a generalization to say that from 1871, when the last Kabyle revolt was put down, until 1919 Algeria was, politically speaking, a land of silence. It had been physically broken, no indigenous political institution had survived the conquest, and the country had never had a traditional urban elite class of the same dimensions as Tunisia or even Morocco. Recuperation was a slow affair and furthermore it was almost impossible to raise a voice even of mild protest, for anything could legally be construed as treason. But after Algeria had made a heavy man power contribution in World War I, a faint realization arose in France, that some kind of reward was fitting. In 1919 a limited right of citizenship was offered to certain Muslims, mainly veterans and those who had received decorations from the French government, indigenous representation in local government bodies was enlarged, and the number of Muslims allowed to participate in municipal elections was increased. These were offered, however, as gifts for past services rather than inherent rights and, in any event, how little they meant in practice was shown in the municipal elections in Algiers in 1920 when, after a list led by the Emir Khaled calling for equality of rights and the abolition of special administrative powers over Muslims was victorious, the results were invalidated. This doctrine of "equal status" was the first nationalist call; indeed, it was the only one that could be voiced, and even this modest demand brought forth violent denunciation from the settlers. Typical was the program of a deputy from Constantine in the same year, who called for the rejection of assimilation, decentralization of the government with the establishment of an efficient administration, increased European colonization, the implantation of strong garrisons, and reinforced security for persons and property.

Bit by bit during the 1920's four separate foci of nationalism and opposition appeared. The first full political movement was founded in France where wider liberties were available; it was the Etoile Nord-Africaine of Hajj Messali, and included Khaled as an honorary president. The ENA was a far left movement whose appeal was mainly to the more evolved Algerian workers in France, and it dared from the safety of the metropole to call openly for independence and confiscation of "stolen lands." A second tendency was that of a group of intellectuals who believed in assimilation, and who, in 1927, formed an association of Algerian deputies, among them Ferhat Abbas. A third group was the Communists, who formed a federation in Algeria in 1924, although the Algerian Communist Party itself was not born until 1935. The Communist audience was restrained because its appeal to those "classes injured in their rights" made no sense to Algerians who had no reason to think in terms of a class struggle, and because Europeans were preponderant from the start in the organization.

A specific Muslim-Arab content was contained in the reform movement which began to grow up around 1930 under the sponsorship of a fourth group, made up of religious teachers (*'ulama*), as part of a general revival of Islamic feeling in North Africa at the time. If the Algerian people were still in the majority indifferent to social and economic appeals, Islam was the one sure way to reach them. The *'ulama* denied that they were a political movement and emphasized their struggle against maraboutism and wayward practices in the faith, but the separation of politics and religion in Islam has always been difficult. The program put forward in their journal Ash Shihab in July 1932, and which said, in part,

What we want to do is to awaken our compatriots from their sleep, to teach them to be vigilant, to demand their part of life in this world, to imbue themselves with the principles of their religion . . .

was as dangerous ultimately to the idea of a French Algeria as any purely political tract, and the administration, realizing it, kept the group under observation and harassment. The authorities unwittingly helped spread their ideas by keeping the educational budget low, thus driving many young Algerians to the Koranic schools founded by the *'ulama*. Another means of propagation lay in the sermons preached in the mosques, and here the government hesitated to interfere at first, but finally in a complete violation of all previous assurances about the inviolability of religion, they restricted preaching to those officials invested by the state who would be politically safe.

As elsewhere in the Maghrib, the Popular Front in France brought hope to Algerians, but in the end they were disappointed. The new government had planned a modest reform in the political status of Muslims to allow a small elite "to exercise the political rights of French citizens without any modification of their civil status or rights." Because of right-wing opposition in France and mass European indignation in Algeria, which included a strike of mayors, the project was never discussed in parliament and remained a dead letter. It has been argued that this was the last chance for France to have brought Algeria into its fold in full integration, but looking back this seems doubtful. Assimilation in the 1930's was only the opening wedge of the battle, and while it was the goal of the intellectuals, it was not accepted by the *'ulama*, or Messali and the ENA (even though the *'ulama* approved it for tactical reasons at the first Algerian Muslim Congress in 1936). Already the sharpening of issues was foreshadowed in two statements made that year. The first was the assimilationist cry of Ferhat Abbas:

If I had discovered the Algerian nation I would be a nationalist and would not blush as if it were a crime . . . But I will not die for the Algerian fatherland because that fatherland does not exist, I have not discovered it. I have asked history, I have asked the living and the dead; I have visited the cemeteries; no one has spoken to me of it . . .

To which Sheikh Ben Badis, one of the leading *'ulama*, replied a few months later in Ash Shihab:

History had taught us that the Muslim people of Algeria were created like all the others. They have their history, illustrated by noble deeds; they have their religious unity and their language; they have their culture, their customs, their habits with all that is good and bad in them. This Muslim population is not France; it cannot be France, it does not want to be France. It is a population very far from France in its language, its life and its religion; it does not seek to incorporate itself in France. It possesses its fatherland whose frontiers are fixed, and this is the Algerian fatherland.

After the beginning of World War II there was little na-tionalist activity in Algeria until the area was liberated by Anglo-American forces in November 1942. The Vichy regime had maintained the status quo, except for condoning anti-semitism and revoking the old decree under which Algerian Jews were French citizens. But in 1943, Ferhat Abbas, moving forward with the winds of history, published his Manifesto of the Algerian People, calling for the end of colonialism, the right of the Algerian people to manage their own affairs, and a constitution with equality for all the inhabitants of Algeria. From assimilation he had now come to the idea of a Franco-Algerian community, but he still did not go as far as the *'ulama* or the Messalists. France was unwilling to make drastic changes during the conflict, but after General de Gaulle arrived in Algiers in 1943—perhaps reflecting that the Free French movement had never been warmly supported by the Europeans in Algeria—the lot of the Muslims was improved. He announced "after examining carefully what is desirable and what is now possible" a wide range of reforms. Several thousand Algerians were given immediate citizenship, and easier access to public posts was promised: the Indigenat was finally abolished and all Muslims and non-Muslims considered equal in rights and duties. But an important provision of the ordinance of March 7, 1944, added that all Muslims who did not expressly indicate their desire to be placed under French law would continue to be subject to Muslim law, and that these would receive French citizenship, "according to the decision of the French Assembly." Thus, only about 60,000 persons were affected by the citizenship changes at the time and, although this move would have been welcomed before the war, it was now opposed by all nationalists including Abbas, the *'ulama,* and the clandestine Parti du Peuple Algerien (PPA) which Messali had founded after the banning of the ENA. Algerian nationalist thought had changed radically in a decade.

If any date can be marked a point of no return in the Algerian tragedy, it is the uprising in the Constantine district in May 1945. On May Day and a week later during the V-E Day celebrations, Algerians demonstrated with green and white nationalist flags, calling for the release of Messali from prison. The police fired, there were casualties, and the demonstrations turned into riots which ended as a general revolt in much of the department. The uprising was savage, nearly 100 Europeans were killed and another hundred wounded; the repression was devastating. Artillery and aviation were used and summary executions at the hands of settler vigilante groups were common. The Muslim death toll is impossible to know with exactitude—official figures of 1,500 are low, and nationalist claims go as high as 45,000. The events went practically unnoticed in the outside world because of their timing, but to those who knew they might have shown how grave the situation in Algeria really was. In retrospect it hardly seems possible that any political concessions could have contained the tide which was beginning to run, and within Algeria after 1945 the two communities were separated by an abyss of mutual misunderstanding, hatred, and fear which fed on itself right down to the end of the revolution and all its horrors. The emotional background in Algeria was much higher pitched than that of its neighbors, and the lesson of the May 1945 troubles was that the legacy of the conquest had not been forgotten but that the stored up wrath would some day explode somewhere.

For a few years after 1945 efforts to find a political compromise continued. In 1946 Abbas founded a new party, the Union Democratique du Manifeste Algerien (UDMA), moderate in outlook, and a proposal made by him to the French parliament that Algeria be made an autonomous republic within the French Union was rejected. Finally, in 1947, the Fourth Republic made a last effort to plaster over the cracks in Algeria. An organic statute for Algeria was passed, after a long struggle with several other propositions some of which were more liberal. Algeria was kept an integral part of France and citizenship was extended to all Algerians. The administration was not much changed but an Algerian Assembly was set up with two sections, one European and one Muslim. Two separate electoral colleges, European and Muslim, chose sixty deputies each to this assembly and each sent fifteen representatives to the French National Assembly, provisions under which a Muslim vote counted for about one-eighth that of a European.

Other sections provided for later decision by the Algerian Assembly on voting rights for Muslim women, the suppression of the mixed communes, and the use of Arabic in schools. A detailed analysis of the Statute is not worthwhile because its promises were insufficient for nationalist demands, much of it was never executed (nothing was done about Arabic until after the revolution began, for example), and what was put into effect was carefully controlled by the European minority. The Muslim majority was not only underrepresented and its deputies in the Algerian Assembly unable to pass legislation without European support, but the elections of 1948 were commonly known to have been "arranged" and a number of Muslim yesmen voted into office.

From 1948 until the start of the revolution in 1954 the history of Algeria is striking for the absence of any meaningful political activity. There were two sides to the drama, however; one was a puppet play being presented on the official stage in which the usual speeches and words were mouthed, and the other was a silent, hidden story of the growing desperation of many young Algerians, of all kinds of classes, who had become tired of temporizing, and were goaded by a landless, undernourished peasantry which was turning into an underpaid urban proletariat. To them the UDMA and Abbas meant nothing, and the MTLD (Movement for the Triumph of Democratic Liberties), the successor to the PPA of Messali, was made ineffective by his difficult personality and his insistence on absolute obedience to himself. The story of the development of these "angry young men" into an insurrectional brotherhood is part of the history of the revolution, but it seems incredible now to think that this clandestine sentiment could have been flowering without anyone in Algeria knowing what was happening—except for the Deuxième Bureau (the military intelligence arm) which occasionally picked up the threads of one or another plot, but which, too, missed seeing the forest for the trees and was finally as surprised as everyone else when the revolution began. In the larger social sense this blindness can only be explained by realizing that the two communities in Algeria had completely reversed roles since the beginning of the century. In 1900 it was the Europeans who possessed the future and dominated the scene, while the Muslims lived locked away in a dream of past glory and an indifference to the present. In 1950 it is they who command politically and economically, not in terms of actual power, of course, but it is their drive and vigor at the lowest level at which they have entered the European world which stand out. They are now the ones working for a future which they see more clearly outlined each day, while the Europeans look back nostalgically to the "belle époque," are interested only in maintaining their privileges, and, having closed the door of their city to the Muslim majority, are unaware of what it is up to in its medinas and douars.

Nationalist action came latest to Morocco, where it showed some unique characteristics. Whereas political activity had begun in Tunisia in 1905–1906 and the first true party was formed by 1920, in Morocco the initial stirrings did not take place until 1926, and even an embryonic party was not constituted until 1937. In fact, unlike the other Maghrib countries, Moroccan nationalism matured only after World War II. Also, the leadership in Morocco was two-headed, divided between that of normal political organizations and that of the palace. Morocco was the only North African country in which the national authority which had existed before the French took control was fully involved with the nationalist movement and successfully made the transition from an archaic institution to an instrument of national renewal. The price has been that to some extent the power and prestige of the throne and the veneration accorded its occupant by many Moroccans have restrained political forces in the country from their fullest play. Another noteworthy feature of Moroccan nationalism is that, having been encompassed in one generation, its founders are alive and functioning today in high government posts, thus offering a continuity rarely found elsewhere.

The nationalist movement began with the founding of study groups by two such young men, Allal al Fassi in Fez and Ahmed Balafrej in Rabat. The groups differed in many ways: the Fez group, which was typical of the milieu of that traditional and learned city, stressed religious reform; the Rabatis were more politically oriented. It is significant that today Allal al Fassi is Minister of Islamic Affairs and Balafrej is Foreign Minister. The results obtained by such formations in the first years should not be overestimated. Morocco was not yet fully conquered and the Rif War, going on almost outside the gates of Fez, was a truer symbol of the resistance of the period. The nation had a smaller urban elite than did Tunisia and has never been so vocal a society; moreover, the heterogeneity of the country hindered the spread of nationalism at all times, and what went on among a handful of intellectuals in Fez did not then much interest the countryside or the workers who were being drawn into the mushrooming city of Casablanca.

Progress would certainly have been slower had the French not provided a *cause célèbre* in the so-called Berber dahir incident in 1930. This was a decree under the terms of which the Berber tribes in certain mountain areas were removed from the jurisdiction of orthodox Muslim law and placed under French criminal law with customary Berber tribunals for civil cases. The situation was complex; there are "Berbers" or at least Berberophones, and many of these had actually never much used religious law, but the subtleties of the situation faded with this attempt by foreigners and non-Muslims to separate the population in such a gross way. In a year which we have already seen marked by blunders of taste, this was a serious political error for it aroused the country and a good deal of the Muslim-Arab world and facilitated the progress of the nationalists, to whom this was an effort to undermine the physical and spiritual integrity of the Sharifian state.

During the 1930's opposition to the Berber dahir and to the many heterodox Sufist brotherhoods was the principal leitmotif of the nationalists. They had formed a Committee for National Action and were active in the newly organized North African Muslim Students League and the Boy Scouts. In 1934 when the sultan visited Fez he was given a rousing welcome, which upset the French authorities, and when they shortened his stay riots followed. It was not until 1937, however, that something like a political party was formed by the Committee and it did not last long. A short period of tolerance was succeeded, here as everywhere in North Africa at the time, by a sharp repression. Al Fassi was exiled to Central Africa until the end of World War II, and some of the others went to Switzerland, while activity was much reduced in Morocco until the Allied landings in 1942. During this period and after, the Spanish zone of Morocco exhibited a nationalist growth of its own which was more adapted to the peculiar circumstances in which Spain found itself than to the mainstream of Moroccan politics: the existence of the Spanish Republic, the revolution of 1936–1939, and the large number of Moroccans who fought on the nationalist side in that struggle. The only party of importance, which represented the bourgeoisie of Tetuán, was the Reformist (Islah) Party founded by Abdelkhalek Torres, which at the time of Moroccan independence merged with the dominant Istiqlal party and claimed that it had always been part of it.

Moroccan nationalists were excited by the prospects held forth in the Atlantic Charter and their hopes were further raised by the visit of President Roosevelt and Prime Minister Churchill to Casablanca in January 1943. At a private meeting with the sultan without the presence of French advisors, the President is reliably reported to have assured him of America's interest in seeing Moroccan freedom restored after the war. The exact words have been the subject of dispute, but what matters is the widespread belief (held not only by Moroccans but by bitter French officials as well) that the commitment was made. For some time afterward American prestige in the country coasted on the grounds of this story, which was known, often with embellishments, to nearly every Moroccan. From then on, in any event, politics was renewed with gusto. A new party, the Independence (Istiqlal) Party was formed, grouping most of the old leaders of the Action Committee. It published a manifesto in January 1944, calling for negotiations to end the Protectorate, but this led only to the usual chain of arrests and riots.

At the end of the war there were several parties in the fray. The Istiqlal, headed by Allal Al Fassi; a new party, the Democratic Independence Party (Hizb ash Shura wa'l Istiqlal, commonly known as the PDI) which had splintered off from it; and the Communist Party, whose appeal was negligible. The Istiqlal had a tacit alliance with the throne, but both the national parties and the palace faced the hostility of the feudal chiefs who had been fortified in their privileges by the Protectorate, of some traditionalist elements in the cities, and of the heads of some religious brotherhoods. They had not yet made much headway in the newer cities like Casablanca, Meknes, or Kénitra (Port Lyautey), but from 1947 to 1951 the principal event was the change of the Istiqlal from an elite organization with restricted admission to a mass movement whose popularity rested on the simple but hard line it put forward, which stressed that it "had no program except independence." The palace took an important initiative in 1947 when the sultan used the more liberal climate of Tangier to make a speech that stressed Morocco's place in the Arab World and omitted a laudatory paragraph about France, which the authorities had inserted in his prepared text. The repercussions of the speech brought a new resident, General Juin, and a tougher policy. Relations between the Protectorate and the Istiqlal declined steadily and while the sultan remained theoretically above the struggle, his sympathies were well known and an increasing coolness set in between the residency and the palace.

As the cities became a bastion of Istiqlalism and nationalism, the French resorted to a variation of the divide-and-rule tactic by stressing the city-country split. The charge was made that the sultan represented only the urban "radicals" and nationalists, and Berber tribesmen from the Middle Atlas, who were mostly unaware of the issues, were brought to Rabat in 1951 to demonstrate and pressure the sovereign into disavowing the party. The sultan temporized but began a campaign of passive resistance by refusing to sign the decrees prepared for him by the Protectorate. An operation of greater scope had to be mounted. First, after riots in Casablanca in protest against the killing of the Tunisian labor leader, Ferhat Hached, the Istiqlal was outlawed. Then a campaign was begun by some of the personal enemies of the sultan among the feudal leaders and the brotherhoods, headed by the Pasha of Marrakesh and the Sheikh Kittani, to convince rural notables and tribal leaders that the sultan had abandoned Islam for political extremism. Throughout the summer of 1953 this movement, which was that of a small minority, was nurtured by the Protectorate with all the potent means at its command. Finally the Resident, claiming that France was unable to guarantee the security of the country owing to the alleged threat of revolution, deposed the sultan and exiled him "for his own safety," first to Corsica and eventually to Madagascar, while a docile relative was put on the throne.

The deportation, in violation of the Treaty of Fez which specifically pledged France to protect the sultan, turned the Moroccan nationalist movement into an open battle for freedom. The whole nation coalesced in opposition, and even a section of opinion in France was hesitant about policy in Morocco. With the main political party destroyed and the sultan gone, resistance turned to violent means, and within a few months sporadic terrorism broke out in the cities. Some of it was in-discriminate, but mostly it was directed at Moroccan police informers and collaborators, or notorious European members of "Présence Française." In August 1955, on the second anni-versary of the deposition, there was a serious outbreak of trouble in the countryside, as well as in Algeria. This was the first time rural Morocco had risen in a generation, and there followed in October the first sparks of what would have been a guerilla war, had not a political settlement been quickly reached.

The Europeans in Morocco were not in the main as much of a problem as their counterparts in Algeria and Tunisia, but they were fully opposed to Moroccan independence and they made as many difficulties as they could. Urban terrorism had unnerved them and in July 1955, feeling on the brink of being abandoned by France, they responded to a bombing outrage in Casablanca by sacking Muslim quarters and killing scores of Moroccans; for a few days the city seemed on the verge of community warfare. But the Europeans harmed mostly them-selves by their action, for it was the last straw in convincing the French government that an error had been made in 1953 and that some face-saving compromise must be arranged to undo it. A conference of moderate nationalists and Moroccan notables was held in France late in August, which led in a very roundabout way to the return of Muhammad ben Youssef, first to France at the end of October, and finally to Morocco on November 16, 1955, where he reclaimed his throne as Muhammad V, in the midst of scenes of genuinely indescribable enthusiasm.

Since it had become obvious to the French government—more so each day in October as resistance spread to the Rif and Middle Atlas under the banner of the Moroccan Liberation Army—that nothing could be done without the consent of the sultan, a protocol was concluded on November 6, by which France agreed to terminate the Protectorate and begin talks leading to Moroccan independence. An interim government, empowered to conduct the discussions, was formed under the leadership of Si Bekkai, an army officer of nationalist leanings but an independent, with a cabinet in majority Istiqlal. Negotiations were completed rapidly and Morocco became independent on March 2, 1956. Legally, once the French protectorate was terminated there was no basis for the continuation of the small Spanish zone, and an agreement was signed in Madrid on April 7, following which the King (as he was now called) entered Tetuán in triumph. Later in the year the Tangier International Zone was also returned to Moroccan administration and reincorporated in the country.

The path of decolonization in Algeria took a very different turn. This had always been a country of extremes; the conquest and the colonial period were excessive and the revolution that aimed at erasing this past was even more so. Since 1954 Algeria has been quite simply made over, as profoundly changed as any society has ever been in so short a time. The transformation was made at an appalling cost: nearly a million dead or missing, two million Muslims uprooted, "relocated" in concentration camps and resettlement centers, or refugees in neighbor countries; the massive flight of 800,000 Europeans and the abandonment of several million hectares of the best farmland; and the disintegration of the Fourth Republic and a series of severe tests for democratic institutions in France. The revolution created a new order in Algeria, a *tabula rasa* upon which anything might be built, and 1954 represented as sharp a break in the Algerian stream of history as had 1830. Indeed, the revolution was almost as much a surprise to everyone, including most Algerians, as the French landings had been a century before.

From 1948 on, Algerian politics had an air of unreality. The status quo was being maintained, stale slogans were repeated, and the best but most discontented young energies were occupied elsewhere—like those of Ahmed Ben Bella, who was robbing a bank to get funds for the activities of his secret organization. Algerian political movements were ossified, and the MTLD was rent by quarrels between the followers of Messali and the Centralists, who opposed his personal dictatorship. Disgusted by these divisions and all the sterile disputes around them, a third group gradually grew up which was impressed by the recourse to force in Tunisia and Morocco in the early 1950's and decided that only armed action would bring a change in French policy. This Revolutionary Committee for Unity and Action (CRUA) was made up of dissidents from the MTLD, ex-French army men who had seen and learned much in Indochina, and a miscellaneous undergroup of dedicated and desperate men who were willing to risk all. Through the summer of 1954 preparations for a revolutionary outbreak were pursued. In July the military organization was set up and Algeria was divided into six provinces (wilayas); liaison was made with agents in Cairo for the supply of arms, and the date of the insurrection was fixed by October 10. At midnight on the night of October 31–November 1, as if it were a Halloween-like attempt to frighten on the eve of All Saints Day, action began, and a proclamation was issued by the National Liberation Front (FLN) calling on Algerians to rise and fight for their freedom.

For a long time there was not much military activity. It is remarkable to think that in the winter of 1954–1955 only a few hundred rebels were in action, but that by the spring of 1958 the National Liberation Army (ALN) had trained a force of 60,000 men equipped with automatic weapons, which was tying down half a million French troops. At first French reaction was one of annoyance and disdain—the bandits would soon be brought to heel, Algeria was and would remain French—mixed with a certain incoherence. The MTLD, which had nothing to do with the outbreak (the French had no idea for some time who was responsible), was outlawed and its leaders arrested. The situation was described as "preoccupying" but "stabilizing itself" and while even the liberal left threatened a pitiless repression, visiting deputies announced that the situation was in hand. The military shared this confusion. In December most of the Aurès was described as under control, but in January 5,000 troops with tanks launched a campaign to clean it out. The rebels in Kabylia were dismissed as "bandits who had always existed in the area."

Like cancer, the revolt spread slowly from the Aurès and southeastern Algeria where it had begun, to the wooded, mountainous Constantinois. There had been 50,000 French troops in the country in November; at the end of February 1955, there were 80,000. But France continued to be deaf to talk of reform. Early in the struggle, François Mitterand, Minister of the Interior, who later became a fervent partisan of discussions, said that "the only negotiation was war," and in May, M. Bourgès-Maunoury, who then held the same post, said much the same thing. A state of emergency was declared—the first of many measures which gradually destroyed all concept of law in Algeria—permitting "assignment to residence" and granting widespread special powers of search, censorship, and the control of persons. By August 20, 1955, however, all France knew that the revolt was a revolution. On that day there were surprise attacks all around Philippeville in which more than one hundred Europeans were massacred, in reprisal, according to the FLN, for French refusal to give combat status to rebels who were captured and sentenced to death. European counter-reprisals far exceeded this figure and the vicious circle of blood in which Algeria finally almost drowned had begun.

The second period of the revolution lasted from then until May 1958. It was marked by stepped-up military operations, together with the gradual loss of control by the government in Paris over its military forces in Algeria and the settlers. Algerian representation in the French Assembly was not renewed in the general elections in 1956. The new premier, M. Mollet, went to Algiers where truculent demonstrations broke out because of his nomination of a possibly liberal Resident. When he backed down and withdrew the nomination, it marked the beginning of a period of five years during which Algiers was the effective capital of France and nothing could be done without the approval of the army and the colon leaders there.

Meanwhile the Algerian revolution was becoming a subject of international concern. The Bandoeng Conference had created a group of nonaligned countries and Prime Minister Nehru made a reference to the Algerian right to independence, but active support was confined at first to the Arab states, now augmented by Tunisia and Morocco, whose newly independent status allowed the Algerians to establish training camps and use their territory as a sanctuary and an arms depot. These neighbors were further involved when a Moroccan plane carrying five leaders of the FLN to a meeting in Tunis, including Ahmed Ben Bella and Mohammed Khider, was forced to land in Algiers. NATO allies of France were disturbed by the withdrawal of forces committed to the defense of Europe, and the United States found itself criticized in some French political circles for its failure to support France wholeheartedly, while the FLN denounced it as an accomplice of colonialism for continuing to supply military equipment, particularly helicopters, to France. In 1957 two statements underscored the heightened United States interest. On June 2, Senator Kennedy noted that Algeria had stopped being an exclusively French problem, and a month later he called on the administration to use the good offices of Bourguiba and the King of Morocco to work out Algerian independence within the framework of North African interdependence. In the interim, Secretary of State Dulles had announced that the United States would not put any pressure on France and that arms deliveries would continue. The most noteworthy developments late in 1957 were uneasiness in France because of repeated allegations of the widespread use of torture in Algeria, which was much later admitted, and the debate in the Assembly on a proposed Basic Law for Algeria, which would have reorganized the country into federative departments with regional autonomy. Although the bill was defeated as first presented after heated debate, it is worth recalling if only to show how far official policy was from the realities of the revolution in believing that such an anodyne measure could now make any difference.

The French military elite in Algeria, spearheaded by officers who were intent on waging the same kind of revolutionary war they had encountered in Indochina, had become increasingly isolated from opinion in the metropole, not to speak of the outside world. It was almost neurotically obsessed with the idea that it could solve the Algerian problem through the simultaneous application of force, persuasion, and propaganda, if only it were not interfered with by the civilian authorities. It felt betrayed on many scores, not the least of which was the government's acceptance of the open support given the rebels by Tunisia. The right to violate the frontier in hot pursuit was exercised and early in 1958 the airforce heavily bombed a small town, Sakiet Sidi Youssef, which was known to have sheltered Algerian forces. The wave of sympathy that went around the world was in itself an indication of how much ground anti-colonialist sentiment had gained in a few years, and the results of this act were decisive in another way. Tunisia and France suspended normal relations and the United States and British volunteered their good offices to heal the breach. In the talks that followed, suspicion grew in Algeria that the cabinet in Paris might be amenable to or lead into indirect negotiations with the FLN under the blanket of Anglo-American mediation. The formation of a new government under M. Pflimlin, who referred vaguely to the possibility of negotiations, was the signal for action. On May 13, a demonstration in Algiers was manipulated by activist leaders into seizing government headquarters and calling on the Army to take power. This the Army did, finally but hesitantly, through the device of forming "Committees of Public Safety" in which colon leaders and army officers were associated. The seizure of Corsica by forces loyal to the insurrection in Algiers and the threat of invading metropolitan France sufficed to bring the shaky new cabinet to its knees, and in unusual circumstances General de Gaulle was asked to take charge of the government, which he agreed to do on condition that he be given a free hand to reform the constitution. Thus the Fourth Republic died under the threat of a military coup and the Fifth was gradually born over the next few months.

General de Gaulle had been welcomed by the Army and accepted, but less enthusiastically, by the Europeans in Algeria. For a time it was not clear what line he would take. In June 1958, from the balcony of the Forum in Algiers, he made the cryptic statement, "I have understood you," but it was more than a year before he revealed his intentions. In September, the FLN constituted itself a government, the Provisional Government of the Algerian Republic (GPRA), a step taken partly for fear that Gaullist policy, which then looked as if it might be tending toward assimilation with full equality for Muslims and Europeans, might draw some support from Algerians who were, understandably, tired of the war. A referendum at the end of September on the new French constitution, which was widely but fallaciously considered to be a vote in Algeria for or against such integration, produced an overwhelming majority in that country, but many abstentions. The balloting in Algeria was under French Army control and while not falsified, as had been other elections, was not free of indirect pressure. During his visit to Algeria at that time, President de Gaulle announced that a large-scale five-year economic development plan would be initiated, and he followed this with a delicately phrased offer of an amnesty to the rebels if they would raise a "white flag." The GPRA construed this as a demand to surrender and rejected it, but the outlines of de Gaulle's thought were becoming clear: with one hand he offered economic betterment, and with the other a promise of political forgiveness with the veiled threat of other, more drastic decisions if his terms were not accepted. This policy was continued with his renewed offer of peace on honorable terms late in January 1959.

Algeria was by now a major international political problem. The GPRA had at once been recognized by the Arab countries, as it was later by the Communist states in Asia and a few of the Afro-Asian group. As African states became independent in greater number they all recognized the Algerian government. The Algerians began taking part as observers in various international meetings, principally of the Afro-Asian group, and sending delegations to neutralist and communist countries. Close relations with some of the Communist bloc, which was supplying part of the Algerian arms requirements, led to a division of opinion in the West, particularly in the United States, on how to treat them. This was reflected in the United States abstention on the United Nations resolution voted in December 1958 by a 35–18 majority, "recognizing the right of the Algerian people to independence and recommending negotiations between the two interested parties."

It was clear though that the solution lay always with the French government. General de Gaulle had already shown when dealing with the greatest powers and personalities that he was not to be persuaded or bullied into anything he did not think in the best interests of France. Thus, every statement he made was carefully watched for signs of a new trend in French policy. These came in the summer of 1959 when informed circles began to bruit about the word "self-determination" with emphasis. Official confirmation came in the presidential speech of September 16, 1959, in which he forcefully stated the right of Algerians to choose among gallicization, association, and secession. The subtlety of this choice became clear in the eventual negotiations, because it was always implicit in the French position that independence for Algeria meant association (the term finally used was cooperation), while Algerian nationalists, even though they were willing to sign agreements binding them quite tightly to France, could consider that they were always fundamentally choosing the third alternative. Only thus could public opinion in France and nationalist sentiment in Algeria be reconciled, and only thus today can various necessary fictions in Franco-Algerian relations be maintained.

The declaration of September 16, 1959, was the decisive turning point in the revolution. It was the first French recognition that sovereignty in Algeria lay with the Algerians and, once that was agreed to, everything was possible. The revolution had won on the crucial point for which it took up arms. Naturally this did not escape the attention of the other participants in the battle, and their reaction expressed itself first in Algiers in January 1960, in a week-long strike and defiance of the government by armed Europeans barricaded in part of the city. The inability or refusal of the army to put down this semi-revolt was the most serious aspect of the affair, and it required a sharp reprimand by President de Gaulle in full uniform to bring compliance. Clearly there was a large part of the officer corps which was shaky if not totally unreliable, and much of 1960 was devoted to weeding these elements out and transferring them from Algeria, not with complete success, as was later proved.

Taking advantage of the momentum gained after the so-called revolt of the barricades had failed, de Gaulle renewed his offer of negotiations early in June, and it was accepted by the GPRA. An Algerian delegation came to France for preliminary talks but there were difficulties—the Algerians complained that their representatives were not treated as equals—and negotiations were never formally begun. There is ground for suspecting that the entire meeting was a Gaullist tactical move to accustom French opinion to the idea of parleys. The President continued to dispense tidbits of information, often to confuse as well as to suggest, in his periodic press conferences. In September he announced that he would not talk with leaders of the rebellion as long as killings continued, but on November 4 he indicated that he would go on pointing toward an Algerian Algeria, and for the first time made an oblique allusion to the "Algerian Republic, which will exist some day."

Having decided to submit his policy of allowing the Algerians self-determination to the French electorate for approval, de Gaulle toured Algeria in December. Violent European demonstrations broke out, with attacks on Muslims which led to ninety-six deaths of Algerians alone, but they called forth other demonstrations by Muslims who openly displayed the green and white flag of the national movement, cheered the names of rebel leaders, and called for an Algerian Algeria (and even more insistently for a Muslim Algeria). If there had been any doubts about mass support for the revolution they were removed then. On January 8, 1961, the Algerian policy of General de Gaulle was approved by a 75 per cent majority in France and a 69 per cent majority in Algeria, following which the GPRA said it was ready to hold direct conversations. These were delayed by the visit of Bourguiba to France and the death of the King of Morocco, but a rendezvous was made for early April. At the last minute the Algerians refused to attend on the pretext that the French delegation had been in contact with supporters of Messali Hadj, whom they refused to have associated in any way with the discussions. The postponement of the talks had serious repercussions, for in an off-hand way at a press conference a few days later President de Gaulle stated that if the Algerians did not come to an agreement with France he would proceed to a regrouping of the people of the country and leave all those who did not choose French protection to shift for themselves. This triggered carefully laid army plans for an uprising in Algeria, which took place on April 22. Headed by a quartet of generals and relying for support on parachutist units and legionaries, a military coup temporarily seized Algiers, and later Oran and Constantine. But it failed to obtain the essential support of the airforce (for a possible invasion of France), or, most importantly, of the draftees who, in some cases, refused to obey their officers. The coup collapsed as suddenly as it had begun and with its demise came the end of organized resistance in the military forces, although diehard individual officers and some deserters went on cooperating with activist groups of settlers who had formed the Secret Army Organization (OAS), which now began a systematic campaign of terror. Negotiations were begun in May 1961, at Evian, but obstacles about the organization of a referendum and the status of the Saharan territories were not easily overcome. Talks had to be adjourned in June, and were unsuccessfully resumed for a short while in July. Part of the difficulties was eased when General de Gaulle announced at a press conference that it was reasonable for an independent Algeria to demand its integral frontiers, which included the Sahara. There was now no doubt that an agreement would finally be reached; it was merely a question of time, and the final accord on a cease-fire was reached at Evian on March 19, 1962. These agreements offered Algeria the possibility of choosing independence in cooperation with France in a referendum fixed for July 1 of that year. The vote was overwhelmingly favorable to this proposition; more than 99 per cent of those voting said, "Yes" and there were 8 per cent abstentions.

As the inevitability of Algerian independence became clear, the opposition of the European minority there turned to a blind rage of senseless violence and, in one of the most extraordinary finales to any event in recent history, a Götterdämmerung of self-immolation accompanied by mass flight. The OAS, which virtually controlled the large cities, gradually turned from the selective elimination of government agents and military figures loyal to the regime to mass murder, and by the spring of 1962 reason had ceased to exist in the cities of Algiers and Oran as Muslim housemaids, delivery boys, and children were shot down at random, trucks filled with flaming gasoline were launched on native quarters, and booby-trapped automobiles killed and maimed workers and innocent passers-by. The alleged and probably true original motivation was to provoke a Muslim retaliation which would then force French troops to intervene, but eventually violence fed on itself and became an indiscriminate slaughter in which one is forced to recognize complex and atavistic desires for suicide and revenge which were the more appalling for coming from a civilized community. When all else failed, the OAS began the destruction of government buildings and offices, records, and cultural property, in fulfillment of a policy of scorched earth. After having forbidden the Europeans to leave because they were to consider themselves soldiers, it encouraged them to do so at the end of May, and a panic flight of unprecedented proportions set in, with as many as ten thousand persons a day arriving in France in mid-June, while other thousands camped at airports and docks awaiting transportation. The last, apocalyptic days of Oran symbolized the close of the European era in Algeria: the city engulfed in a great pall of smoke from the exploded oil tanks in the port and empty of everything save death and hatred. The only fitting epitaph for this ending was that the colonial period died as it had lived, in violence and incomprehension.

III. Independent North Africa

GOVERNMENT AND POLITICS

If we look at the problems of government in the independent countries of North Africa in an order of ascending difficulties, we find that Tunisia made the transition from dependence to independence with a minimum of shock and discontinuity, and has functioned since with remarkable smoothness. Arrangements had already been made during the autonomous period for elections to a Constituent Assembly and these were held on March 25, 1956, only five days after Franco-Tunisian protocol recognizing Tunisia as an independent state had been signed. The neo-Destour ticket, a national union front grouping together labor, commercial and agricultural organization, won an overwhelming victory (97 per cent of the vote). The Assembly was convened and Bourguiba elected presiding officer, but he resigned shortly to become Premier of the first Tunisian government.

The principal task of the Assembly was to draft a constitution, but as it got down to work it became evident that there was strong sentiment among the deputies and throughout the country to change the regime from a monarchy to a republic. In fact, the eventual disappearance of the Beylical system had long been planned by Destourians and taken for granted by most Tunisians. There had never been any deep feeling among the people for it, although it had been accepted without rancor. But the whole political evolution of Tunisia, from the earliest days of the nationalist struggle, had taken place outside the monarchy, which had remained a fossil institution incapable of inspiring affection or admiration. The neo-Destour had been the focus of national life and Bourguiba the national hero. Accordingly on July 25, 1957, the Assembly unanimously passed a resolution abolishing the monarchy and proclaiming Tunisia a republic. Premier Bourguiba was entrusted with the duties of head of state until the constitution was ready. That was not until June 1959, and national elections were not held until November that year, so that for two years Tunisia functioned provisionally with Bourguiba as head of state and head of government without a legislative assembly in existence. This meant a heavy concentration of power in the hands of one man, and it is significant that almost all the social reform legislation was promulgated in the period between 1956 and 1959 by executive decree and bears the stamp of the presidential personality.

The constitution as adopted established Tunisia as a republican state, with Islam its religion and Arabic its language, which forms a part of the "Greater Maghrib." The choice of regime was influenced both by American ideas—Bourguiba has always been an admirer of Franklin D. Roosevelt, whom he resembles in many ways—and, negatively, by the example of the Fourth Republic in France, the weakness of which was fully demonstrated while the document was under study. Thus a presidential regime was chosen which gives much power to the executive but provides a legislative check as well. The President is elected directly by universal adult suffrage for a period of five years and can hold office for three terms. Like the American president, he appoints his cabinet (whose members are titled Secretaries of State rather than Ministers), is Commander-in-chief of the armed forces, declares war and makes peace, and ratifies treaties with the agreement of the Assembly. The President can introduce legislation which then takes precedence, can issue orders in council while the assembly is not in session, subject to certain restrictions, and, finally, can take exceptional measures if the safety and independence of the Republic are threatened.

Compared to that, the prerogatives of the Assembly are somewhat restricted. Its members are elected at the same time as the President for five years, and all deputies represent the country as a whole instead of a particular district. The Assembly can pass bills over presidential veto by a two-thirds majority on second reading, but its most telling power is that of fixing the final figures of the budget. In practice the legislature has been overshadowed during the seven years of Tunisian independence by the executive, but that is not too unusual in the first stages of a new country which is tempted to dramatize the national will in one personality, especially when the magnetism of that individual is such that it is impossible to imagine the country without him.

Grouped around the presidency is the executive office, beginning with the cabinet which has been staffed with little change by members of the neo-Destour. The Secretary of State to the Presidency functions as a vice-president and is also responsible for national defense. The forces under his command include a small army of about 20,000 men, which has enhanced its reputation in the Congo, a naval contingent for coastal defense, a parachutist elite unit, a few officer pilots, and the gendarmerie. Military service is compulsory, but the rate of rejection is high and many trainees are enrolled in a civil corps which has done excellent work in the economic development program.

On the regional level, the country is divided into thirteen governorates, with each governor assisted by an elected advisory council. These have limited powers but provide a useful testing ground of local opinion. It is in the competence of its regional administration that Tunisia has particularly distinguished itself. On the whole the governors have been able and conscientious younger Destourians, and a neat balance between centralization and decentralization has been kept. The governor has wide latitude to make decisions on the spot—something which has been capital in handling the large public works unemployment program—but he cannot get too much out of hand because the smallness of Tunisia, and its facile communications allow for frequent consultation with the capital and the shadow of the central government is kept at just about optimum intensity.

All the governments of the new Maghrib states could legitimately be considered reform governments, for each has made significant changes in the legal, judicial, and social structure of its countries, but in Tunisia reform has been perhaps the most notable among many accomplishments. Many of the details are discussed later under the heading of social change, but mention should be made here that Tunisia has made a sweeping renovation of the legal basis of society which far exceeds that of any other North African or Arab country. When the Personal Status Code went into effect in 1957 Tunisia became the only Arab state in which polygamy was unconditionally abolished and women granted full equality with men in all domains. Marriage and divorce were reformed and regulated by new civil laws, while summary repudiation of the wife by the husband was terminated. Religious tribunals for Muslims and Rabbinical courts for Jews were abolished, placing everyone under the same secular jurisdiction. These reforms were completed by a Civil Status Law which made registration of births and deaths obligatory for the first time and insisted on a specific identity for each individual to replace the anarchic anonymity which prevails in many Arab countries where people do not have surnames. All things considered, the reform of justice, the secularization of the law, and the removal of inequality between citizens were probably the most important steps taken by the Tunisian state along the path to becoming an integrated, modern nation.

In Tunisia it is common to hear it said that the government is the party, and vice versa. "We are all Destourians" is a standard statement. This is almost, but not completely, true, and it may be getting less so very recently. But it is often hard to separate the two, and although Tunisia is not in any sense a one-party state with totalitarian harshness, it does have the unexciting air of a country in which one party is very dominant indeed. Aside from the neo-Destour today, there are only the Communists with a minuscule following, some young independents of the left, and the unorganized conservative remnants of the old Destour. Individuals sometimes quarrel with Bourguiba personally or break with party doctrine, but they have almost always returned to the fold, and no real foyer of opposition has developed since the ben Youssef split in 1955 and early 1956. Once again the smooth social contours of Tunisia must be given credit. The party owes much of its success, frankly speaking, to the quality of the men who make up its top and medium leadership. The advantages of the age of civilization in the country begin to be seen; the relative richness of human resources in Tunisia compared to many new countries is something it can be proud of and an asset which has been a leading factor in the country's successful adjustment to the modern world. The backbone of the neo-Destour has come from the hard-headed merchants of the Sahel, dour and practical peasant individualists, artisans and craftsmen, the brightest lights among the professional classes in the cities, with a dosage of intellectuals to give it sauce. Its cornerstone has been, rather than the brilliant verbosity of many political movements, a quiet, pragmatic flexibility, and it has followed the rule that the art of politics is to know what is possible. From this spirit emerged the gradualist techniques of Bourguiba, to advance step-by-step, never to break contact with the interlocutor, to continue negotiating at all times, and to compromise tactically but never on principles.

The top party leadership is homogeneous, too; some might almost say inbred. Most of the high officials are graduates of the Sadiqi College, and there is a nucleus from the specialized schools in Paris, particularly the Ecole Libre des Sciences Politiques. A clubby and familial atmosphere prevails among them. They see much of each other; it is not uncommon to come across half a dozen important government figures lunching together for no special reason other than that Tunis is small and their society is limited. (The extraordinary difference between the school-tie government of a very little country like Tunisia and the normally impersonal administration of a large country like the United States may not at first strike most Americans but it is a vital political reality.) Bourguiba's place at the top of this intimate hierarchy has never been disputed since the early 1930's, and he is now consecrated as the first citizen of the country, even though criticism of some of his actions is heard on a rising scale. His popularity with the average Tunisian—maintained by a boundless energy, numerous public appearances, regular radio talks, and a fine popular touch—is still great, although it has somewhat declined since the Bizerte fiasco in 1961. The ill-conceived plot against the life of the President at the end of 1962 is less symptomatic of this than is the vague popular discontent owing to the slowness of economic progress and the growing realization that Bourguiba is not infallible. Still, there is a general recognition, even among intellectuals who often show impatience, that it was he who first lit the lamp in Tunisia and kept it burning at all times. Around him is a group of distinguished men touching fifty years of age: Mongi Slim, now Foreign Minister after having served as President of the United Nations Assembly; Bahi Ladgham, in theory the second man in the country; and a half a dozen other old companions-in-arms. But they are aging and a new generation is behind them, men arriving at forty, of whom the able Minister of the Interior, Taieb Mehiri, is an example. With others, like Masmoudi, Bourguiba has quarreled over religious and personal issues, or like ben Salah, over the degree of socialization in the economy, but most of these disputes have ended in reconciliation, that word which always comes back in a discussion of Tunisian affairs.

If it is hard to see the party breaking apart from within, another danger faces it, that of withering away through indifference. To qualify this, it should be said that this is not an immediate danger and that the neo-Destour, more successfully than most parties, has crossed the bridge from being a revolutionary force directing national energies toward a clearly defined goal to playing the role of a formally organized political party supporting a government which overshadows it and has pre-empted many of its functions. There are at least three problems here: one is the difficulty the party has in recruiting new members and maintaining interest at local cell levels; a second is the diffuse nature of the party structure, which was desirable when flexibility and the capacity to survive political repression was important but is not now adequate to the needs of a state which feels it must control and direct a complex socioeconomic battle on many fronts; and a third is the result of having many talented party members in government jobs which inevitably take all their energy. Certainly a crisis in party-government relations has been smoldering for several years, and now there is an incipient crisis in the popular response to the party. Efforts to solve the first by reinforcing central authority over regional party federations do not seem to have been too successful, and as to the second, it is notorious that the party is unable to summon up mass enthusiasm; that is a task which has to be left to the magic of the presidential appeal. It is too early to say that there is a crisis of generations in Tunisia, but it looks as if the next five years or so will determine whether the elan that has so far carried the country along can be maintained as power moves into the hands of another age group.

It is not easy to sum up political nuances in Tunisia. The state is paternalistic and verges on authoritarianism without openly espousing totalitarian methods. Up to now it has been a relatively free country without much sense of oppression; almost anything could be criticized save Bourguiba, and if criticism did not get very far neither did it bring down more than minor sanctions. Quite recently there has been a noticeable tightening of authority and an increased severity in punishments. Whether this is a temporary phenomenon or not will be more clearly seen when the present term of the President comes to an end in 1965—a time when many of the problems mentioned above: authoritarianism, the conflict of age and power groups, and the results of economic sacrifices, seem likely to come to a head. The present paternalism can be justified, and seems to be accepted by the people, on the grounds that the President's energy and vision have pushed and cajoled the country into progress which it would not have made on its own. The people tend to be inert, something which is at once a strength and a weakness, but the danger is that continuing paternalism will make them more inert. On the other hand, Tunisia has been buttressed by other rare values. Its long-standing social cohesion has been translated into political unity, and, as the result of long and patient indoctrination since the mid-1930's by a highly organized political formation, national values have permeated all important sectors of the country. Time has also been useful; Tunisia had a generation to ripen before plunging into independent life and this maturity now shows. For these reasons, although it is likely that a period of uncertainty is ahead in the not-too-distant future, when one considers the proved Tunisian capacity for accommodation and the ability to subordinate petty problems of the moment to the pursuit of the principal goal, there is much reason to be hopeful.

In Morocco, a large and more complex country than Tunisia, the transition period just after independence was more unsettled but since then there has been more variety and movement in the texture of political life. Until 1953 two forces had shared the leadership of the nationalist movement: the palace and the Istiqlal Party. After their temporary effacement, a third force came on the scene, the so-called "resistance," made up by the various terrorist groups in the cities and the Liberation Army in the countryside. The story of independent Morocco reduced to its simplest political terms has been the sorting out of relations between these forces and the search for a system in which each will have its proper place. This was first exemplified by the problem of incorporating all the undercover elements of the struggle into the national political structure, and later by the growing polarity between the throne and various political groups, with each seeking a mandate from the Moroccan people for the eventual shaping of a new framework. After the King had become the symbol of national resistance in 1953, there was an assumption in many quarters that he would on his return stay aloof from any political involvement, that he would reign and not rule, and that he would remain the representative of a precious but precarious national unity. The prestige of the monarchy was overwhelming and its latent power immense, as it still is. But between 1956 and 1960 that prestige was transformed into active political power as well, although the step was not taken until the inability of the normal political organizations of the country to produce a needed stability had been demonstrated.

At the beginning of 1956 Morocco faced a host of problems, but none was more pressing than the insecurity and turbulence which reigned in both town and country. The several resistance movements which had come into being after 1953 had grown up, as it were, on the streets without proper guidance. They had siphoned off, especially toward the end of the underground period, most of the active and aggressive young men in the country. With the return of normalcy many of these were unwilling to return to ordinary jobs or, in many cases, unemployment and dreary poverty, and they turned to gangsterism, extortion, and various kinds of illegal activities. The field was almost clear because Morocco was dependent on French security forces, which were reluctant to intervene in purely Moroccan affairs, until the national police was formed in May 1956. Even as late as that summer, however, the police had to fight pitched battles in Casablanca with the Black

Crescent, one of the underground groups that had Communist affiliations. Individually the resistants were heroes, however, and the movements were judiciously signaled out for praise in royal speeches although less favorably viewed by the Istiqlal, which did not intend to lose the fruits of its generation-long campaign. Only gradually was urban order restored as the police got the upper hand, and as some of the resistants themselves were incorporated into the police while others drifted back to their ordinary occupations with the assurance that they would be given a gamut of veterans' benefits and special consideration.

The reintegration of the Liberation Army in the countryside was more delicate. In the spring of 1956 it was continuing attacks on French outposts and government offices, and presented a serious threat to order in rural areas where dissidence was an old habit. If the new state was unable to control all its territory, there could be serious consequences. A Royal Army was created, mainly with volunteers who had served with French forces and on the basis of personal and tribal loyalty to the King. It was possible to integrate some of the rank-and-file of the Liberation Army, who themselves came from rural backgrounds, into the Royal Army after careful screening. But the Liberation Army had also recruited urban resistants and political leaders whose ideas did not seem suitable to the force the palace was building up, and so good parts of it were never incorporated. Regrouped in the far south of the country, they were patronized for a time by Allal Al Fassi and his wing of the Istiqlal, which began making claims to large parts of the Sahara in French and Spanish hands, and they unsuccessfully tried to seize Ifni from the Spanish in November 1957, a move which was meant to emphasize the intransigence of their outlook—for they had originally considered themselves part of a unified force meant to liberate all North Africa and had close ties with the Algerian rebels—and embarrass the government. Although this was the last major enterprise of the Liberation Army, it lingered on in the southern border regions and caused minor incidents until French troops were withdrawn a year later. Late in 1957, however, ex-leaders of the Liberation Army formed a new political party, the Popular Movement, which stressed a vague doctrine of "Islamic socialism," and has shown strength in rural and Berber areas in which the Army had previously operated.

After the restoration of public order, which was completed by the end of 1956, Moroccan political life blossomed. Since independence there have been six governments, four of them political cabinets and the last two formed and presided over by the King. The first government of Si Bekkai lasted until October 1956, but was under constant attack by the Istiqlal, which wanted all the cabinet posts instead of a mere majority. In fact, the cabinet was a governing institution in name only at this time because of the unlimited nature of royal power, and the separate political activity which flourished in the palace with all its ramifications, plus royal control of the Army and the police. When the second, all-Istiqlal government was formed, the King retained Si Bekkai, personally loyal to him, as head of government and formed a crown council to handle certain matters that he did not want to go through the cabinet. Thus, the Istiqlal did not ever have full power and it was, moreover, beginning to show signs of internal strain. The enthusiastic support it had received from a majority of the people just after independence was giving way to disillusionment as the economy slowed down and the standard of living dipped. Also there was a basic cleavage between the old-guard leadership which had come from and represented more conservative circles and a minority group headed by Mehdi ben Barka, Abdallah Ibrahim, and Abderrahim Bouabid, which accused the party of having lost contact with popular reality and which turned to the urban proletariat for support. The quarrel was noticeable in 1957, when the tone of party publications controlled by each faction started to clash. After the Istiqlal ministers had resigned and brought down the second

Bekkai government, the conservative wing of the party formed a government under the stewardship of Balafrej. This lasted from May to December 1958, and made an indifferent record. It was a period when events in the Middle East like the Iraqi Revolution made the palace sensitive, while labor disorders increased in the cities. Late in the year an uprising in the Rif, stemming from both economic and political discontent, was forcefully put down by the Royal Army led by Crown Prince (now King) Mulay Hassan. It was also a time when intraparty disharmony came to open rupture. The government was forced to resign and, after three weeks of consultations, the King chose a cabinet directed by one of the leaders of the opposing faction, Ibrahim, although members were to serve, according to royal decision, on a personal and not party basis. The purpose of this cabinet was to prepare for elections and resign, but in fact it lingered in office well over a year, during which time political confusion reached a climax. The Istiqlal split into two segments, and in the summer of 1959 the "progressive" wing, as it termed itself, organized a new party, the National Union of Popular Forces (UNFP), which united Istiqlal secessionists, dissidents from minor parties, and leaders of the Moroccan Labor Union (UMT). Chaos was the only description of the events of early 1960. The government refused to resign voluntarily and signs of impatience and hostility multiplied from the palace, particularly from the Crown Prince, who was politically very active. To compensate for the defection of the UMT, the Istiqlal had formed a rival labor union which did not attract a large clientele, but private political and union strong-arm squads brought a return of violence to the cities. The government was powerless since the palace had control of the security forces, and it refused to intervene. The situation was such that in fact the leaders of the government were the chiefs of the opposition, and an uprising in the Atlas was attempted not against but in favor of the government. To check further degradation, the King stepped in to end the mandate of the Ibrahim government. He announced in a nationwide speech that he was assuming control of the government himself with the Crown Prince as Vice-premier, and asked individuals of all tendencies to help him form a cabinet of national union. All groups except the UNFP agreed to participate in this stabilization effort.

Since 1960 Morocco has been governed as well as reigned over by its monarchs, Muhammad V until his sudden death in February 1961, and Hassan II thereafter. In that interval, although there have been few changes in political structure, a clear division has emerged between the palace and its supporters in groups representing conservative and rural elements, and the opposition entrenched in the industrial cities along the Atlantic coast, where in municipal elections in 1960 (the only elections yet held in Morocco) its candidates won a majority.

The monarchy is the point of departure for any understanding of modern Morocco, and it is more than just one of many political ingredients. The 'Alawite family has ruled for three centuries and has by now forged a strong affective bond between itself and the people, which makes the throne as close to the heart of the continuing tradition of the nation as possible. Thus the King, who wields power not only as the malik, or temporal executive, but also as imam, the spiritual leader of the Moroccan Muslim community, is the evocation of the national personality. His popularity among simple and rural people approaches adulation and if in the cities there is a newer, sophisticated view of him as a political figure, he can still never really be looked on by any Moroccan as an ordinary individual. The decision of the royal family to step into the arena of politics was a fateful one. It raised cries of arbitrariness and "personal power" from the UNFP opposition, and caused discussion in many circles, but until now there has been no sign that any other force in the country is capable of assuring national solidarity.

Until the end of 1962 Morocco was an absolute monarchy in

which the King held an accumulation of executive, legislative, and judicial power as he chose to use or delegate it. But in December, a constitution prepared by the King and his advisors, which had been promised when Muhammad V first took over the government, was presented to the people in a referendum and accepted by a vote of 3,733,816 to 113,199. By its terms Morocco is a constitutional, democratic and social monarchy, an Islamic country whose language is Arabic, a part of the Maghrib and an African state which looks toward the achievement of African (but most significantly nothing is said about Arab) unity. Very great power is retained by the King. He names ministers, who are responsible to him, although they may be censured by parliament and the government brought down; he may decree the dissolution of parliament, although not more than once a year; legislation passed by the parliament is "left to the decision of the King," but the sovereign may himself submit projects, which have not been voted upon by the houses, to the people directly by referendum. A bicameral legislature is established, the lower house (Assembly) elected for four years by universal suffrage and the upper house (Councillors) for six years by a restricted electorate formed of members of prefectural and provincial assemblies, chambers of agriculture and commerce, syndicalist representatives, etcetera, substantially the urban middle classes and rural notables.

As the power of the throne has expanded in recent years, that of all the political parties has diminished correspondingly. However, the parties have lost the flavor they originally had of being simple clusters of individuals with more or fewer adherents depending on the passions of the moment and have emerged into a reasonable representativity. Today they stand for the principal social divisions of the country: the Istiqlal is the party of the traditional urban bourgeoisie and the religious; the UNFP that of the city workers; and the Popular Movement, still in nebulous growth, that of Berber particularism and generalized rural discontent. All overlap somewhat but the lines are now more rationally drawn, because the interests of these sections of the population seldom coincide as Morocco is run today. In this difficult and many-sided country it is a natural division, although it may be regretted that national consciousness has not yet overcome regionalism. One reason is that there has never been effective nationwide work by a political organization—which may not be the fault of the parties entirely, given the handicap they have to work under of competition from the dynasty—and the failure of the Istiqlal in the crucial years of the late 1940's to get a foothold in rural areas (as the neo-Destour did so well) is perhaps a key factor, added to which was the fact that Istiqlal leaders were too much drawn from one source in a diverse culture to make a lasting impression on all classes and regions.

Early in 1963 the above political alignments were further clarified when the Istiqlal ministers resigned from the government and a new royalist party, the Front for the Defense of Constitutional Institutions (FDIC), was formed by persons close to the King, headed by Ahmed Reda Guedira, the Minister of the Interior, with the backing of the Popular Movement. The predilection of the regime for continuing the Gaullist pattern stands out, and the line is drawn more sharply than before between those who place first loyalty to the monarchy and the King, and those who are trying to develop political organizations with coherent and appealing national aims while attempting to push the throne back off the political scene. At the same time it is probable that the split between rural and urban political attitudes will be reinforced by this move.

Today Morocco is a paradox, but so far a very successfully functioning one. The position of the King is described in the constitution as inviolable, and his hand is ceremoniously kissed on state occasions, but the opposition attacks him and his government as ordinary political opponents in strong terms. Compared to many new, underdeveloped countries, Morocco is surprisingly democratic and shows a political variety and vigor which can only be healthful. A charter of public liberties promulgated in 1958 guarantees free expression, the press is unrestrained by censorship, and the labor movements are among the most highly developed in Africa. On the other hand, there is that constant threat of violence or the possibility of it which runs through Moroccan life as much as it is absent in Tunisia. Opposition leaders complain of attempts on their life, the UNFP printing plant was destroyed by a mysterious explosion, and interpolitical warfare is as physical as it is verbal. The eclecticism of Morocco extends to economic life, with its mixture of the public and private sector, and foreign policy, in which Morocco has on the whole avoided extreme positions and hence enemies—except in the impasse over Mauritania. It is the lack of social cohesion in Morocco which has made for political division, and the question now is whether the monarchy, by having become an active political entity, will sharpen these differences and tarnish its own great prestige or whether it can continue to serve as a stabilizing force which will help eventually to turn the internal contradictions of the country into enriching contrasts.

In its turn, the building of the Algerian state has proceeded on entirely different bases from those of its neighbors. Algeria had no core of civilization or dominant elite to draw on. Durable institutions, tradition, and leadership were absent or deficient and the only images on which the organs of the revolution, which eventually became the new state, could model themselves were those of the semiclandestine political groups from which they sprang, or the ancient structures of rural Algeria which had shown a lasting power of resistance. For the Algerian revolution was basically a peasant and popular movement, to which only later the middle-class political and religious figures adhered by necessity. The atmosphere of this revolution was that of a clandestine brotherhood shared in a spartan peasant environment, and Algeria today has been molded by this ethic into a politico-military state in which the social qualities of equality and fraternity in a collectively oriented community are given precedence over liberty. This is the main theme but there is a counterpoint in the tendency, inherent in any collegial activity, to one-man rule. The cult of personality may be denounced by a collective leadership in Algeria as elsewhere but the group finds it useful in the early stages of a revolutionary state to use the charisma of a popular leader in order to charm the masses emotionally where it cannot persuade them intellectually. But these two entities are inimical and sooner or later the single leader or the group, whichever is better able to identify with what in Algeria today is called "the only hero, the people," must destroy the other.

The organization of the PPA, and later the less undercover MTLD, presaged the National Liberation Front. The cell was the base of operations, elastic enough to expand or contract in accordance with the degree of police pressure. Revolutionary habits and techniques were implanted in the leadership, particularly those who were in the Special Organization (OS) formed in 1948 as an underground terror and sabotage arm of the MTLD. The OS was tracked by the police in Algeria and France from then until 1954, but despite many arrests its nucleus was never destroyed and the activity and training of its paramilitary commandos broadened in the early 1950's. It was the OS that gave birth to the CRUA, which was the core of the revolution, and from it most of the "historic chiefs," the founding fathers of Algeria, came.

The FLN was busy just keeping alive early in the revolution, and it was some time before it felt the time ripe to lay a firm groundwork for the Algeria it was working toward. Through 1955 there had not been much change in the leadership, but by the spring of 1956 it had attracted much outside support. In April, the UDMA ceased to exist and Ferhat Abbas and Ahmed Francis flew to Cairo to join the FLN. They were followed by Tewfiq al Madani and some, but not all, of the 'ulama group. At the same time the PCA Communists began to collaborate with the revolutionary group, and from July communists were integrated into the National Liberation Army (ALN) with the understanding that they came as individuals without party label. Earlier that year two support groups had been secretly formed: the General Union of Algerian Workers (UGTA) and the General Union of Algerian Merchants (UGCA). The labor group, which was a rival to the USTA union of Messalist obedience, was admitted in July 1956, to the International Confederation of Free Trade Unions with the backing of international representatives of American labor unions.

With the broader background available to it, the FLN held its first congress in August 1956, under rather trying conditions in the forests of the Soummam Valley in Kabylia. The ALN was organized in detail on paper, and the direction of the Front was confided to a National Council of the Algerian Revolution (CNRA) made up of seventeen full members and seventeen alternates. The list was headed by the historic chiefs, the heads of wilayas and the higher ranking politicians who had just joined. This Congress of the Soummam had been called by the leaders of the "interior" who had not given all their counterparts outside the country enough time warning to attend. This was a first sign of tension between those who were actively fighting inside Algeria and the political and military figures outside the country; the problem never wholly disappeared and came out again in the tension between the wilayas and the externally based ALN when it returned to Algeria from Tunisia and Morocco after independence in 1962. Because of the unwieldy size of the National Council, executive power was delegated to a Committee of Coordination and Execution (CCE), composed at the beginning of five men. Of those, two are now dead and enshrined as national heroes, and the other three (Krim, Ben Khedda, and Dahlab) all played important roles in the GPRA after it was formed in 1958. The Soummam

Congress also consecrated the principle of collective leadership, the supremacy of political considerations over military, and the precedence of the combatants of the interior over those of the exterior. The platform adopted had a neo-Marxist ring to it, and spoke of the future state as a "social and democratic republic" while making a slighting reference to "outdated theocracy and monarchy" which, it was stressed, was not what the revolution was fighting for.

The kidnaping by the French of four important leaders of the Front (Ben Bella, Bitat, Khider, and Ait Ahmed) in October 1956 temporarily weakened the external group and the newly arrived politicians were unable to move into high posts. In 1957 the CNRA met in Cairo and expanded the Council to fifty-four members and the CCE to nine. A year later the provisional government headed by Abbas was formed, both because the revolution was unsure of developments in Algeria and sure of considerable recognition outside. The third full meeting of the CNRA was in Tripoli in December 1959, and it was important because it reaffirmed the provisional character of the power it was holding in trust for the Algerian people, describing itself as the "depositary of the national sovereignty." It noted that only universal suffrage could validate this power when Algeria was independent, but in the meantime the CNRA could make decisions by a two-thirds majority vote. It further stipulated that members of the GRPA; of the general staff; the leaders of the external federations of the Front in France, Tunisia, and Morocco; and the heads of wilayas were all members by right of the National Council. Two years later, after the breakdown in the first two rounds of negotiations with France, the CNRA met in Tripoli in August and reorganized the government. The politicians and late joiners like Abbas had been dropped for what seemed to be a more homogeneous and tighter cabinet, headed by Youssef ben Khedda, a younger man and a pharmacist who had been a militant in the PPA and the MTLD. There was speculation that although the new government was considered to be on the whole farther to the left, it might prove more tractable in negotiations because it had, from the revolutionary point of view, a less disreputable past to make up for than did the government headed by Abbas. The Council developed national theory a bit further by stressing that it would continue to "mobilize the masses" to raise the level of the struggle and build a modern nation and "an economy at the service of the people," but a formal doctrine of socialism was not elaborated.

Early in 1962 the CNRA met once again and ratified the proposals which were to be agreed to at Evian in March. But meanwhile the structures of the revolution were undergoing severe trials, and it speaks volumes of the ingrained habit of dissimulation which the Algerian leadership had taken to practicing that almost nothing about them was known until much later. The origins of the split in the movement are ancient, profound, and complex. They relate partly to the fractionalization of nationalism, with its enduring bitterness between Messalists and anti-Messalists, in the period before the revolution. They have something to do with Kabyle regionalism and the old antagonism of Berbers and Arabs, no matter how much that may be denied by pan-Arabist partisans, and so they are connected with the early division between the internal group, strongly Kabyle, and the external group influenced especially at the beginning by Cairo. From this comes, too, the split between the Cairo group and those closer to a doctrine with social ideology, between the military and the civilians, and between the early, classless Front members and the later bourgeois arrivals. Mix this up a bit and there is more than enough material for a fine schism. There had already been strains; in one of these Lamine Debbaghine, the Foreign Minister of the GPRA, was eliminated from the government and remained in Cairo; in an earlier one, the Kabyle maquisard of the CCE, Abbane, was physically liquidated; and there had already been one sharp discussion between the ALN and the

GPRA long before the final break. The Front, in short, was just what its name implied and no more, and the closer victory approached in 1962 the more it creaked.

When the Evian agreements were signed in March 1962, the kidnapees of six years before, who had always been honorary members of the GPRA, were released to the Moroccans who had been their hosts. The aura of this group had been dimmed during the years and the GPRA had just successfully completed negotiations for independence; time and events threatened to pass them by unless they made themselves felt. Thus, shortly after his release Ahmed ben Bella criticized the GPRA for having "confiscated the revolution," a statement from which some of his co-detainees, Boudiaf and Ait Ahmed, disassociated themselves. But he found allies among the military who were irritated by GPRA treatment of the army, and from the old UDMA men, like Abbas, who did not feel warm toward those who had replaced them. This group succeeded in having the CNRA convoked for May, theoretically to prepare for the return to Algeria and to go on record with the fundamental program of the revolution. The GPRA directorate, which then included Ben Khedda, Krim, Dahlab, and Yazid, opposed this for fear that their direction of affairs during the past year might be challenged. Ben Bella and his supporters were in a minority in the government, but, with the backing of some wilaya leaders, the army, and assorted political figures hostile to the Ben Khedda group, they seemed likely to have a majority in the Council.

At the conference the GPRA was charged with having established a "fractionalist dictatorship" and charges of personal despotism were particularly hurled at Krim. A lengthy platform was then presented for approval. It was not difficult to agree on such matters as the reconversion of the Front to a party, or the decision to make it a "preponderant party" but not a single party (a doctrine which was rapidly revised after independence when all opposition was eliminated), or the agreement that the movement should continue to be one of a restricted elite and not a mass organization. But the key issue was who would form a Political Bureau charged with the task of designating candidates for national elections. Ben Bella presented a list which included the five ex-prisoners plus one member of the GPRA, Said Mohammedi, who was notoriously anti-Krim. This did not obtain a majority, nor did another more balanced selection which included the five main figures of the revolution (Ben Bella, Ben Khedda, Krim, Boudiaf, and Abbas), whereupon the majority group within the GPRA withdrew. A statement was then issued by its opponents, including Ben Bella, Khider, Bitat, the ALN leaders, and the ex-UDMA heads, roundly condemning them.

Since all deliberations were clothed in secrecy, no official word of any of this came out at the time, although observers close to the scene suspected that something had gone wrong. In the month between the Tripoli conference and independence, a race developed to win over the forces inside Algeria. The ALN sent propaganda teams to visit the wilayas and Krim dispatched his own lieutenants to work on them. Krim widened the breach by antagonizing purists in the opposition when he sanctioned negotiations in the latter part of June with European OAS terrorists, thus granting them a political recognition which the Front had categorically denied them before. At the end of June the GPRA decided to take action, either from growing weakness on its part as the ALN tried to undermine its position, or because it genuinely misread its own strength and thought it would be obeyed. It arrested one prominent ALN officer, the only one it could get its hands on, and ordered in all three chiefs of the General Staff, including its commander, Colonel Boumedienne, stripped of rank. This brought the government to a dead end, however. It began to come apart as Khider resigned and Ben Bella, in an unusually theatrical move, jumped aboard a waiting plane at the airport in Tunis and fled to Tripoli, where he withdrew his support from the GPRA. Moreover, the ALN refused to obey and the General Staff, except for the arrested Major Slimane, remained as it was. The legal basis for opposition was the fact that the GPRA could not take such executive action because it was merely an agent holding power from the Council, but the true reason seems to have been little more than a naked struggle for power. The next day, Algeria became independent in the midst of popular rejoicing tempered by disillusionment, as the people inside the country received the news that the unity forged in seven years of war, and which had been an immense source of pride to them(as well as to all Arabs conscious of their own divisions), had been destroyed on the very eve of victory. Certainly no state has ever acceded to independence in more bizarre conditions than Algeria—in a state of complete economic collapse, social disorder, physical insecurity, and with nearly a tenth of the population having fled. These difficulties were an unavoidable part of what was a real tragedy and therefore some allowance must be made, but the additional burden that it had to carry, that its only political formation was hopelessly split, was unnecessarily self-imposed by ambitious and selfish leaders whose people during the next few months judged them more severely and eloquently than any outsiders could.

The history of the first months of Algerian independence is divided into two distinct periods: first, the continuing institutional crisis, the lack of a government, and a power fight which put one foot over the brink of civil war; this was followed by a compromise solution in September which permitted the formation of a national constitutional assembly and a central government, and the belated appearance of Algeria on the international scene with its recognition by all countries (many, like the United States which waited until September 29 to grant recognition, were concerned that there was no effective government body to whom to transmit it) and its admission to the United Nations.

Although the country was independent as of July 1, it was a state with no functioning mechanism of any sort. The transitional executive established at Evian was to hand over power within three weeks (when elections were scheduled), but it was not until September 5 that the Ben Bella group finally succeeded in imposing itself by force, and elections took place only on September 20. While the orthodox members of the GPRA returned to Algiers in dubious triumph on July 3, Ben Bella was installing himself in Western Algeria, near his birthplace, from where, supported by the well-armed forces of the ALN which came in from Morocco, he announced the formation of a Political Bureau which declared itself the supreme political authority in the country. Leaders of the wilayas, who had met a few days before to try to effect a compromise, had been unsuccessful. Later in July Ben Bellist forces seized some cities in eastern Algeria, resistance was organized by Wilaya III in Kabylia, headed by Boudiaf and Krim, and almost no one was left among the shreds of the GPRA in Algiers except Ben Khedda himself. A temporary accord was then signed between the Ben Bellist and Kabyle factions and for a time Ben Bella held power in Algiers. But soon he was criticized by his opponents and by the heads of Wilaya IV (Algiers region) because he wanted to reduce the ALN, then swollen to well over 100,000 men, to a size in keeping with Algerian need and capacity. Once again, Ben Bella left without warning, and from Oran ordered troops loyal to him to march on Algiers. These forces, under the command of Boumedienne, after some skirmishes with the more lightly equipped men of Wilaya IV, convinced the adversary of the strength if not the justice of the Ben Bellist cause and a second agreement was reached to end combats, organize elections, and demilitarize Algiers. Within four days the National Popular Army (ANP), as the ALN was now renamed, entered the demilitarized city. Under its protection and surveillance the Political Bureau prepared a single list of candidates for the elections, from which almost all the opponents of Ben Bella were eliminated. With no opposition the elections were a formality which meant to the Algerian people only the end of the political infighting and the privations which had lasted long enough—a sentiment they expressed with touching sincerity at Boghari earlier in the month when civilians interposed themselves between the warring factions, and later in the streets of Algiers where they demonstrated by calling out the single word, "Enough!"

The Assembly met on September 29 under the speakership of its new president, Ferhat Abbas, and invested a government headed by Ben Bella by a vote of 159 to 1. Boudiaf refused to accept his election as a member of parliament, while a clandestine socialist revolutionary party announced its formation and violently attacked the government in handbills. The government announced a priority program for agriculture and education, in both of which domains the exodus of Europeans from farmlands and administrative posts had caused problems, and promised to deal with the unabated insecurity reigning throughout the country. The Premier then turned for two weeks to international affairs, traveling to New York, Washington, and Havana. After his return in November, insistence on adherence to the single party increased. Pressure was put on the UGTA labor leaders who were trying to retain a separate nonpolitical identity, and the Algerian Communist Party was outlawed at the end of the month. By the end of 1962 Algeria was almost entirely without funds. In preparation for the definitive separation of the French and Algerian treasuries at the end of the year, separate accounts were kept beginning in November. Previously France had been advancing nearly two million dollars a day for current expenses, since Algerian receipts covered less than 20 per cent of expenditures, partly owing to European departures and a collapse in tax receipts. Talks were begun with France late in November for emergency aid to tide the state over till the beginning of 1963, when further sums were to be advanced as part of the economic aid stipulated in the Evian agreements.

Six months is not a long time in which to get a country going, and Algeria had unprecedented problems for which no government in power would have been wholly responsible. After the political power struggle died down temporarily, the new leaders showed signs of inexperience and uncertainty. They were hampered by the lack of structure to guide them; by the physical absence of so many indispensable civil servants, from technicians to stenographers; and by the fact that economic pressures kept them from being masters in their own house. Under the circumstances, a return to the traditional refuge of the society was predictable, and this seems to be happening. The Islamic content of the new Algeria was growing daily at the end of 1962. The Premier was careful to attend public prayers at the ex-Cathedral of Algiers (restored to its original status as a mosque with an unseemly haste which irked the French government), and the strictures of the Soummam platform were forgotten as Tewfiq al Madani said, to Assembly applause, that "We are all Muslims before everything else." The pressure of public opinion, always exercised on leaders in Muslim countries in the direction of greater piety, was forcing a backtracking from the idea of a lay state in Algeria open to all. While the Islamic revival waxed, socialism waned, or at least it may be said to have occupied a subsidiary position during this time of uncertainty and stress, and Ben Bella announced in November that it could not be built "in a few months or even years." But in the spring of 1963—whether the government felt that national convalescence had advanced enough so that it could tackle this problem, or whether it was pushed into action by unfavorable comment—important new measures were taken nationalizing many large European landholdings, as well as numerous cinemas, restaurants, and hotels which in most cases had been bought by Algerians from departing Europeans at bargain prices. Early in April it was claimed that the area under the control of management committees totaled 1,500,000 ha. Among other important trends in the new state were the consecration of the single-party system, completed at the end of 1962 by bringing the UGTA to heel, and a delicate balancing of power among the civilian Political Bureau (all of whose members were not in agreement among themselves), the military which shored it up, and the as yet unheard from but potentially crucial forces of farmers and workers who will judge the regime not on its dogma or diplomatic successes but by its bread-and-butter results.

By early 1963 Algeria seemed to have weathered its worst initial crisis; the patient had not died—largely owing to continued French financial assistance and American relief shipments—but he was still gravely ill and only beginning to convalesce. Every branch of activity in both the public and private sector had been seriously touched, but the all-pervading problem as the country touched bottom was the lack of a solid structure from which to begin to construct the new nation. The top leadership varies enormously from brilliant and dedicated to mediocre, but it is in almost all cases inexperienced. The gravest lacunae are found in middle-level positions and among technicians, and the national government is far better staffed than are regional offices. If the administration is faulty, the government and the military together have largely restored order, a by no means inconsiderable task. The most disappointing feature perhaps is the inability of the FLN to develop and function as a peace-time political party with roots in the countryside. It is not yet clear how this vacuum will be filled, but less than a year after the end of the war it was evident that a natural decline in revolutionary spirit had not been matched by the growth of a new ideology accepted by the whole country. It will likely take some time before this can be built— like socialism and Rome it will not be the work of a day or a decree—and it is tempting to predict that it will not happen until meaningful power elites, each with a sound idea of its own needs and position, have been formed out of the amorphousness of a revolution to which respect is still paid but which as a driving force for the future no longer exists; for only in the tension between such groups can the country generate enough energy to leap forward. National unity as demanded by the authorities may be valid for a while but it is doubtful that it can serve as a positive force in the long run. Because of all these factors, to which might be added the fact that full national unity is far from prevailing at present—what with some of the best talents in the country either without responsibility or in silent opposition—while many skilled Algerians have left the country and continue to do so in disillusionment, it is hard to make anything but a negative prognosis for Algeria for some time to come.

ECONOMIC PROBLEMS

There are several ways of looking at the North African economy. The conventional encyclopedia description goes something like this: The economy is based primarily on agriculture of the Mediterranean type, and agricultural products make up the bulk of the exports, with wine, citrus fruit, cereals, olive oil, and winter vegetables heading the list. Secondarily, the area has extensive mineral deposits, and the extractive industries, with phosphates, iron ore, and now oil in great quantities in the Sahara, help to balance trade accounts which are usually adverse. In all three countries in the past two decades light industries have been developing, including fish, fruit, and vegetable canning; cement making and glass making; tobacco growing; and paper and textile industries. The infrastructure is highly developed: excellent roads; an integrated railway system linking Algeria, Tunisia, and Morocco; an extensive air network; and a large number of automobiles and trucks per capita have made communications a minor problem. Agricultural expansion has been furthered by dam-building in

recent years and irrigated areas have been extended. Health
and sanitation are generally good, and are improving. There
are few endemic diseases, and the major scourge is trachoma
in rural regions. The death rate has been much reduced in the
last generation and is now about 15/1,000. Per capita income
ran around $190 for Morocco in 1958, $200 in Algeria in 1960,
and $130 in Tunisia in 1956. While these figures are lower than
for any European country, they are two to three times as high
as standards in India and many parts of Asia and Africa.

All of that is exact, but there are other facts which are mentioned less often. North Africa is an underdeveloped area,
whose economic, social, cultural, and demographic factors are
intertwined. The population is largely rural, more than 70
per cent in each of the three countries, whereas the share of
agriculture in the gross national products is approximately half
that; thus productivity is low, and disguised or seasonal unemployment high. But the population, driven by pressure on
the land, is urbanizing with increasing rapidity, and undis-
guised unemployment is rampant in the cities. In foreign trade,
the Maghrib is at the mercy of its markets overseas, particularly
in France and Western Europe whose inhabitants are overwhelmingly its principal clients. The ton of exported raw
materials is worth much less than the ton of finished goods
brought back in exchange. Population pressure varies from
moderate in Morocco, to heavy in Tunisia, and it is almost
unbearable in parts of Algeria. Natality ranges from 40-50/1,-
000, the population is increasing by more than 2 per cent each
year and will double in thirty years. Undernourishment is
common and the average calorie level is slightly under 2,000
a day in rural areas, higher in the cities, but with both groups
oversupplied with carbohydrates and deficient in animal pro-
teins. The orientation of the economy is external and its
structure colonial.

All those facts are true, too, but even when the above two
paragraphs are put together the essence of the economy of

North Africa is missing. This essence is that it is a dual economy of unique proportions in which a modern economic
sector has been superimposed on a traditional one. The modern
sector is a testimony to the efforts of two million European
settlers who inhabited the Maghrib in the 1950's, and the
results, while brilliant if judged for themselves, have not led
to the construction of an economic ensemble but rather have
created a grave disequilibrium, which is the economic equivalent of the other imbalances caused by the European entry into
the Maghrib. The sclerosis from which the traditional North
African economy was already suffering in the nineteenth century for historical reasons was aggravated as it was bypassed
and isolated by this intrusion. The Europeans developed a
superior commercial-type agriculture and invested in the mining industry, both of these for export purposes; they repatri-
ated capital and invested part of it at home while using some
to import manufactured goods which they sold, with tariff
preferences and good profit margins, to their own large, self-
sufficient European community. The whole system formed a
closed circuit with which the bulk of the native population
had nothing to do.

There are other, perhaps more important aspects of the
dual society that deserve explanation. Granted that there are
many kinds of dual economics in other parts of the world—in
colonial countries in Africa, in the differences between effendi
city life in Cairo compared to Egyptian peasant squalor, or
even in the gap between the developed north of Italy and
Spain and the backward southern parts of those countries. But
the situation in North Africa was different in many respects.
It involved a larger part of the population than in other
colonial regions (in the Algerian case just before independence
it is estimated that the modern sector contained the million
Europeans at the top and middle levels, and about two million
Muslim Algerians who had infiltrated it and formed the modern
proletariat—a third of the total population). The economic

differences between the two sectors were correlated with, and sharpened, all other social, cultural, and religious differences. There was less mobility between the sectors than usually found in the case of a developing country, and strict limits beyond which the mass (although not always the individual) could not rise. And finally, the entire ethos of the economy was, until independence in Morocco and Tunisia, and until the Constantine Plan was evolved very late in the revolution in Algeria in 1958, centered around the minority and its ties to another homeland and way of life, while the needs and aspirations of the majority were considered only in passing.

To understand the true nature of this dual economy one must imagine what it was like to live in French Algiers—and still is, to a lesser extent, in Casablanca today. The example of Algiers is the most striking because it was a city with 200,000 Europeans and 164,000 Muslims in 1954 (in 1926 it had 160,-000 Europeans and only 55,000 Muslims, showing the drift of jobseekers in the latter group into the city, which picked up sharply after 1954). Muslims, with the rarest exceptions, entered the economy at the lowest levels. They were the runners, doormen, scavengers, dockworkers, minor clerks, factory hands, but the higher functionaries and white-collar employees were all European. In factories, department stores, and banks throughout the city the two groups mixed economically but maintained this balance even though they both might belong to the same socialist union in a factory bottling soda water. Muslim salaries were poor by European standards but remarkable compared to the earnings of millions of Algerians in the traditional sector. This is why the idea of a national per capita income is meaningless. The $200 average for Algeria really meant an income of around $600 to $700 and up for the Europeans, $250 to $300 for urban Algerians in the modern economy, and perhaps $60 to $70 for the rural Muslims who formed 65 per cent of the population. For the European, it was almost like living in France. His salary might be paid by his office, the branch of a French firm, and his apartment was rented from a French bank with offices in Algiers and was furnished with Louis XV or Empire pieces which did not have to be brought with him but were available at good shops. The only language seen written in public or taught in the schools was French, and the radio, the films, or the Museum of Fine Arts on Sunday all reminded him that he was at home. His wife dressed herself in copies of Paris originals which she bought locally and shopped in branches of metropolitan department stores, or alternatively at the corner (usually European) grocer where she got cheese, pâté, butter, flour, and a stream of incidentals which came from across the Mediterranean. It might be that the only Algerian product she invariably consumed was local wine, grown almost exclusively by Europeans, and the only Algerian service she used directly was her household help. One can sympathize with the dislocation of an Algerian Muslim in this strange world of half-dream, half-reality, in the fringes of which he participated if he had a job, but which he saw flourishing all about him even if he were jobless and penniless. In this reproduction of Europe on an immense scale, treasures beyond the wildest imagination of a countrified Algerian, and beyond the reach of all but a few urban Algerians were displayed tantalizingly. Looking back, one realizes how strong the separation of the two groups was, not by any kind of legal segregation—this was not South Africa or even the American deep south—but for socioeconomic causes. The Muslims did not participate in the true life of the city because they knew instinctively it was not theirs, and one of the greatest shocks in postindependence Algiers, or any Algerian city, is to see Algerians everywhere for the first time. Thus, Algeria was not India or Egypt, where one had to go and seek out the British in certain clubs and hotels if he wanted to see what their life was like, it was . . . France. And it represented to the North African the ultimates in hope, envy, and despair that the poor feel living close to the inordinately rich.

Let us see how this dual economy functions. In agriculture the two sectors exist alongside each other throughout the countryside. They differ in the quality of the land farmed, in equipment and techniques, crops, and yields. The modern sector, which includes all Europeans and a few Muslims (in Algeria, for example, there were approximately 540,000 traditional Muslim holdings totaling 7,000,000 hectares; 22,000 European farms with 2,700,000 hectares; and 15,000 modern Muslim properties of 750,000 hectares in 1954), is mechanized and often irrigated, uses selected plants and seeds, and studies its market. Citrus fruit growers follow a precise calendar because a delay of a few weeks in shipping their produce means losing out to their competition from other Mediterranean lands. Modern sector farmers experiment with new species and learn quickly about the modern appurtenances of cultivation. Finally, their operations are rounded out by facilities for stockage, trucking to port, dock warehousing, and transport to Europe, which makes a unified commercial system. Often, in fact, the proprietor lives in town or overseas, and the running of the farm is entrusted to an overseer.

Traditional agriculture, on the other hand, is that of the simple wooden plow which just scratches the surface of the soil—and much of the problem begins right there. It is dependent completely on adequate and propitious rainfall which is seldom available, and it is unencumbered by scientific calculations, although it is blessed by a peasant canniness. The donkey is the universal helper and carrier, and tools are rare and rudimentary. There is no provision for the disposal of a surplus; usually there is none, but a part of the crop must be saved to trade for the essentials that cannot be produced on the farm: tobacco, salt, sugar, tea, and a bit of cloth. Holdings are small—in Morocco, where the average European farm is more than 150 hectares, the normal Moroccan holding is about 6 hectares, and three-quarters of all Algerian Muslim traditional properties are less than 10 hectares in area.

With such contrasting backgrounds, yields naturally vary; the Europeans hold better land normally and, where they do, yields tend to run from three to four times that of traditional farmers, but even where they share the same kind of soil, their technical superiority and know-how brings in about double the traditional harvest. Finally, the specialization of the modern sector has led to concentrating on those cash crops which bring in more per hectare. One hectare of a vineyard is roughly ten times more profitable than one of wheat, and one of tomatoes thirty times more so. The Europeans dominate the specialty fields in the heaviest proportions. They grow from half to two-thirds of the soft wheat in all three countries; 90 to 95 per cent of the wine; 90 per cent of the citrus fruit in Algeria and Morocco and 75 per cent in Tunisia; half of all cereals in Algeria and Tunisia; two-thirds of the garden vegetables in Algeria. Traditional farming, unable to compete, is relegated to the production of hard wheat and barley for self-consumption or local trade, figs, and dates. These, with olives and a little oil added, make up the basic diet of the peasant.

Nothing illustrates the involutions of the Maghribi economy better than the wine industry. Winegrowing is widely practiced in all three countries. In Morocco and Tunisia, however, the proportions are reasonable; wine represents about 15 per cent of the value of agricultural production in Tunisia. But in Algeria it has reached such a scale that it has become the principal economic nightmare of the country. Nearly 400,000 hectares are cultivated and wine production reaches nearly half a billion gallons. Until independence about 6 per cent of this was consumed in the country, mostly by the Europeans. New prohibition laws for Muslims since Algerian independence and the drastic reduction of the European population will cut even that figure down. The balance is exported and represents, year in year out, half the value of all Algerian exports. It goes to France, the world's leading producer of wines, where some of it is mixed into cheap table wines and the bulk distilled into commercial or inferior brandy products and re-exported, often at a loss. The upshot of all this is that some 200,000 hectares of the most fertile land in Algeria is devoted to a product which cannot be consumed in the country, is unneeded abroad (and it might be noted that French wine consumption is decreasing), is looked on with religio-cultural prejudice at home because it is "impure" and is occupying land which otherwise might be used for food production in a country which has had to import food regularly. But the dilemma is that if wine exports were suddenly stopped, especially with the precarious state of finances in independent Algeria, the country would suffer a loss of precious hard franc currency. In addition, the vineyards provide employment for a considerable working force, and engage seasonal labor as well. If the experience of Morocco and Tunisia is a guide, Algeria will inveigh against the tyranny of this monoculture, will make periodic efforts to popularize domestic consumption of the grape and its unfermented juice, and will end by proudly organizing sales campaigns abroad for the fine vintages of its soil. But, then, Algeria in 1962 is not Morocco or Tunisia, and more drastic solutions may follow heavier social pressures.

The last great refuge of traditional agriculture is stock raising, except for swine and some cattle. The Muslims possess the great majority of the sheep, goats, camels, and horses. But it is a precarious livelihood. The shepherd is at the mercy of an unreliable climate, badgered by the steady encroachment of cultivation and the restriction on pastures, and condemned by his own habits. The ordinary Maghribi stock raiser feels that his prosperity and prestige are determined by the size of his flock, which is therefore often oversized while individual members may be undernourished. Then a drought arrives and the lack of facilities for storage fodder or for speedy large-scale slaughtering and preservation, condemn him to sudden massive losses. One of the most useful but little-remarked moves by the Food and Agriculture Organization of the United Nations in the countries of North Africa has been to aid in developing slaughter and cold-storage chains for such emergencies.

Turning to the industrial economy, we find the same general division lines as in agriculture. There is a traditional sector, which has handicrafts as its principal activity, with some milling and oil-pressing. It touches on food industries on a small scale, and there is a modern sector of secondary industries such as fruit, vegetable, and fish canning; wine and soft-drink bottling; tobacco, cellulose, and paper-making factories; and glass, cement, textile, and leather industries about complete the list. Here again there has been the ruinous competition of one with the other, with the help of the outside world. Handicrafts occupy a large part of the active population; in Morocco, about 800,000 people are supported by the more than 160,000 craftsmen. And that number has already dwindled sharply since the beginning of the French Protectorate in that country. In that fifty-year period, Fez lost three-fourths of its slipper-makers, and more than half its tanners and weavers. The traditional shoemaker cannot compete with the branch of a European shoe factory in the modern town, and the weaver cannot hold his own against imported textiles from the Far East, and today faces for the first time competition from nascent textile industries in the country itself. Strenuous efforts have been made, notably in Morocco, to keep the artisan afloat at least temporarily (for there seems little hope in the long run) by rationalizing production through cooperatives, and the rapid progress of mass tourism in the country may stave off disaster for a while longer.

The extractive industries play a large part in the North African economy. Morocco is the world's second producer of phosphates with 20 per cent of world output, while Tunisia is the fourth producer. In Morocco the phosphate industry has been long nationalized, is the country's leading export in value and tonnage, and the revenues from it are used for state economic investment. Moroccan phosphates are of unusually high quality and are much sought after. During the period of the French rule in North Africa, marketing was managed by a joint bureau for the three countries, but Morocco has now withdrawn from the arrangement to its advantage and to the distress of Tunisia. Up to now the phosphates have been exported raw or washed, but work has begun in Morocco on a chemical complex at Safi which will produce sulphuric and phosphoric acid and triple-superphosphate. Algeria mines considerable iron ore, but until recently the poor quality of local coal and the lack of industrial opportunity caused it to be exported, mostly to England. Among other metals, Morocco produces sizable quantities of lead, manganese, and cobalt (10 per cent of world production of the last), and both Morocco and Tunisia have substantial reserves of iron ore and moderate production. The mining industry is important not only for the direct employment it provides for nearly 100,000 workers, but for the additional jobs and activity it stimulates in rail transport, port loading, and shipping.

By far the most important mineral resources in the Maghrib, however, are the oil and natural gas deposits which have recently been found in the Sahara. The deficiency of energy sources everywhere in North Africa had until then been a severe handicap and now at least Algeria's economic potential should change radically. Petroleum deposits in the Algerian Sahara have been estimated at about four billion barrels of reserves, roughly one-eighth those of the United States. There are two main fields, one at Hassi Messaoud, the other in the Edjelé area near the Libyan frontier, and pipelines connect each with the Mediterranean. The Hassi Messaoud line terminates at Bougie and lies entirely within the Algerian territory, but the Edjelé pipeline crosses Tunisian territory and ends at Skhira on the Gulf of Gabes. Total production in 1961 amounted to more than 110 million barrels and is expected to rise to 170 million barrels in 1963 and 190 million barrels in 1965. The Algerian government is part shareholder and the revenues it will receive from oil will play a large part in its economic accounts. Since independence, Franco-Algerian co-operation in the oil and gas industry in the Sahara has been more noticeably successful than in other domains, something which underlines the independent existence which the industry enjoys almost everywhere. Under the Evian agreements, a Saharan Technical Cooperation Organism is to be established, and France has been guaranteed that it will continue to enjoy its present mining rights, will be granted preference on an equal basis in new exploration permits, and will be supplied with all oil and gas needed by France and the franc zone with payment to be made in French francs.

Natural gas, however, is as likely to become as important, or even more so, to Algeria and its neighbors. The huge deposits discovered in the western Sahara at Hassi Rmel are now estimated to hold about 2,000 billion cubic feet. A pipe-line to the coast at Arzew was completed in 1961; it has branches to carry gas to the cities of Algiers and Oran. Arzew, where the port is being modernized, a gas liquefication plant is starting, and other chemical factories are being considered, is one of the few bright spots in the postindependence Algerian economy. The cost of Hassi Rmel gas is low and this cheap energy can change the outlook for industrial growth in Algeria in the long run, and for all the Maghrib if cooperation can be arranged. With plentiful reserves of iron ore in all the countries, steel can now be manufactured; in fact, gas is to be used in the steel complex at Bone. But the full potentialities of the reserves of gas cannot be realized in the foreseeable future in North Africa alone, and undersea cross-Mediterranean pipe-lines have been planned: one from Mostaganem, near Arzew, to Cartagena in Spain and thence to France, the other from the Cape Bon region of Tunisia to Sicily. Arrangements have already been made in France and the United Kingdom for the purchase of gas beginning in 1964. The long-range political implications of this connection may be as noteworthy as its economic importance. One obstacle that must be overcome is the Tunisian claim to parts of the Algerian Sahara which include the Edjelé fields and which were expressed forcibly in the summer of 1961 at the time of the Bizerte incidents.

The last distinguishing feature of the economy in all the North African states is the way in which it is tied in each case to the ex-mother country. In the case of Algeria, more than 80 per cent of its imports and exports came from or went to France. Tunisia received 54 per cent of its imports and sent 55 per cent of its exports to France, while Moroccan commerce with France in these categories was 49 per cent and 37 per cent, respectively, slightly less because the open-door policy of the Algeciras conference had partially prevented a full integration of Morocco into the French economic system. More striking perhaps in terms of the future is the fact that the principal subsidiary trading partners are the other countries in Western Europe, particularly those in the Common Market. Tunisia is the only exception, but this is because 15 per cent of its imports come from the United States as part of the American aid program. In the case of Morocco, 60 per cent of its trade is with Common Market countries. Algeria, as a territory included in the geographical area of the original treaty, has the option as an independent country of remaining within the organization. At the end of 1962, Algerian goods were being treated as French, but this cannot continue indefinitely and a decision must be made. Morocco and Tunisia are much preoccupied with the necessity for working out a permanent agreement with the European Economic Community which will not infringe on their sovereignty or other treaty arrangements, but they have taken no steps other than to renew agreements with France for the continuation of trade preferences for limited periods.

Algeria is now, and under the Evian agreements is bound to stay, within the franc zone. The position of the other two North African states is anomalous. Tunisia seems at times quite outside it for practical purposes; it has made bilateral agreements without going through franc zone clearing procedures, for example, but it has not formally withdrawn. However, the customs union it had with France has been abrogated. Morocco has a similarly tenuous connection, and has instituted exchange controls on transfers to the rest of the franc zone. Both countries have unpegged their currencies from the franc, but again both have flexible credit arrangements with the Bank of France. All three North African countries have had habitual adverse trade balances. Since 1956 Morocco and Tunisia have made strenuous efforts to equalize the balance of trade, but have only rarely succeeded, although coverage is now much higher than before. The case of Algeria, where deficits have been extremely high in recent years (in 1961 exports amounted to only 38 per cent of imports) promises to be even more difficult in the future. The lessons of the complicated economic maneuverings of Morocco and Tunisia in recent years, which are likely to be repeated in Algeria, are that while it is difficult for an underdeveloped country to change the pattern of its trade with an industrial group of nations, an elastic membership in monetary and trading area like the franc zone can be made to cover almost any contingency.

An analysis of the specific economic problems of North Africa and the attempts being made to overcome them must start at the beginning of a vicious circle common to many underdeveloped societies. The basic problem is the lack of employment, which goes back to the crisis on the land: too many people are doing too little on land insufficient in quantity and often inadequate in quality. Because of the rapidly increasing population the situation in the countryside goes from bad to worse, and there are only three general ways to escape. One is to make the relationship between the population and the land more bearable by the adjustment and redistribution of existing acreage (land reform). A second is to make better utilization of existing areas (increased cultivation) through improved techniques (increased productivity). Another is to increase the available amount of land by the reclamation of unused or marginal regions or added irrigation. These solutions employ agrarian measures exclusively, but they may be combined with a fourth—a process already being initiated by the population itself in most cases—that is, providing employment in a new urban environment. This means the development of an industrial economy and a planned campaign of investment to achieve it. Usually the investment capital is not sufficient locally, and what there is of it does not necessarily go into investments which are the most job-productive. In North Africa and all countries undergoing decolonization, what capital there was, mostly of local European origin or coming from European sources in the homeland (in Morocco the European share in private investment in 1956 was about 95 per cent) tended to dry up in the critical period after independence when it was most needed. The flight of capital in Tunisia and Morocco in 1956–1957 was serious; that in Algeria has been catastrophic. The final obstacle comes from the fact that the purchasing power of the market in underdeveloped countries is, and will be for some time, too limited to provide a probable profit on investments.

Broadly speaking, each country in the Maghrib has made a choice for the moment which puts more emphasis on one or the other of these "solutions," although the decisions have generally been tentative and limited ones which do not engage a final responsibility or rule out future changes. Tunisia has put most of its stress on the first and second alternatives, with some experimentation in the third. Morocco has confined itself almost exclusively to the second. Algeria in some ways is not a case in point because it has not had a chance as an independent nation to make a full choice, but the broad lines of the Constantine Plan for economic development, started under the French in 1958, were based on the assumption that the fourth solution was the only possible answer in Algeria, and political pressures since independence have led to the beginning of an agrarian reform more sweeping than anything planned in either neighbor country. These choices reflect the acuteness of the crisis within the economy of each country (as well as the determination of the authorities to face it). Thus the situation in Morocco, while far from brilliant, can stand more temporizing for a while in terms of population-land resources than can the explosive and desperate state of Algeria, while Tunisia falls between the two in the direness of its plight.

Land reform has become an article of faith in the social planning of nearly every underdeveloped country, but, as has been seen in the example of the Algerian vineyards, it is not so easy to put into practice. While conditions in each country vary, it would seem that in North Africa the mere shifting around of people on the land, however politically useful or necessary it may be, is only a temporary palliative and may, as has happened elsewhere, reduce productivity disastrously. The breakup of the large, mechanized operations in Syria during its unhappy period in the United Arab Republic comes to mind as an example not to be followed with the same kind of efficient exploitations in Algeria.

In any event, in Morocco until now there has been little done about land reforms. The holdings of European settlers have not been touched although the continued existence of some questionably acquired property is a delicate political issue; and only the most flagrant collaborators with the old regime were inconvenienced by confiscation of their sometimes extensive property. Perhaps the most important step yet taken in Morocco was the decree in 1962 which begins at the beginning by organizing a cadastral survey with a view to reunification of fragmented holdings. (One of the principal problems created by Islamic law is the excessive subdivision of inherited property.) In 1957 Morocco began a cooperative farming experiment, "Operation Tractor," in which the state provided mechanized equipment, seed, and fertilizer for private lands which were to be plowed and sown without regard to individual lots, although the land itself and the harvest remained private property. This compromise solution increased the yield on the 300,000 hectares where it was carried out but ran into serious problems of social psychology and did nothing to solve the basic land issue. Since its inception with great fanfare it has dropped into obscurity, and plans to extend the area thus cultivated seem to have been shelved.

Tunisia has gone farther and deeper. A fundamental modernization of property laws, a program to buy out all foreign-held land, and an agricultural reform program with interesting social overtones have been combined in an effort to make a real dent in rural stagnation and poverty. The undermining during the Protectorate period of the *habus* system through the practice of *enzel* leasing has already been described. This breach and the generally inefficient and discredited management of the *habus* enabled the Tunisian government, with its secular orientation, to move boldly in this field. It sequestered all public *habus* land in 1956 and in the following year other *habus* types were taken over. In all, about one-quarter of the cultivable surface of Tunisia was affected, and public lots were put up for sale to would-be proprietors. Thus land which had in many cases been unproductive and outside the normal commercial circuit was restored to full use. Simultaneously, the Tunisians attacked two extreme cases, that of collective tribal lands, some 2,000,000 hectares of which were reorganized for division into individual holdings, and lands of "extreme fragmentation" which were consolidated. The division of collective lands were associated with the plan to settle nomads on the land. Then in 1958 President Bourguiba announced the intention of the state to repurchase all settler-held property eventually, and the French government agreed to the principle. An agreement was signed in October 1960, for the restitution with compensation of a first lot of 100,000 hectares, but this was never implemented and during the Bizerte crisis the Tunisians expropriated without payment 60,000 hectares. Negotiation on this whole subject were continuing in 1962, but in the light of Tunisian determination it seems likely that in a few years there will be no substantial European holdings left in the country.

In Algeria the agrarian situation after independence turned into near anarchy and the future is unclear. Much of the European-owned farmland was abandoned, at least temporarily, by proprietors in the flight of 1962. In many cases Algerian peasants moved in as squatters and the Algerian Army was used to bring in harvests that otherwise would have rotted. In other instances Algerian employees on large estates took over operations and felt that their labor and the principles of the revolution gave them rights to the property on which they had been salaried workers. The Provisional Executive threatened to confiscate abandoned property of owners who did not return by October, but this was not made effective. Later, however, the Algerian government instituted "management committees" composed of three members elected by workers in the enterprise, for "all vacant agricultural enterprises" which employed more than ten workers. The text does not exclude the return of the property to the original owner and provides that it is a provisional measure, but it hardly seems possible that popular sentiment could be made to accept a return to prerevolution status even if many of the proprietors were willing to come back. The principal problems involved, if this kind of empirical socialism continues, is that of disposing of the farm produce in European or, if they can be found, other markets. It is no surprise that the Algerian government has decided to nationalize foreign trade, beginning with agricultural export products like wine and citrus fruits.

The new Algerian state has for imperative economic reasons

given priority to the maintenance of productivity on vacated farmlands. This has meant that holdings have been kept integral instead of being redistributed or split up. The management committees do not have title to the land and, in Kabylia for example, the new collectives resemble *sovkhozes* on which salaried workers are paid as before at the regular farmhand rate (about $1.35 a day), in addition to which they share in the profits. The Minister of Agriculture and Land Reform expressed the wish that the committees should become a new type municipality in which both the estates and new model villages housing the workers would be administered by them. It is too early to judge the effectiveness of such steps, and, indeed, the government's action so far should perhaps be viewed as a desperate attempt to avoid in agriculture the kind of disaster that has overtaken the industrial and financial sector. But there are already signs that the collectivist trend is meeting hostility from peasants who expected that the revolution would bring them a plot of land all their own and who are now showing the same distrust of a cooperative system that their fellow farmers in Morocco did. However, with five state farms already in existence late in 1962, a determined government effort may be in the making to break old habits, and the struggle between collectivization and redistribution promises to be bitter and crucial for the future of Algeria.

Throughout North Africa there is a great amount of hidden unemployment in the countryside. In Morocco and Algeria studies indicated that in the 1950's rural idleness among the active population reached around 50 per cent. Figures oscillate from time to time because unemployment is difficult to calculate with exactness, and there are many peasants who have work for fifty days one year and one hundred the next. But with one adult in two lacking full-time employment, and a growing number of young men coming into the rural labor market with little hope of finding work, a mass migration to the cities has been taking place for the past generation. The

city of Casablanca has added 25,000 people a year for the past
twenty-five years, which means an annual increment of the
city's labor force by more than 10,000 workers or would-be
workers, and the story is the same in all the principal cities of
Algeria and Tunisia. In Tunisia and preindependence Algeria,
one person out of three in the urban sector, and in Morocco
one out of five was normally unemployed. In 1955 living conditions were in keeping with the general poverty. Slum towns
had grown up around the cities, and in Morocco such *bidonvilles* were estimated to hold nearly 300,000 persons, or one in
five, in the chief industrial towns of the country. During the
postwar boom, which lasted until 1953 in the two protectorate
countries, and till the end of the war in Algeria, with its attendant construction and military spending, some of the labor
surplus could be taken up, although the steady backlog mentioned above continued in existence. But independence brought
with it a slackening of the economy in all fields. European
business closed or reduced the number of personnel employed.
Particularly hard hit was the construction industry which had
been flourishing. In Morocco 100,000 workers were laid off in
a few years following 1955 and the same pattern was repeated
in Tunisia. Private investment there dwindled by 1957 to a
third of what it had been in 1953 and industrial activity declined sharply. By 1958–1959 some stabilization was achieved,
and in a few fields some advances were made, but on the whole
there has been no real progress and the economies of both
countries are becalmed partly through lack of funds for investment and partly because of indecision as to exactly how to
go about constructing a rational economy.

Meanwhile, though, the human problem would not wait.
Recognizing this, Tunisia took the lead in 1959 with a program
called the "Battle Against Underdevelopment." The audacious
format planned to substitute labor for capital by using the
unemployed in large numbers on works projects which would
add permanent value to the national wealth while changing

the face and the spirit of the nation. The unemployment program had an important secondary aim, that of putting an end to the urban slum towns, for migration to the cities is now firmly discouraged and individuals are sent back to their province of origin where they are put to work. Since 1959 Tunisia has become a fascinating workshop in which these ex-unemployed are engaged in urban renewal, road-building and well-digging, construction of small-scale earthworks and dams to retain rain waters, erosion and flood-control work, building irrigation canals, and carrying out a reforestation scheme which will hopefully some day make Tunisia as attractive as it must have been in antiquity. Out of an estimated 300,000 unemployed or underemployed (nearly 8 per cent of the total population and the equivalent of more than 14,000,000 American jobless in 1960), more than half have been put to work paid partly in cash and partly in surplus agricultural products provided by the United States aid program. A similar program was undertaken beginning in 1960 in Morocco, but on a smaller scale, employing about 100,000 workers. The National Promotion in Morocco has not done so much to revitalize the society, but this is not the fault of those in charge, for the goals were more modest and there are more social and cultural obstacles in Morocco than in Tunisia. If any single factor were to be cited for the Tunisian success, it might relate to the balance between local autonomy and central power previously mentioned. The initiative in using workers and instigating projects at local level without interference from above has been most praiseworthy, but some of the credit must also go to the political unity of the country as the result of the work done long ago by the neo-Destour in kneading the rural component into the national dough. Thus the peasant and nomad have learned that the well dug and the trees planted will eventually benefit him and his collectivity, and the all-important step of projecting a semiprimitive into a new dimension of time, authority, and security has been taken.

In Algeria the situation has evolved otherwise. There, as part of the psychological war effort, and possibly because of a genuine concern to make up in the last years for what had not been done before, General de Gaulle announced a plan in 1958 for the intensive economic development of Algeria, stressing industrialization, housing, and schooling. The Constantine Plan planned at the end of five years, by 1964, to have built new housing for a million persons, to create 80,000 jobs a year instead of the 20,000 hitherto generated annually, to put two-thirds of all Algerian children in school, to accelerate the development of Saharan oil and natural gas, and to establish metallurgical and chemical industries as a base for further industrialization. This has been the only attempted solution so far in North Africa using the fourth alternative.

The Constantine Plan did not change the course of political history and today, of course, Algeria is a very different country from what was foreseen in 1958. Generally the plan is regarded as a failure and has been criticized because it concentrated its investments in sectors of the economy which were already partly modernized and in urban or advanced geographical regions. This is valid criticism, for the Plan made no real provision for the six million rural Algerians, except for a minor redistribution of land. It is also true that the Plan failed in some of its objectives, especially in the last two years, 1960–1962, when private investment in Algeria not only stopped but a massive capital outflow took place, estimated at about $800 million in that period. Yet, all things considered, the results are not unimpressive. In 1961 half of Algeria's children were in school, housing plans were being fulfilled, oil and natural gas installations were operative, and the chemical industry complex was under construction, although the steel mill project was in trouble. The gaps had been, significantly, in providing anything like enough jobs and in stimulating sufficient investment from internal sources in Algeria. What are the lessons of the Plan then, in the end? First, a warning that if anything is to be done in an overpopulated and backward country like Algeria, far more money must be provided than is usually associated with development. The Plan called for spending roughly $4 billion in five years, and while it did not effectively disburse that sum, a total of $506 million was spent in public and private monies in 1960 and figures the next year were higher. And second, that even such astronomical sums will not get full results if an integrated effort to activate both rural and urban sectors is not made. And third, that political solutions must perhaps precede economic ones, and it is doubtful if any effort by a body external to the society concerned can provide the same impetus and morale as that generated from within. The problem remains, then, of finding sufficient external resources, stimulating enough internal drive, and learning if the two can be harnessed together.

Thanks to the Plan in large measure, Algeria is today in one way very unlike other underdeveloped countries. It abounds in schools but has almost no school-teachers, is endowed with modern hospitals without doctors, and has a physical infrastructure of which many advanced countries would be proud, but which it cannot use because the motor force of the country, the trained European element, has gone. Nothing like the collapse of Algeria has occurred since the fall of Germany in World War II, and there the country was materially destroyed but basic talents remained, whereas Algeria, despite minor destruction, is intact and gleaming with new construction but without human resources. As an example, almost all the 1,800 doctors have left, and nearly 20,000 of the 27,000 teachers, including 3,500 of the 4,000 secondary school instructors. Emergency aid in many fields has been sent by various countries, but it is not a permanent remedy. The wholesale departure of the Europeans reduced the active population by 30 per cent (in 1960 there were 350,000 Europeans and 790,000 Muslims in nonagricultural activities) and deprived it of practically all its higher personnel and the heads of establishments who, by leaving, multiplied unemployment among workers dependent on them, so that unemployment at the end of 1962 was almost total. Statistics have been difficult to get since independence, but it is commonly assumed that there was an active Muslim population of about two and a half million in rural and urban areas, of whom nearly all the city workers and about half the rural population (large numbers of which were being held in resettlement camps) are now unemployed: a total of nearly two million of whom the one million in the cities have little immediate prospect of work unless there is—and how can it be avoided?—a mass national mobilization. Premier Ben Bella stated in December 1962 that half the country's population of over 9,000,000 was without jobs or resources, and dependent on state aid. Even then, the resources of the Algerian treasury will have to be supplemented considerably, not only by continued economic aid, to which France pledged itself at Evian, but simply to meet ordinary expenses. When treasury statistics exist, which is rare because of OAS destruction, it seems that tax receipts will cover only about one-sixth of expenditures for 1962, and prospects are not likely to improve much in the near future. Even so, in the kind of ultimate poverty in which Algeria finds itself today money becomes rather meaningless, and the credits budgeted for Algeria by France, which in 1962 amounted to around $400 million, are certain to be underspent because the state machinery to handle them does not exist.

Underspending of budgeted credits, including those in the American aid program, has been common in Morocco, where much remains to be done before the industrial economy of the country is more than paper plans. There have been achievements: an oil refinery, an assembly plant for trucks, the phosphate complex, firm decisions seem to have been made about a pharmaceutical industry, and progress is being made on the projected iron and steel complex in the north. But Moroccan industrialization is being carried forward with gov-

ernment participation through its Bureau of Studies for Industrial Participation (BEPI), which approves projects and
becomes part shareholder, and so far it has been marked by
caution and slow decisions, for which reason many projects are
still only under study and others have fallen through. The
handmaiden of this prudence is a conservative budget policy
which has been decried in some quarters, in keeping with
which only health and education this year received substantial
increases. Rightly or wrongly, in its economic as in its political
life, Morocco has chosen to make haste slowly and maintain a
solid financial position.

The discussion might be concluded by looking rapidly at
some other problems which deal more loosely with the social
orientation of the economy. Once again colonialism will be a
whipping boy, for one of the legacies of the dual society in
North Africa is that the general train of modern urban life is
too high for the resources of the countries and out of balance
with the rural sector. The French left a heritage of high prices
and wages; the cost of living is almost equal to that of Paris in
all respects and salaries for waiters and servants begin around
$50 a month, while starting civil servants may well receive $300
(almost what their American equivalents begin with) and
higher civil servants in Algeria were drawing the same salaries
as top American government employees. Added to this is a
system of fringe benefits, escalator clauses, family allocations
and pensions, the last of which was a French device to stimulate the birth rate in France but was copied on a modified
scale in North Africa where, if anything, incentives should
be offered to restrict family size. (In fairness, it would be
added that in both Tunisia and Algeria official salaries and
some of the extras have been reduced since independence.)

Urban salaries are also excessive in return for value given.
The young functionary with a limited education is simply not
yet as competent as the colonial civil servant he replaced, and
standards of honesty as well as efficiency have declined no-

ticeably, except in Tunisia. The quality of labor in general in North Africa has been criticized—and defended. The average worker does have low productivity, and is often an inefficient worker, but it is not always his fault. Adaptation to new norms is difficult, and working under foreign direction is trying. Moreover, taking the society as a psychological whole, it was crippled because so many tasks it should have been doing were performed by others, from governing to working as shoe clerk. Many North Africans are highly skilled and competent workers in their own fields, such as handicrafts of all kinds, metalworking, gardening, and sundry specialized farming. The quality of mine laborers, for example, has often been denigrated because of the high labor turnover. But it is the lack of incentive that matters here, for most of the workers come to earn a little extra money, or to save for a specific purchase after which they return to their traditional ways. They see no reason to go on working, for the inner reasons behind the existence of modern industrial society escape them, and one must in a way envy them. The effect of incentive on performance was shown by Tunisian ditch-diggers in the national public works program who functioned, from personal observation, several times as efficiently as their Moroccan counterparts, because in some deeper way were sharing in the mystique of national redressment.

We finally arrive at the critical question of entrepreneurship —whether it exists in the area and how it might be stimulated. No one has been more incisive on this point than Guedira, who said,

The triptych we have cited above (work, saving, investment) comes in the end from a certain philosophical attitude, a certain conception of existence. It stems from the conviction that man is metaphysically free in his choices and his destiny; it results from the cult of effort, the sense of the future, of a very real importance accorded to material values, to earthly goods. If one does not believe in the absolute value of possession because one is deeply penetrated with the quite transitory and relative character of our life on earth;

if one does not want to think of tomorrow, because the future escapes us and has too much uncertainty in it; if one does not feel the pleasure of amassing because, once immediate needs are satisfied accumulation is a burden and time spent in this kind of activity is lost for meditation, then, really, what good is it to save and invest?

Put otherwise, the material success of western civilization today (that of the machine) is the salary of a resolutely materialistic, or at least "earthly" view of life; on the other hand, a spiritual conception of existence which professes even a certain disdain for tangible goods, carries inevitably with it the drawback of backwardness in economic development compared to those on the other side.

This is, we believe, the real heart of the problem, and the center of all our difficulties. Everything else is an accessory and a consequence.

It is true that there is no exact word for "enterprise" in Arabic, the same term serving triple duty for "institution" and "foundation." Bourgeois Islamic society has always been one of small merchants, who favor direct exchange and the close, personal control of family-size business, and who invest in the solid values of land, houses, flocks, jewelry, and precious metals. The joint stock company is not favored in North Africa, not even on the scale on which it has begun to emerge in the Levant and the Arab Middle East. But again the chloroforming effects of settler colonialism must be weighed. For all the odds were against the Maghribi merchant who tried to compete with the technical skills and the financial and political connections of a European business rival. Now that this handicap has been removed, there should be only two possible obstacles: an inherent lethargy in the society or its lack of resources. Islam may have been very slow to adapt itself to modern economic conditions, but there are many signs that it is giving way to new pressures. Perhaps "giving way" is not the right word, for any great religious and social system which has endured as long as Islam is quite capable of encompassing and developing within itself some variation of the idea of entrepreneurship just as it has accepted banking and insurance practices which half a century ago were considered generally unacceptable by orthodox Muslims. And, apart from the subtle changes in Islamic practice, there are important shifts in thought going on almost daily among the younger generation of North Africans, over two million of whom are now receiving a basically French-inspired education which is inevitably and insidiously injecting them with a new value system, in which modern economic views of life are implicit. While the Maghrib has had a long history of spiritual activity, it also reflects a good amount of gross materialism, as in any other society. The emphasis, if any, on otherworldliness may have come more than a little from the paucity of material blessings, a condition which most North Africans this writer knows are only too willing to change.

SOCIAL PROBLEMS

In a sense there is only one social problem in North Africa today but it is multifaceted and everything revolves around it. This is the battle by the Arab-Muslim community to preserve its fundamental patterns of life and thought within an Islamic framework from the destructive impact of the alien society of the West. The Western attack is, here as everywhere in the non-Western world, total, but the struggle is sharpened with respect to the Arab world where Islam has for so long played an all-pervading role as religion, state, and legal and social system. It might be put that the social problems of the Maghrib are indistinguishable from a crisis in Islam, if that institution is thought of as the regulator of all the material and spiritual aspects of the society.

As part of the Arab World, North Africa has shared in the traditions which have shaped Arab-Muslim society for the past thirteen hundred years. From the bedouin life of the pre-Islamic period of Arab history has come the individualism and the mobility of nomadism, the association of honor and manliness, the love of horses, war, and the ideal of the purity of the Arabic language—a romantic and excessive, hedonistic view of life. But an alteration to this in the Maghrib was the stamp put on this complex of open-ended characteristics by the indigenous Berber element which contributed shades of quiet rusticism, the stubborn silence that contradicts the extremes of verbalism, and a peasant frugality which is the opposite of the lavish hospitality of the bedouin tent. The Maghrib is Arab in many ways, but compared to the Middle Eastern heartland, North Africa is a much more cautious, almost furtive society of compromise, a quality which has been forced upon it by history. This amalgam has been tempered by the Islamic contributions of resignation to the will of God, piety, and the concept of the straight path of rectitude. Asceticism was added to romanticism and frugality and a composite quality was born,—something like the *mesure* which the French brought intellectually much later,—which became the standard for the cultured society of the cities of North Africa. The religious note of the *shari'a*—the way of the golden mean—dominated this life, from the family in which polygamy was permitted but limited, and the great houses whose excessive luxury, concealed behind huge cedar doors, was mitigated by the charities dispensed in front of them, to the business world in which it was neither seemly in the eyes of God nor perhaps wise vis-à-vis the rulers to become too wealthy. It was a closed and static system, but one in which there was faith and security, even for the poorer members to whom the consolation was offered that the pious would receive their reward in paradise. In the countryside this atmosphere gave way often before extremes of violence, exuberance, and stinginess, but faith was no less. In fact, a more burning and personal, although often imperfect view of God and the religion of his Prophet usually flourished, anthropolatric in its addiction to holy men, xenophobic in its exclusiveness and its confounding of local virtues with spiritual righteousness. In both areas however, Islam was the center of all existence and the Islamic community was the best and only world. Then, as throughout the Arab World, the arrival of the "new" Europeans in the nineteenth century raised grave doubts in Muslim minds, as it became clear that material and technical superiority belonged to the foreigner and not to the community of God. The impact grew and was felt in every detail of life, so that the believer who wanted to hold fast to the Islamic order had continually to square his memory of a venerable past and his sense of moral superiority with this material degradation; to adjust his belief in Islam as a system of divine justice to the realities of social and economic inqualities which were revealed to him by the foreign intrusion; to struggle with powerful new ideas about the state and its authority placed outside the totality of Islam, and the meaning of a national entity as opposed to the community of believers; and finally, he had to consider unconsciously the advantages and dangers of becoming the autonomous man which he found in the post-Renaissance European, so unlike the European that Islam had known at the time of the Crusades, and whose sharply defined personality was contrasted for him to the anonymity of his own.

The methods and effects of the political and economic attack of Europe on North Africa in the nineteenth century have already been looked at, but in the final analysis it is probably the socio-intellectual invasion which has caused, and goes on causing, the greatest dislocation. It has led to a reform in the legal bases of society, to marked changes in political structures and institutions, and to the recasting of many of the values and goals which the society held. The overwhelming majority of the population still "believes" formally, and it is extremely rare to find any overt withdrawal from Islam. In fact, as noted before political gains in recent years have resulted in a temporary stimulation of assiduousness, if only by association. There are many depths of belief today, from the "rigorism in ignorance" with which a French scholar succinctly described rural conformity, to an urbane placing of Islam in a Friday pigeon hole in the same way that many Christians isolate their Sunday morning devotion, just as there are extremes of religious intolerance noted particularly in Algeria today but balanced by the antireligious zeal of young Tunisian supermoderns in conspicuously breaking the Ramadan fast and eating prohibited food in public.

As to whether Islam is vigorous or moribund in North Africa today, it is certainly true that attachment to it in the country generally and among most older and middle-aged persons in the cities is as profound as ever. There is also a new class of young Maghribians who genuinely feel a link between religion and nationalism or Arabist pride. But this sentiment is not that of the true believer, for it uses religion in a way that the pious cannot permit himself to, and it indicates an inner doubt in the validity of either force if it is unsupported by the other. There is to be considered the fact that Arab society always draws renewed strength from religion in time of stress. All the nationalist movements were accompanied by some degree of revivalism and puritanism (even the neo-Destour in the 1930's took some unusual turns), and as late as 1961 Tunisia, which had shown the most secular tendencies, took on an increased Islamic coloration after Bizerte. There is also the defensive reaction of Muslims which comes out most fully when non-Muslims comment on their faith. Yet, a flaw exists which may turn into something grave in time—the spearhead of all change and progress in North Africa is non-Muslim, European (and hence largely French) thought and culture. In this, North Africa is different from the Middle East, where many renovation movements have their roots in local soil and Islamic tradition. While French control was physically present, the cultural influence of France was absorbed but resisted; in recent years it has made deeper inroads than ever, to the dismay of many keen observers among the religious leaders who decry this. The new wave of North Africans that comes out of lyceums and universities each year becomes more neo-French —are we seeing a repetition of a constant in North African history? This French-molded elite is moving away not only from many of the bases of traditional Islam, but also from the orthodox masses. One would be tempted to say that its fate would not be bright under those circumstances, except that it is increasing its numbers so rapidly because of mass education. It is possible that some synthesis between a secular and scientific-oriented European education and a sound revivified Islam could be made—but it will not be done by adding on an hour a day of Koranic recitation to a program which has been basically conceived in a ministry in Paris and inspired by 1789 and the Declaration of the Rights of Man, and it seems more likely that one or the other must give way, at least tacitly. The most that one can say definitely is that at the moment the one-way direction of change from traditionally oriented families to indifferent or agnostic individuals, and the speed of this change among the young are so remarkable that whatever transformations of Islamic thought and practice do appear in the future, they will certainly be directed by this growing new body and not by the orthodox theologians working in old channels.

The social structure of North Africa does not fit Western classification in many domains such as status and mobility, any more than it does Marxist stereotypes about class divisions. The entire society is, in the largest sense, mobile because it has lost its anchor and is drifting or rushing without much control into a maelstrom. The most valid approach might be to consider the key groups within the society and look at them through the mirror of social change in their structures and their attitudes. One such group is traditional rural society, which is both changing within a rural environment and is in part turning into a new urban proletariat. The other pattern of importance is the modernization of the city middle classes and aristocracy as they turn into the new leading class. But, before sketching them and their movements in outline, the reader should be warned of two things: One is that with a society in movement as this is, different changes are of course taking place at different speeds so, in effect, we are looking at hundreds of railroad tracks on which individual trains are moving at different speeds but going mostly from and to the same direction. The other is that each type sketched here is an artificial composite, made up of norms and tendencies rather than specific items of change, although we find a high degree of homogeneousness in the over-all pattern, whether dealing with a seminomadic Zlassi who moves to Tunis, a Kabyle villager settling in Algiers, or a Doukkali farmer who comes to Casablanca.

Typical of traditional rural life everywhere in the area have been poverty and until quite recently, physical insecurity. This has produced a tough, indrawn population which values armed strength, virility, and boys over girls. It depends on patriarchal, authoritarian rule for cohesion and holds property in common to keep the group strong and together. Reliance upon oneself in the group sense and upon group institutions is marked. In Berber areas, customary or tribal law prevails but even elsewhere unofficially the judgment of the group chief or the elders is usually definitive. Agnatic family descent through the eldest surviving male is practiced widely for obvious security reasons. The economy also tends to be autonomous and the use of money is limited. Local products can be exchanged for the few goods that are needed from the outside or the specialized services such as tinkering and masonry which are unobtainable except from itinerants. Everything else is produced within the group. Food comes from fields, orchards, and flocks; and clothing and footwear from sheep (woolen robes) and goats (mocassins). Furnishings are limited to home-made mats, blankets, wooden chests and vessels, and low-fired pottery. The family is a closely knit unit which arranges marriages for the children and prefers early marriages because life is short, young men are particularly apt to die, and male children are always needed. Polygamy varies, but is not common, except for taking a second wife if the first one is incapacitated. Women are unveiled and freer in the country than in the city, but are worked very hard. They do the cooking, weaving, field work, gather wood, and carry water and heavy burdens. Both infant natality and mortality are high. Girl children are often not counted, and in some areas surreptitious female infanticide is practiced. The diet is Mediterranean, with dried staples like chick peas, lentils, and beans, plus grain, oil, and curdled milk, with almost no meat. Religion is widely practiced but not deeply felt in an orthodox sense; attention is often more centered on the rite than the spirit, and occasional unconscious pagan survival practices connected with nature worship, such as sacred groves and springs, are to be found. In most parts of Algeria and Tunisia this kind of description might be valid until the beginning of this century in true rural areas, and in Morocco it lasted until around 1930.

By those dates the effects of French authority were felt everywhere and important changes started taking place. For one thing, security brought a gradual loosening of tribal and familial bonds. French law favored and native custom relaxed toward the division of property now that it was no longer a matter of survival to hold it in common. With divisions came the growing notion of accumulating personal property on a modest scale by individual family members. Government interfered with tribal and local institutions mainly through tax collection, occasional forced labor, and in the gradual extension of external kinds of justice, either Koranic law, which might have been ignored or rejected before, or French administrative penalties; in all cases self-regulation declined. Young men began to volunteer for military service as a substitute for lapsed vendetta warfare. This had multiple results: it acquainted them with the outside world and was a factor in the growth of nationalism, it allowed them to save a small amount of money for marriage, and it delayed marriage. Meanwhile the economy was moved toward a cash basis more and more. With roads opened in the countryside, more vendors came through selling material, old clothes, and specialty items like tea, which gradually became necessities. Because of the economic advantages of buying such products, many local skills, such as weaving, were slowly abandoned and the costume changed. Cheap rubber and leather sandals replaced skin mocassins, and women preferred simple sheet-like garments to traditional woven cloth. Changed, too, were dwellings among sedentaries, where items of furniture occasionally appeared and plaster or cement tended to replace mud and straw on floors and walls. Family life evolved toward later marriage, but still arranged. With the spread of hygiene, epidemic diseases declined, infant deaths were reduced, and life expectancy rose, although natality remains high. There is a resultant overpopulation which is "felt" for the first time. Women have more leisure in a very relative sense and tend to have marriage contracts with more stipulations in their favor. With this leisure, the village woman may even pass into rural lower middle-class status and adopt the veil paradoxically as a sign that she has no need to work, something like the long fingernail of the Mandarin. The sensed crowding and impoverization on the land; the widened horizon created by officials, traders, and sons back from the wars; and the tales of economic opportunities in the towns, finally combined to start migration to the cities, which, once it began, fed back to the country in a growing stream of communication and swelled into a torrent.

The members of the new urban proletariat thus created have aptly been called urban nomads. Like them, they are camped in and around the city rather than living in it in a civic sense. Through no fault of their own, they are usually rootless and propertyless, and tend to come and go, drift to other slums in the same city or a nearby town, or occasionally but not often drift back to the country in failure. Socially, the poor city family is distinguished from both the rural family and the urban bourgeois family in that the extended family pattern is broken down. Most families in this category are conjugal, with only husband, wife, and children; there are many broken families, the remnants of divorces, and fewer children. The main social scourge of the new proletariat is not polygamy, economically difficult, but repudiation, whereby the husband divorces his wife by unilateral statement. The ease of this kind of divorce, coupled with frequent remarriage if there are no children, has led to a kind of successive polygamy which adds to family instability. One factor in curbing this excess is the growing number of working women, in factories or as domestics, who often with acerbity demand better treament once they have financial independence. The stereotype of the timid, cloistered wife of the harem is not at all applicable here. One important social development is the decline of religious practice. Neglect of prayers is common in the industrial cities and excused on the grounds that strict Islamic practice and modern life do not go together. Yet the ideal remains often and it is felt that some explanation is required. Men are more active religiously than women, to whom the subject often becomes a social activity, such as the Friday visits to cemeteries. Poverty and the lack of living space further splits the family. The husband spends much of his leisure time at a cafe which becomes his club; there, for the price of a cup of tea or coffee, he passes the evenings with friends and the radio, discussing politics and listening to music. Among the younger generation a wholesome association between the sexes is becoming more common, but it is ordinarily still restricted to modest walking and conversation; prudery inhibits dancing, and poverty stands in the way of going to the movies. But the real passion of North African youth everywhere is soccer, followed by bicycle-racing, swimming, and boxing, to a degree that one of the most effective propagators of European culture at the moment is certainly sports. A speech by President Bourguiba in 1960 on the "Role of Sport in the Battle against Underdevelopment" paid tribute to the Hellenistic ideal of the healthy body and mind and the pre-Islamic Arab sporting tradition, but contrasted these to the doctrines of Christian and Muslim mystics who taught men "to despise their bodies." Judging by the actions of the young, these remarks did not fall on deaf ears.

A picture of the traditional well-to-do family can be drawn from a prototype in Fez, the epitome of Muslim city life in the Maghrib, but similar patterns would be found in any of the traditional towns. This, too, is an extended patriarchal family, and a well-to-do household may include as many as fifty persons: the head of the family, his wife or wives, the children and their wives, and the grandchildren, with perhaps a widowed mother or aunt, and scattered indigent relatives who have been adopted out of charity, plus several servants. The head of the house is an autocrat, who owns all the property and makes the decisions. He supervises all important purchases, the comings and goings of family members, and the education of the children. The atmosphere is one of strictness, sobriety, and respect, with a formal segregation between the sexes and an informal one between age groups. The women live apart and eat separately, keeping the younger children with them. The young boy associates with the male members of the household after circumcision, usually after his sixth or seventh year, but daughters remain cloistered with the women. Family stability is high and, although the caprice of the patriarch can make everyone miserable, there is usually a solid sense of affection to hold the group together. The houses are built around a courtyard, usually tiled and often with a fountain; they are well-constructed in stone and furnished with rugs, divans, and furniture of local make. A general air of religious piety warms the house; customarily, father and children pray together, and in the evening there may be religious tales or readings to close the family day. People do not go out because there is little public life, and gentlemen are not seen in places of entertainment. For special occasions storytellers or dancers may be brought in, and for the wedding of a daughter, arranged between the heads of families, no expense is spared. This kind of household is usually well off enough to afford polygamy; there is a division of labor among the women, but much free time is available for music, cards, and chatting on the interlocking rooftop terraces which are reserved for them. Education for the children is limited to Koranic learning and simple mathematics. The son often enters his father's business or shop at adolescence, or if the family is prosperous and he has shown a bent for learning, he may go on to a religious college to study the classical language, composition, and poetry—the hallmarks of the gentleman—following which he leads a life of indolence until one day he is informed that a bride has been chosen for him. He then enters on the full cycle of manhood and repeats the pattern of his father.

As in the rural world, this kind of society has been changing in two ways: One is a slow adaptation in which the essence of traditional life is maintained and selected cultural elements from the West are added; the other a headlong plunge into Westernization with considerable rejection of old ways; and, of course, there are intermediate types. The first group is still in the majority for all those over forty, but among the young the tendency to a more complete break grows all the time. Adaptation is a matter of several stages. The first is a reform of religion, with the substitution of a more severe orthodoxy in place of membership in brotherhoods and with greater participation by women in religious life. Then comes a physical transformation as the products of the house reflect the Europeanization of commerce. This began in the nineteenth century with the appearance of the grandfather clock and the four-poster bed, and continues now with furniture, a radio, and a stove. Contemporary to this is a reduction in household size as sons become more independent and live apart after marriage, and as there is greater monogamy. Husbands divorce their wives less brusquely, girls are accepted as offspring with greater grace, and the women's lives become less secluded. In the intermediate stage, the sons may be given a double education, French and Koranic, which it is hoped will allow them to prosper materially under new conditions but retain their faith. Wives in the slowly adapting family usually remain veiled but they go out unaccompanied, they send their unveiled daughters to school, and the girls will be asked for their consent, somewhat as a formality, when they are to be married. A step beyond that is the family which wears European clothes at home but as a concession to opinion puts on traditional dress for the street.

The focus of adaptation in this kind of family is material change for practical and physical reasons. They have concentrated on what is more comfortable, useful, pleasant, or likely to improve their lot. But they have not on the whole looked for an internal evolution and still less for a revolution in their philosophy of life which holds fast to much of what seems good to them in their culture. But this traditional-modern group is in constant movement, and the direction of that movement in almost all cases is toward greater modernity. It is perhaps the most interesting but most unstable fraction of Maghribi society. Beyond it, in the sense of having reached what it feels is a new stability, is the completely evolved Western-type family. This is now found in small but growing numbers among young businessmen; government officials; and figures in the world of art, letters, and journalism. The modern society of Tunisia is the fullest example, but the others are not far behind. Here we find an almost complete acceptance of Western ways in clothing, food, housing, and amusements (of which food is possibly the most telling example because there a few societies where there has been such a complete abandonment of local cuisine as among the neo-Western elite of North Africa.) The model in all cases is French, and that language will generally be used in proportion to the depth of change. The house is usually Western, but sometimes with typical local decor, or it may in a few cases contain an Arab salon revived as a period piece to add local color. Wives usually have their own budget, handle household monies, and on occasion do charity or social work, but they rarely hold jobs. In the main, the traditional family was not too far from the atmosphere of an autocratic establishment in rural parts of the Occident in the mid-nineteenth century. The modern North African household is close in spirit to the home of Latin Europe, and so full equality and partnership in marriage is not a goal. Educational differences help account for the fact that the husband spends more time away with his friends than at home, but the gap between men and women is being gradually narrowed here. Needless to say, the children of already modernized families have almost nothing of the traditional left in them. There are few such who are over twenty-five today, but they are beginning to make up the ground swell of a *nouvelle vague* whose life is centered on their modern education and passing the baccalaureate examination; having a chance to go overseas (especially to France); on sports; scout movements; vacation colonies; the cinema; clothes; and automobiles. As in any group, some individuals are frivolous and others are hard-working, but in all cases their background and interests are hardly different at all from those of French youth in the 1960's.

The vast changes in North African society which have been fleetingly touched on here have been accompanied by and reinforced through changes in the legal structure and the very basis of legal principle, the importance of which can not be overestimated. The problem of Western influence has always been particularly acute in the field of law in the Arab world, for Islam was predisposed to a legicentric attitude and considered itself a universal system of divine jurisprudence designed for all worlds and purposes. Moreover, to a traditional city threatened with destruction, its system for regulating behavior is all the more vital, and as the institutions of Arab society came under fire after 1800 so did the legal foundations become suspect, and a need was felt to revise the law in accordance with the conditions of modern life. This progress started in the Middle East (and has been carried to completion there, notably in Egypt) but there was a flurry in Tunisia in the reform period after 1850. It took the French presence, however, to serve as a necessary stimulus.

In Algeria, as a part of the indivisible republic, French law prevailed, and the only concession to Muslims was to allow them to continue to use Koranic law for questions of personal status, or customary law in Berber areas. Algeria has not been independent long enough to have made any irrevocable decisions, but it seems unlikely that there will be any great break from modern European law, despite the need for Islam which the state feels in its critical gestation period. The FLN called repeatedly for a lay state and Algeria may soon be in the position of not wanting to appear to be going backward legally when compared with its neighbors. This makes it all the more useful to look at the evolution of Tunisia and Morocco, both of which preserved their legal institution on paper during the Protectorate.

Tunisia had three kinds of courts during most of the Protectorate period. There were religious tribunals for personal litigation, both Muslim and Jewish; French courts which handled all cases in which European nationals were involved; and secular Tunisian courts dealing with matters involving Tunisians which had been relatively independent since 1921. After independence, Tunisia moved rapidly to unify its system of justice by abolishing French jurisdiction, although granting some concessions in cases to be tried in Tunisian courts which involved French citizens. It also abolished religious courts and adopted a Nationality Code, a Code of Personal Status, and new Civil and Criminal Codes based on European models. With all citizens of both sexes equal before the law and with only one law in operation, Tunisian justice is the equivalent of that in most European countries, and has fully broken with Islamic guidelines.

In Morocco the situation was more complex and reforms have consequently been slower in realization and the steps taken less bold. As in Tunisia, French courts had functioned in regard to foreigners, but Morocco had no locally constituted courts. Penal matters were dealt with by the executive authorities, the pashas in the cities and the *cadis* in rural areas, just as they had always been in Islamic lands, while personal matters were determined by judges (*cadis*) according to the Holy Law. After independence, French courts were turned into modern Moroccan tribunals, but because there were too few qualified Moroccan jurists, French judges continued to sit on them as temporary assistants. The religious tribunals have been incorporated in the unified system and continue to function, although their style has been modified by the introduction of modern paraphernalia and the subsidiary personnel of modern court practice. Then in 1959 the religious courts were provided with a modern Code of Personal Status which contained many reforms but was far behind that adopted in Tunisia. Polygamy is still sanctioned but is made somewhat more difficult in that it is not permitted if "inequality in treatment is feared" presumably by the judge deciding, and contractual stipulations can be made by the first wife to bar a second marriage, from which in any case she has the right of appeal to the cadi. A minimum marriage age is fixed, and girls cannot be constrained to marry against their will. Perhaps most important of all is the narrowing of the right of repudiation. Again, less daring than Tunisia, where divorce is now treated as a matter for court hearing on demand by either party, the Moroccan law allows repudiation but restricts the right by requiring a cooling-off period and instituting a form of alimony for the divorced wife, something which will clearly reduce the frequency of the act among the poor. The contrast between the two codes shows how different is the representative ethic of each society: the Tunisian stress on republican equality and trenchant reform, the cautious infiltration of religious law in Morocco, and the timidity with which social change must be tackled. But, when one looks at the laws of North Africa today, one sees that where they have not been fully Europeanized they have begun to tilt toward that direction, and one finds that the men who plead and judge are either Europeans or Maghribians whose outlook is being increasingly formed in the legal schools and traditions inherited from the West. If law is a reflection of the deepest instincts of a society and what men think is right, then traditional Islam is slowly but surely giving ground in North Africa.

Much of this description of social upheaval has touched on the change in the lives of women. This is paramount because they are attempting to redress an inequality from which they have long suffered. Few societies have discriminated against women as much as Arab-Muslim culture, despite the rash of apologetics which issues from reformist theologians about the theoretically blissful position of women in the early days of Islam. Women have been discriminated against in the Koran, according to which men are placed above them, by the law that their testimony is inferior in value to that of men; in matter of inheritance, where they receive lesser shares than male heirs; and by custom, which has on the whole turned them into near beasts of burden or hidden and pampered objects of pleasure.

Today their emancipation in the Maghrib is progressing rapidly. Tunisia leads the way, not only in the legal measures mentioned previously but through the efforts of the Tunisian National Women's Union (UNFT) founded in 1955 at the personal insistence of Bourguiba, whose part in the advancement of women has been capital. The spectacle of the President, kissing women voters and encouraging them to remove their veils at the elections in 1957, when women first voted in Tunisia, was a show of political acumen but also a mark of his social concern. The results have repaid him in the form of the bloc feminine vote. The UNFT has more than 35,000 members in Tunis alone and over 100 local branches, which serve as training centers where girls are taught reading, writing, the household arts, civics, hygiene, and maternal care. Subsidiary organs of the UNFT use unemployed women to make clothing and run an orphanage (Tunisia is the only Arab country to have legalized adoption of children) and a cultural club. At least as important as this formal effort, though, is the social evolution of the country, where alone in the Maghrib one finds numbers of Tunisian wives working and leading public lives, or attending functions with their husbands, dressed in European clothes and indistinguishable from their French counterparts.

In Algeria it has been the revolution which opened the road to emancipation. Algerian women served as couriers, nurses for the guerrilla fighters, terrorist agents, and bomb throwers in the cities. Theirs was a hard school, but it led, through imprisonment and often torture, to the status of national heroines, and they became objects of admiration everywhere in the Arab World. Today Algerian women, "Sisters of the Revolution," sit in parliament and are active within the revolutionary elite. But full equality is far from realized in Algeria, and women in the cities felt patriotically obliged to resist French attempts to modernize them in recent years. Thus nationalism for some was equated with traditionalism, for others with the sharing of the hardships of men, and now of their rights. The danger in Algeria lies in the imbalance within feminine society, and the possibility that an understandable lethargy will follow the dynamism of the revolution. This would slow further advances but cannot prevent them ultimately.

Such postrevolution lassitude best describes the Moroccan feminist movement today. In 1956 there was much talk of women's rights in the air, and the eldest daughter of Muhammad V was a leading feminist. But the weight of conservative tradition is still heavy and in recent years progress has not been nearly as much as expected. Except at factory level, working women are almost nonexistent, and the veil is still the badge of all city women, although their daughters in a few cases are beginning to shed it. If the influence of the royal princesses in favor of female emancipation was noticeable, to be fully accurate about the state of modern Morocco it should be pointed out that it was not even announced that Hassan II was married until his wife gave birth to their first child, that even now her name and background are never mentioned, she has never been photographed or seen in public, nor does she hold any title or carry out any function.

Of equal importance with the problem of women is that of the children. Nothing illustrates better than the field of education the complex problems facing the countries of North Africa in delineating a cultural policy for the future. As the result of strenuous effort in the past decade much progress has been made toward educating the coming generation, but some very basic decisions relating to the self-image of the societies have not yet been fully faced. Tunisia and Morocco, which shared much the same legacy from Protectorate days, have gone roughly the same direction since independence, but at different speeds, whereas Algeria had the advantage, and disadvantage, of a more unitary French system of instruction. In this, however, as in every field, Algeria suffered great dislocation during the revolution from which it has not yet begun to recover.

Tunisia possessed a tripartite system of education under French rule, consisting of a completely French program similar to that employed in France; a Franco-Arab system whose "assimilated" curriculum provided instruction which mixed local culture and language with French elements, but with standards lower than those in the French-type schools, to a student body which was overwhelmingly Tunisian Muslim; and traditional religious instruction leading to higher theological studies at the university-mosque of Az Zeitouna. The complexity of the divided system tended to undermine cultural unity, which has now become a principal goal of Tunisian educators, and it favored the European population with the best instruction, to which Tunisians were admitted but at the price of divorcing themselves from any notion of their own background and traditions. The French record in education everywhere in North Africa was far from brilliant, although a genuine effort to remedy the situation in Tunisia began shortly after World War II. Still, in the year of independence, only one out of four Tunisian Muslim school-age children was in school, whereas the great majority of European and Jewish Tunisian children were receiving instruction in French-type institutions, public or private.

For a few years after independence extreme shortages of teaching staffs made drastic moves impossible, but Tunisia during that time integrated traditional religious teaching into the national education system; in any event it had already been declining steadily in student numbers for several years. In 1958 a general reform announced as its goal the unification of instruction and the attainment of universal education within ten years, by 1968–1969. Two-shift sessions and the elimination of one primary year were sacrifices to this end. The third objective of the plan was Arabization, but so far a de facto bilingualism has been operating, within elementary schools, almost equal hours of instruction in Arabic and French (history, geography and ethics are taught in the former, mathematics and science in the second), and with French as the vehicle of instruction in all subjects except religious studies in the secondary. The secondary program is divided into a shorter technical education cycle and a full cycle leading to the baccalaureat and higher studies, the latter conceived of as an elite program. In 1960 the Tunisian University was organized as an administrative unification of the former Institute of Higher Studies and was staffed with largely French faculty. Although more than a thousand Tunisians were studying there in 1959–1960 a larger number was still receiving its higher education abroad, almost exclusively in France.

Progress in enrollment has been steady since independence. By 1962 about 60 per cent of the children of elementary school age were attending school, and in 1960–1961 there were 27,000 secondary school students. If one considers that the proportion of boys to girls is about two to one, this means that enrollment for boys in the cities and villages of northern and coastal Tunisia is about total.

The evolution of Morocco has been much the same, except that it began more slowly than in Tunisia—in 1955 only one Moroccan child out of six was in school—and was delayed by a hasty venture into Arabization immediately after independence. Unprepared in texts and staff capable of teaching in Arabic, the move ended in disaster in 1958 when only half the students that year passed the examination given for the Certificate of Primary Studies. Authorities backtracked in confusion and had to compel several classes to repeat the year under a new system which followed the main lines of the Tunisian reform program. The first two years of the elementary cycle were devoted to the study of Arabic as the national language, after which French, as the vehicle for mathematics and science, was given equal instruction time with Arabic, the number of new students was by necessity sharply limited, an accelerated program to form qualified teachers was begun, and France was requested to help supply additional teachers and training materials. Results since then have been encouraging in general, although overcrowding and the quality of instruction in many rural schools leaves much to be desired. As the result of a particularly intensive construction program in the summer of 1962, Morocco went over the hump in the 1962–1963 school year by placing nearly 1,200,000 children in school, just over half of the school-age population, and whereas only 300 local teachers had been turned out by the normal school in 1958, some 2,000 were expected to graduate in 1963. In the number of secondary students, Morocco is still behind Tunisia but ranks will soon be swelling with the greatly increased number of primary students. The University Muhammad V, first organized in 1957, has faculties of letters, sciences, and a new medical school, all of which held nearly 1,000 aspirant doctors, scientists, and engineers as students in 1962. Religious instruction continues to be given separately at the Qarawiyin University in Fez, with annexes in Tetuán and Marrakesh.

Both Tunisia and Morocco have signed cultural cooperation agreements with France and depend heavily on French assistance in education. Part of this comes through French teachers who are engaged directly by the national Ministries of Education but are paid extra compensation and allowances by the French government while serving in North Africa. Another part is provided by the University and Cultural Mission, which is designed primarily to service the French minority, but in whose classes nationals of the country and foreigners are accepted. In both Tunisia and Morocco, many nationals attend Cultural Mission schools (in Morocco half of the 40,000 students are Moroccan; in Tunisia there are 15,000 Tunisians) whose standards are generally considered higher than the national education system. The contribution in teachers is considerable: 8,500 of a total of slightly more than 20,000 teachers in Morocco in 1962 were French, and in Tunis where the Mission was technically nationalized after the Bizerte incidents, some 2,500 out of 13,000.

In Algeria, education has not benefited from the same kind of development in the past decade. As in Morocco, about one child in six was in school in 1954—and this fact alone after 124 years of French presence explains something about the reasons for the revolution—but during the war schools were often closed by strikes and boycotts on nationalist orders. Thus, enrollment actually dropped for a while and by 1957 was not much higher than it had been three years before. In addition, the instruction was almost exclusively French, with little or no difference from that provided in France, and therefore Arabization did not make even the moderate advances noted in Tunisia and Morocco. It was not until the Constantine Plan was under way that Algeria began to move ahead and by

1960 around 40 per cent of Muslim children were in school. But the chaos of 1962 seriously compromised the educational future as well as all other activities in that unhappy country. Before independence there had been only 2,000 Algerian Muslim teachers, compared to 20,000 French; of the latter group a little more than half left for good, and the administrative staff and organization also withdrew in great numbers. In 1962 the school year opening had to be set back to mid-October and the university, almost destitute of professors, could not begin until early December. Even then, government statements that 80 per cent of the children who had been in school would be able to return should be accepted with reserve. In any event that figure would represent a serious setback, for given demographic growth not more than one child in three is now receiving instruction.

Algeria faces unprecedented obstacles in the shortage of trained teachers. It has called on all available sources for help (notably the Arab countries of the Middle East—Egypt, Lebanon, and Syria—who have adequate numbers of teachers), and it is expected that several thousand volunteers from those countries will be working in the country in 1963. Early in the same year the number of French teachers working for the Algerian government had increased to 13,000 as the result of special recruitment inducements, but administrative and payment difficulties make it uncertain how many of these will stay on permanently. In any case, Algeria is caught in a dilemma between the physical need of the moment to accept any aid it can get—and the fact that such aid is Arab reinforces the political and emotional drive to Arabize the system—and the appalling difficulties of changing over a unitary system on short notice. Not only are there no texts available but the language of the Middle Eastern teachers is not sufficiently close to the Algerian dialect, and children cannot move overnight into the difficult, written classical language without some disturbance. It is estimated that if, by choice or necessity, Arabization is quickly carried out in Algeria it will set the country back about a decade and seriously reduce the efficiency of students who will form the cadres of the early 1970's. But, and this statement applies to so much of what is happening in Algeria today, there may be no free choice.

With this background in mind, we can look more closely at the long-range aims of educational policy in the Maghrib. The stated goals have been unification of systems, total scholarization, and Arabization. None has yet been attained completely, but good progress has been made everywhere toward the first two in Tunisia and Morocco. There only the Cultural Mission exists outside the national framework and it is essentially dispensing a temporary service which is destined to disappear slowly while much of its staff might hopefully integrate itself into the national teaching corps. Algeria, as seen, already has a unified system but it is most doubtful if it can or wants to keep it. At present rates, both Tunisia and Morocco should achieve universal education by 1970 or shortly thereafter, but Algerian progress depends too much on political vagaries to make a prediction.

The self-proclaimed goal of Arabization is a touchier subject. Arabization is part of the Arab national myth in the Maghrib and a symbol of deep feeling about Arabic which is itself connected with religious sentiment. So it cannot be divorced from the whole crisis of Islam and the individual, which has already been touched on. In Morocco a Bureau of Arabization has been established in Rabat to translate foreign terms into the language and prepare textual materials, but so far progress has been slow. Today in both countries there is a bilingual reality, not only on the educational level but also in urban society and government—about two-thirds of the written communications in government departments are still in French and it is necessary to know French to have a superior administrative post in most departments except those dealing with religious affairs and justice. But this reality has to be played down because of national sentiment and that tangential relationship of language and religion. A good case could be made out for each of three possible solutions to the impasse. It has been soundly argued that only Arabization in the long run can permanently solve the whole gamut of sentimental, spiritual, and practical needs of the countries. Conversely, there have been some voices timidly raised recently for the frank adoption of bilingualism as the vehicle with which to achieve that balance between Islamic and Western thought and function which remains an imperfectly expressed ideal of many in the society who inhabit both worlds. And, it is possible that the current self-deception serves a useful purpose for the nonce in hastening the Maghrib along new paths of thought while permitting it to retain respect for itself and its past.

But, when all this is said, the drawbacks to each course must also be pointed out, for the linguistic problem is close to the heart of all Arab problems. The disadvantage of present practice is the near impossibility of making long-term plans, for the situation is something like the individual who is always going to start dieting tomorrow but meanwhile continues to eat abundantly while denying that he is doing so. Added to this is the uneasiness that surrounds the subject of education today, because this somewhat underhanded policy is being followed, and the vulnerability of politicians always open to attack by intransigent conservatives. The drawback of bilingualism itself resides in the strain it puts on the student of learning different material through different vehicles. The empirical, objective view of the world taught in French for the pure sciences contrasts necessarily with the subjective approach to history and culture given in Arabic (even more unsettling must be the official Tunisian description of the sociologically critical study of Islamic thought as taught in the country's secondary schools.) These differences are compounded by the very genius of the languages themselves, for where French prides itself on the precision of one word having one meaning, Arabic delights in the abundance of its synonyms and their nuances. While it may be true that one is eminently suited to logical analysis and the other best fitted for poetry and prophetic declamation, it is hard for one person to flourish in two such disparate spheres. And, finally, the central problem of Arabization is the danger of cutting off the individual from direct contact with the modern West and the intensity of its scientific and technical movement. Arabic is not at this writing a suitable vehicle for the understanding of any modern science and ultimately the crisis of a language is the crisis of its thought. There has been no major original work by any Arab scholar in modern times in any scientific or technical field, and this lacuna could probably be extended to history and philosophy as well. The renaissance of the past century has seen the appearance of remarkable works of the imagination (and innumerable tracts of political passion) but literature has always been the supreme Arab genre and classical Arabic a language excelling in subjective and sensuous expression. The vitality of a language is kept up by the exercise of its thinking muscles, just as the word follows the invention. In this race, Arabic is not only far behind, but it keeps falling further back as the translation of modern terminology—which has become the affair of academicians without ties either to the scientific thought processes behind the formation of the terms or to the genius of the speakers of the living language—lags hopelessly behind in volume and exactness.

In North Africa, moreover, the problem of bilingualism might better be described as trilingualism, for the spoken dialects, particularly those of Algeria and Morocco, are as different from written classical Arabic as, roughly, Portuguese from Latin. The child who begins to speak naturally at home and in the streets, must adapt to two new formal tongues in school, and if he should be one of the several million Berberophones, he will often be dealing in three languages other than his maternal one. Perhaps for this reason North Africa has never shared in the literary and intellectual ferment in modern Arabic which has marked the Middle East in the past century. Its only writer of stature in that tongue has been Mahmoud Messadi, significantly the Tunisian Minister of Education who put through the 1958 reform. That Algeria has produced almost exclusively a literature in French by Muslims (which excludes Europeans from that country like Camus and Roy) is not surprising under the historical circumstances, but what is striking in it is the amount of social wrath expressed by the best writers—Kateb Yacine, Mohammed Dib, and Mouloud Mammeri. All of these use French as the means of their protest, as does the foremost Moroccan writer Driss Chraibi and the Tunisian Jew, Albert Memmi. All of them, too, have surged up in the postwar nationalist-revolutionary period as the harbingers of a new North African type: an unsure mixture of East and West, dissatisfied with both, and trying to establish his identity. A crisis of identity, in fact, is probably the best description of the central North African problem today.

As a still largely illiterate area, the Maghrib would not be expected to do much reading, but it is in keeping with its tradition of nonintellectualism that where it does it prefers the polemics of the press and mundane affairs. The outstanding political weekly in the Arab world is probably *Jeune Afrique,* typically written by Tunisians in French for an audience that encompasses ex-French Africa south of the Sahara, the Maghrib, and France. Circulations of dailies and weeklies in the area are not high (the most widely read papers in Morocco are French dailies whose 30,000–40,000 circulation is mostly made up by the European community) but the public reached is often greater than would be the case in the West because of the custom of one man reading articles aloud to a group of friends. In fact, North Africa remains an area in which oral communication predominates. The tradition of the storytellers in the market place is still alive and the society has jumped through a preliterate stage into the modern world of the radio, and now television, which have become the preferred means of communication, and, along with the cinema, of entertainment. Popular oral literature in the dialects and in Berber is still very lively and political indoctrination campaigns rely much more on the spoken word than the written. Folk music, often consisting of unaccompanied singing, or of the simplest plucked string instruments, flutes and small hand drums or whatever scraps of metal are on hand, is happily improvised on all occasions and is a deeply felt part of life in both city and country. In this kind of music, which has nothing in common with the Arab orchestra of the Middle East, or with the court music of Muslim Spain carefully preserved by Andalusian orchestras in Rabat and Tunis, the Maghrib expresses much of its inner soul, as it has begun to do recently in the fine and applied arts. The primitive painters of the early part of this century have begun to branch out into diversified patterns and artisans have more lately turned to wood and stone sculpture as the prohibition on the graven image fades. North Africa, while disdaining some of the refinements of literature in the formal sense, more than makes up for this in its popular arts, still vibrant with the sure touch of the primitive but flowering now also in other more individualistic paths.

IV. North Africa and the World

When the independent states of North Africa look at the rest of the world today, there are three principal areas with which they have close ties. The influence of two of these, the Arab Middle East and Europe, has been long-standing, and continuing interests in these areas mark the smooth transition from history to current affairs. In the third case, although there had never hitherto been relations of any scope with Black Africa, a movement in this direction began a few years back and has become an important segment of the foreign policy of the states of the Maghrib, the psychological cornerstone of which may be that it marks the first opportunity North Africa has had to exercise its influence on another area.

Nevertheless, there is not much doubt that the paramount concern of North African statesmen at all times lies in relations with France. Independence has meant a changed relationship with the former ruler and protector but not necessarily a diluted one. About as many bonds have been reinforced as have been weakened, and above all, the intensity of the relationship, which was always one of its most apparent aspects, has not diminished. Like the family tie between parent and rebellious children, it has matured into a contact between older and younger adults as equals who are beginning to replace the anger of the past with a more sentimental nostalgia, but whose estrangement is mitigated by a new understanding. The protocols of independence which were signed with Morocco, Tunisia, and Algeria stipulated in all cases that this be accompanied by interdependence or association. From what has been observed so far in seven years in the first two countries, this interdependence, although it has been far from amicable at all times and has raised problems which were not foreseen, is a reality.

The relations of Tunisia with France have been quite complex and stormy, contrary to what might have been expected. It would have seemed in 1956 that a more advanced, secularist, tolerant and republican-minded society would be more likely to establish harmonious new patterns of cooperation with its former tutor. But in practice, although the long-range future is perhaps brighter than anywhere else, there were endless obstacles to overcome. For one thing, the reformist zeal of Tunisia led it to attack all entrenched positions, foreign and indigenous, and the ferment of a population closer to the threshold of modernity and better qualified to occupy positions held by the colonizers made for friction. Also at fault was geography, which made Tunisia the gateway for supplies of arms to Algeria and a haven for rebels, thus causing frequent skirmishes with the French military. Most important, however, was the attitude of the activist regime led by a dynamic President who was eager to play a leading role on the world political stage, particularly in ordering the future of the Maghrib by mediating the Algerian conflict. Oddly enough it was the desire of Bourguiba for a rapprochement between the ensemble of the Maghrib and France that led him to take positions which inevitably brought conflict with France. Accompanying this attitude was the Bourguibist technique of continuing negotiations to gain one's ends and using each point gained as a stepping stone to another. Independence had been associated with many restrictive conditions for Tunisia and he regarded it as only the beginning of real freedom. Thus in mid-1956 Bourguiba pressed for a separate army and diplomatic corps, and when they were granted he began a campaign for the withdrawal of French troops from the country. This was an issue which piqued the French military at a sensitive time, for they felt their presence in strategic areas of Tunisia was the only guarantee against unlimited outside support reaching the Algerian rebels. The presence of the Algerian government-in-exile and its troops on Tunisian soil meant unavoidable incidents. Relations were broken for several months in late 1956 after the kidnaping of Ben Bella and his companions, and in 1957 France suspended economic aid to Tunisia in retaliation for Tunisian aid to the Algerian cause. The Sakiet Sidi Youssef bombing in early 1958 was the next great crisis, and its connection with the end of the Fourth Republic has already been mentioned. After General de Gaulle came to power, it was agreed that French forces would evacuate all Tunisia except for the Bizerte naval base and its attached installations. A detente was noticeable, partly because the characters of the two heads of state had much in common and Bourguiba correctly had faith from the beginning that de Gaulle would eventually find a solution to the Algerian question. Thus, Tunisia signed an agreement which allowed a pipeline to be laid across its territory for the delivery of Algerian oil to France, to the intense irritation of the Algerian rebel authorities, and with minor tactical exceptions Bourguiba approved Gaullist policy from the announcement of self-determination in 1959 on. Bourguiba's role was played largely on the sidelines, but he did perform valuable services in helping to interpret the thought of each party to the other, and his interview with de Gaulle in February 1961 might have helped bring about an earlier settlement if it had not been immediately succeeded by the sudden death of Muhammad V. As it was, delays in Franco-Algerian talks that Spring and continuing concessions to the nationalist viewpoint in speeches by de Gaulle weakened the Tunisian position in all respects. Popular discontent about the continuing French occupation of Bizerte was simmering and the economic situation was unfavorable. Moreover, Bourguiba sensed the danger of being caught short by the arrival of peace in Algeria, for that would have left Tunisia, which had

been complacently but vainly willing to negotiate the disman-
tlement of French military installations, in an unfavorable light
compared to Algeria, which won its points by force of arms
and intransigence. At least partly owing to the necessity of
safeguarding Tunisia's reputation from charges of softness and
cowardice, Bourguiba began a hasty and vocal campaign for
the immediate evacuation of Bizerte, which he coupled with
claims to good parts of the Algerian Sahara, an issue raised
juridically with France but which infringed on the rebel concept of the integral territorial unity of the Algerian state.
Bizerte was certainly Bourguiba's greatest mistake, and the
campaign ended in disaster when unprepared Tunisian irregu-
lars attacked the base and provoked an unnecessarily heavy
retaliatory response which left more than 1,200 Tunisian dead,
in addition to discrediting Bourguibism which had violated its
own principles of moderation. Not until the end of September
was an agreement to maintain the status quo signed, but in the
interim the effects had been considerable, internally and externally. The stability of the government was visibly shaken
for a while, as it was criticized both for initial rashness and
subsequent passivity. The outflow of Europeans was accelerated and the number of teachers and technicians reduced,
while the economy suffered a bad blow. Tunisia in some disarray turned for sympathy to the Arab countries, the neutral-
ists, and for a moment looked warmly at the Communist bloc.
Relations with France were broken and the pipeline to Skhira
closed by the Tunisians to their own financial disadvantage.
Economic ties continued on an ad hoc basis until late 1962,
when negotiations were begun on all outstanding questions
after France had announced the willingness to evacuate
Bizerte by January 1964 at the latest. Today, Tunisia has just
begun to recover from the bitterness and shock of the incident
and the two countries are finding their way back to a path of
cooperation, which is economically more urgent for Tunisia
each year. The new climate is subdued but more realistic, and

with the end of the Algerian war, which was responsible for most of the friction, it gives another chance for the well-proved Tunisian receptivity to French civilization to blossom again without impediment. One of the reasons that Tunisians were so taken aback by the violence of the French riposte at Bizerte was that unconsciously they had felt themselves so close to France that this kind of sharp slap was unthinkable. It will take a long time for the total effect to wear off, but in the end the depth of Tunisian immersion in French culture and the unique gentleness of the Tunisian character give hope that the intimate ties built up in the last half-century will not be abandoned.

Franco-Moroccan relations have reflected the same general rhythm of crisis, although with lesser intensity, and for the same basic reason: the Algerian fight for independence which was wholeheartedly supported in Morocco as in Tunisia. As with Tunisia, France signed special conventions with Morocco in the year following independence covering technical cooperation, educational aid, and judicial matters, and these continue in force. Franco-Moroccan relations came quickly to their lowest point at the end of 1956, with the Algerian kidnaping incident. This was most deeply felt in Morocco as an insult to King Muhammad V, who had been the host of the rebel leaders traveling on a Moroccan plane. Riots broke out in the Meknes region in protest and cost several Europeans their lives, but it should be understood that this was the only occasion in post-independent Morocco where the European colony was molested or has had any reason to complain about treatment in the new state.

The establishment of the Fifth Republic was greeted with renewed hope of ending the Algerian war, but repeated efforts to arrange a meeting between Muhammad V and General de Gaulle came to naught. In September 1960, France agreed to withdraw all its military forces from the country, but Moroccan pleasure at this announcement was offset by the establishment of Mauritania, under French sponsorship, as an independent republic, for Morocco had claimed this as part of its national territory. Moroccan flirtations with the Communist bloc countries further alienated France and relations cooled considerably at the end of the year. However, a change in atmosphere became noticeable soon after the accession of Hassan II in early 1961. Again, personality played a part, for the young king has been widely considered a filial admirer of the French President, something borne out in deed by the quite Gaullist Constitution which he presented to Morocco in 1962 and in manner perceptible even in the details of his speech-making. Relations became slowly warmer as the Algerian question inched toward a denouement—and Morocco, despite numerous incidents, had never been on the spot as Tunisia had, because the bulk of the rebel forces were on the eastern borders of Algeria and most arms shipments came via Tunisia. The question of restoring face to the Moroccan throne was solved when the Algerian minister-prisoners were released to house arrest and put in the custody of the Moroccan ambassador in France; after the Evian agreements were signed, they were returned via Switzerland to their original point of departure six years before in Rabat.

With this point of honor cleared, Hassan II met de Gaulle in France in May 1962, a visit which marked the beginning of a second honeymoon between the two countries. In July, France renewed economic aid which had been suspended for several years; about $70,000,000 was allotted in the form of credit facilities in banking and direct aid for specific development projects, and agreements were continued by which Morocco, like Tunisia, disposed of its agricultural products in France on advantageous terms. The number of French teachers and technicians in the country was stepped up to a record high since independence, and these were given increased overseas allowances by the French government. On the human level as well, the situation of the Europeans in

Morocco was never better than at the end of 1962. The legal status of foreign workers was much more favorable than in Tunisia, and monetary transfers to the metropole were made easier. Unlike Tunisia, there have been no sequestrations of European farmlands in "strategic areas" or forced removal of their owners. In explanation, it should be stressed that skills in Morocco were not so available and competition not so keen as in Tunisia, but even beyond that there must be conceded to Moroccans a simpler but fuller sense of hospitality, which holds the foreigner to be a guest under protection as long as he behaves, a concept close to the Islamic idea of the *dhimmi* protegé of another religion. The number of Europeans still engaged in humble occupations is proof of this liberal policy, which reminds one that Morocco is still a traditional enough country so that the personal decisions of men outweigh the harsh impersonality of the law.

Relations between independent Algeria and France have in many respects not gotten to the point where the two can be recognized as separate entities. The legal basis differs from that of its neighbors for in the Algerian case the Evian agreements were negotiated in detail as part of the cease-fire arrangement. The later referendum which approved independence also accepted these agreements, and Algerian sovereignty from its inception was limited in many ways. Already in the space of a few months the over-all situation in Algeria is so unlike that foreseen in the accords that talk of revision has become common, and in any event most of the complex arrangements drawn up early in 1962 no longer are relevant to the actual state of affairs. At the end of 1962 the principal areas of discussions and contention between the new state and France were in the domains of the security of persons and property; monetary questions arising from the desperate state of Algerian finances; technical assistance of an emergency nature to keep Algeria afloat; the transfer of French state holdings and assets in Algeria to the new government; and the thorny issue of

Algerian retribution against Muslim collaborators and soldiers who had fought with the French Army during the war.

At the end of 1962 security was far from restored in most parts of Algeria, and where it was it threatened to break down without warning. The departure of Europeans continued and the colony was reduced to not more than 150,000 persons, with the probability that the final figure would be much lower. This exodus seems irremediable and the Algerian state will have to learn to live without the European minority. Inevitably the limited number of Europeans in the country will reduce French interest in, and guilt about, what happened to Algeria. France is committed to spend for economic development in Algeria for three years a sum equal to that allocated under the Constantine Plan in 1962, about $210,000,000 from metropolitan public funds. In addition, France was forced to support the Algerian treasury for current expenses in extremis at the end of 1962. Negotiations near the end of the year reached no final decision on further aid but France was willing to provide reimbursable sums to provide for the resettlement and housing of Algerian refugees. The decision by the Algerian government to follow a policy of austerity was welcomed in Paris, but the stability of that government was being increasingly compromised. Of supreme importance in French eyes were the claims of French citizens to large amounts of property in Algeria, most of which was vacated or abandoned in 1962, and which has been either put under temporary administration by the Algerian state or occupied in various unofficial and technically illegal ways by squatter groups and individuals. The problem of technical assistance is linked to that of security, for no recruitment program can be successful for long if technicians cannot be assured of their physical safety. The question of the *harki*-s, however, is one in which French responsibility, and particularly that of the Army, is deeply engaged. It is estimated by reliable sources that in the six months following independence as many as 10,000 of these Algerian auxiliaries who had served

with the French Army were killed, often by lynch mobs or
vigilante summary execution, while many others were tortured
and numbers were put in concentration camps to do forced
labor. While many of the excesses were the settling of personal
grudges and some might even have been justifiable (for the
brutality of Algerian troops in repressing the rebels often exceeded that of metropolitan forces), such acts violated the
Evian agreements which specifically outlawed all reprisals.

This atmosphere has given birth to a new class of refugee.
The Muslim who is accused of collaboration with France—
which was legally his obligation before independence—or who
fears being charged with lukewarmness toward the revolution,
or who cannot produce some evidence of having aided the
FLN, is often threatened with arrest or worse. In many cases
this is the work of gangsters and extortionists who are rife in
Algeria today, but the decision by the government to institute
a formal purge has added to the panic. So many have fled to
what they think is safety in France, where in the few months
after independence the number of Algerians rose from around
400,000 to 600,000 and was increasing steadily at the end of
1962. There are several categories of Muslim refugees and
emigres: landowners and conservatives who see no future in a
state which says it is moving toward socialism; politicians compromised with the old regime; soldiers, often with their families, who fear reprisals; unemployed who have come to France
looking for work which does not exist in Algeria, often paying
the passage to Marseille with their last franc; and a smattering
of dissident or disappointed ex-rebels and intellectuals. In
many cases the difficulty of determining who is a genuine
refugee, and thus entitled to free transportation to France, is
considerable. French policy varied from an initial effort to
escape responsibility to acceptance late in 1962 of the right
of any Algerian who felt menaced to put himself under French
protection and leave. Freedom of movement between the two
countries is guaranteed by the Evian accords, and the Algerian

government is not averse to seeing some of its vast numbers of jobless fed by someone else. It is rather the French government which feels that a labor convention regulating traffic is necessary. Even in metropolitan France personal safety and tranquillity are not assured to Algerians who fled because of the presence of many militants of the revolution among the Algerian residents of France. The French government started clearing the problem away in part by requiring that Algerians in France choose French citizenship before January 1, 1963, failing which they automatically became foreigners, and as such were deportable or otherwise more manageable than if they were citizens.* While so much attention had been focused on the dwindling European minority in Algeria, it should be kept in mind that about 7 per cent of the Algerian population (at least one male in ten) is in France, a fact which will bind the two countries together, for better or for worse, for some time to come.

In sum, the main point in Franco-Maghribi relations at the end of 1962 was that decolonization had been completed, and on the whole quite successfully. The birth pangs of Algeria were unusually painful but aside from that there was much ground for hope. In France the final amputation had not produced the trauma that some had feared, and it was reassuring to compare the present situation with that at the end of 1957 when there seemed no way out of the Algerian impasse. As had already been the case in other European states which ended their colonial career, like Belgium, the Netherlands, and Italy, the laying down of the burden came as a relief; the state was never more prosperous and its institutions were solid. In Morocco and Tunisia there was a fresh scent in the air—and it might eventually be caught in Algeria—which hinted at all kinds of interesting new perspectives. The principal problem between the countries concerned had been transferred to a social and

* Early in 1963 it was reported that approximately 20,000 Algerians had availed themselves of the opportunity to become French.

technical level where they might be handled, as befits this phase of the twentieth century, by economists and applied anthropologists rather than politicians and soldiers.

Such was not the case with Spanish relations with North Africa. Spain is the last and only European colonial power in the area, and there is a strong impression here that the drama is still being played out in a nineteenth century setting of pride and power. It is hard, in fact, now that French links with the Maghrib have evolved so radically, to envisage anything more unlike them than Spanish ties. They are, of course, ancient and deeply intertwined, most of all with Morocco. At no time have official relations ever been warm, but a basic human understanding has always survived. For centuries each culture has contributed much to the other, but for centuries each was a dreaded enemy with whom a more or less constant state of war was maintained. But war, like trade or any intercourse, brings together as well as divides. Although Spain and Morocco are much alike in many ways—climate, culture, aspects of peasant life, and even similarities in ethnic stock abetted by later intermarriage—they have also been separated by the walls of their religious civilizations. It is not unfair to say that Muslims of the Maghrib may never have "liked" the French— they tend either to love or hate them but all the while they respect them enormously—whereas they get along famously in many cases with the Spanish but without strong emotions and without admiring them. The appeal of French civilization is overwhelming, but it is directed to the *évolués* and intellectuals who are seeking something new, whereas the call of Spain is muted, but benefits from a popular sympathy shared by those who are poor and devout and, in large measure, respect the values of a closed, foreign society without understanding them.

Since the end of World War II, Spain had been pursuing a policy of wooing the Arabs for multiple reasons. The recall of historic ties with the Islamic World was often used in explanation, but power rivalry with France in Morocco and jealousy were more to the point. Madrid also compensated in this way for its ostracism by the European concert and took petulant pleasure in corroborating the adage that Africa begins at the Pyrenees. Not least important was the desire, hearkening back to the days of empire, to play a great role and one which was peculiarly Spanish. Thus, at the time of the Suez Users' Conference in 1956, Spain took a position of its own midway between the protagonists but carefully separated from the neutralist viewpoint, which satisfied no one in the end. The value of this policy had certainly been brought into doubt in Spain in 1956 when it had no alternative but to surrender control of its protectorate zone in northern Morocco a month after the French agreed to grant independence to the country, and later that year it was forced to agree to the abolition of the international regime in Tangier in which it had, along with France, a preponderant interest. The integration of ex-Spanish Morocco proceeded in the following years to the detriment of Spanish influence, which had been guaranteed on paper but which was unable to compete with French prestige in practice. The peseta was withdrawn from circulation early in 1958 and linguistic unification meant the replacement of Spanish by French as the second language. Economic integration brought hardship to many Spaniards as prices in the north spiraled up to the levels of the former French zone, and numbers of them left for home, notably after the Spanish economy began its upward climb after the 1959 stabilization moves.

The overriding issue between Spain and Morocco, however, has been an old-fashioned territorial one. After having handed back the northern zone of its protectorate in Morocco, Spain still held several bits of territory which the Moroccans claimed as theirs with more or less historical justification and varying degrees of self-confidence. On the Mediterranean coast are the so-called presidios, the fortress cities of Ceuta and Melilla, and a sprinkling of small off-shore islands and rocks. Inlaid into the Atlantic coast of Morocco is the 600-square-mile enclave of

Ifni. A southern zone of the Protectorate, known as Tarfaya, occupied an area of 10,000 square miles and extended to the edge of the Spanish Sahara territories from which Tarfaya was administered. These territories, sometimes known as Rio de Oro, are now officially titled Spanish Sahara and cover an area of 105,400 square miles. Ceuta and Melilla have been Spanish possessions since the fifteenth century and have at all times since had a heavily Spanish population (now about 140,000 Spaniards and 10,000 Moroccans.) They are attached administratively and ecclesiastically to the mainland provinces opposite them and function as normal Spanish towns in most ways, but they are dependent on outside sources for the necessities of life, including drinking water. Ifni is an oddity of history, a relic of a fifteenth century fishing settlement which was ceded to Spain in 1860 but not effectively occupied by it until 1934. The inhabitants are mostly Berber-speaking sedentaries and the area is geographically and historically a part of southern Morocco. Spanish Sahara, on the other hand, which is almost uninhabited (34,000 nomads in an area the size of Colorado) is culturally linked more with Mauritania than Morocco proper and should be considered part of the "Mauritanian question." In both cases the establishment in January 1958 of Ifni and Spanish Sahara as provinces of metropolitan Spain seems an anachronistic refusal to come to terms with the modern world.

Trouble broke out in November 1957, when an uprising of tribes in the Ifni enclave was touched off with the help of the Liberation Army, then occupying the southern border areas of Morocco. Spanish reaction was sharp and, after much difficulty bringing in supplies from the Canary Islands to the harborless enclave, the revolt was beaten down. Morocco disclaimed official responsibility for the attack but a period of tension ensued between the two countries and Spain refused to discuss the transfer of the southern zone of the protectorate until Morocco showed it could keep order in its southern regions. Spanish policy began to harden and change, and early in 1958 Spanish troops and French forces from Mauritania cooperated in eliminating roving bands who styled themselves the "Liberation Army of the Greater Sahara." The success of this operation put an end temporarily to Moroccan irregular forces in this desolate area. When, in April 1958, the Moroccan Royal Army occupied the southern extremities of the country, Spain made a gesture of reconciliation by transferring Tarfaya to sharifian authority. This did not fully appease Morocco, however, and the Istiqlal Party, through its leader Allal Al Fassi, who was at that time Minister of Saharan Affairs, continued to voice claims to all the Spanish territories as well as Mauritania with an occasional reference, made without much conviction, however, to the Canaries.

Since 1958 there have been intermittent periods of tension because of the irridentist sentiment in Morocco, but the only physical manifestations of this have been the unofficial boycott of Ceuta and deliberate transit slowdowns and nuisance regulations at the presidio frontiers. In the summer of 1962, however, Morocco extended its territorial waters to a six-mile limit and there were incidents with Spanish fishing boats. To discuss this, visits were exchanged, with Moroccan Foreign Minister Ahmed Balafrej going to Madrid, and the Vice-president of the Spanish government and second figure in Spain, Captain-General Muñoz Grandes, returning the courtesy soon afterward. This was the first visit by a high Spanish official to Morocco since independence, and it indicated a slight thaw in relations. The unofficial attitudes of both parties are so extreme when taken as a whole that compromise would seem unlikely on the surface, but each has some justification for part of its position. The incontestable validity of the Spanish presence in Ceuta and Melilla is counterbalanced by the fact that Ifni clearly belongs to Morocco. Since the latter is economically useless to Spain, it is not unthinkable that it might be traded in return for a firm guarantee by Morocco to respect the presidios, about which Spain is doubly sensitive because it is unable to get rid of a similar outpost on its soil, Gibraltar across the Straits from Ceuta. As to the Spanish Sahara, oil is being intensively searched for there and Spain seemingly considers the economic advantage worth the political risk, but it is difficult to see how such vestigial territories can remain indefinitely in foreign hands, when the high temperature of modern African nationalism is taken into consideration.

The relations of the Maghrib with Italy during the Middle Ages were much like those entertained with Spain, and Muslim Sicily was, like Muslim Spain, a center of learning and a bridge between Arab and Latin civilization. But in recent times similarity has ceased. Italian ambitions were centered on Libya for lack of anything better, and after the Italian debacle in World War II, the large Italian colony in Tunisia turned to France for protection. Italy gained an advantage in being forced out of the colonial game as early as 1942, for its unsavory record in Libya tended to be obscured after the war by the Afro-Asian concentration on latter-day colonial powers. Much of Italian energy had to be devoted to internal reconstruction until late in the 1950's, and the country was not eager to be accused of having neo-Fascist expansionist designs in the Mediterranean, so it was slow to renew contacts with the Arab World. In the past few years, however, both in its own right and as part of the Common Market, Italy has become an important commercial partner for Tunisia and Morocco and is beginning to give substantial development aid. In November 1961, Tunisia and Italy signed a general agreement for technical cooperation which includes training and scholarships for Tunisians in Italy. So far, the agreement has produced $16 million, part of which covers the transfer of a portion of the assets of Italians leaving Tunisia. The visit of the Italian Prime Minister to Tunisia in the summer of 1962 confirmed the new interest of his country in its neighbor. At present, Italy takes about 10 per cent of Tunisian exports and supplies 6 per cent of its imports, but it is noteworthy that Tunisian trade with

Italy is rising faster than that with any other country. In Morocco, the principal field of Italian activity has been oil; in partnership with the Moroccan government, the Italian state oil monopoly ENI has built a refinery at Mohammedia and is prospecting in the Tarfaya region, so far without success.

Another country which has made considerable headway recently in broadening the base of its relations with the area is Western Germany, especially in its growing links with Morocco. Germany is now Morocco's second customer, importing $40 million worth of its products annually, mostly citrus fruit. The ever larger number of Moroccan workers going to Germany in construction, mining, and metal industries, led to negotiations in the fall of 1962 for a labor agreement. German tourism and investment are also rapidly spreading in Morocco, and it might be recalled that the road Spain took to economic recovery consisted of the hard currency brought in by foreign tourists and the remittances of Spanish workers abroad. The opening of Europe to North African workers, already a fact for Algerians, and now becoming one for Moroccans and Tunisians, could be one of the most profound influences of the times on these countries.

The history of relations between North African states and the Communist bloc countries has been marked since 1956 by hesitancy, then a growing friendliness, and most recently a stabilization of relations on a basis of nonalignment accompanied by a certain coolness. There are differences of emphasis in each case: Tunisia always showed the least interest in the blandishments of the East, while the Algerian revolutionary movement was heavily indebted to the Communist countries during much of its fight for independence.

For two years after Morocco and Tunisia became independent there were no formal contacts. The Algerian revolution was the opening wedge for Communist activity, but it had to be carefully handled for fear of offending French public opinion, including many French Communist supporters who were not particularly disposed to Algerian independence early in the revolt. At that time success seemed distant or unlikely for the rebels, and the Soviet Union refrained from all overt statements, preferring to play the card of a popular front in France which would include the French Communist Party. Power in France for a long time took precedence over sympathy to Algeria. The constitution of the Algerian government-in-exile in September 1958 gave the then united Communist world a chance to keep two irons in the fire. A few days after the GPRA was formed, Communist China and the satellite states in Asia, who had no relations with France, recognized it de jure. The USSR and the European satellites were more circumspect and only gradually extended de facto recognition. They sent weapons, however, beginning in 1957, and deliveries built up until massive shipments of automatic arms and heavy material came from Communist China after 1959. Peking was host to many Algerian leaders, including both the men who were at different times its chief ministers, Ben Khedda and Abbas. When the Evian agreements were signed, the USSR extended de jure recognition at once, an act which much displeased France. Since independence, Algeria has not had time to reveal a clear-cut line of foreign policy, but nonengagement has been officially espoused and no economic or political commitments of any scope have been entered into with the East. With Bulgaria in the forefront, emergency help in food, medical supplies, and some specialists has come from the Communists, while Yugoslavia has continued the large-scale aid which it has given since early in the revolution. Algerian sympathy and identification with Cuba led to frigidity in relations with the United States, but in the wake of the Cuban Crisis of 1962 there were signs that these ties were being soft-pedaled by the Algerian government, at least for the moment. At the same time, the suppression of the Algerian Communist Party brought protests from the Soviet Union and other Communist countries.

Morocco exchanged ambassadors with the Soviet Union in September 1958, after leading members of the left-wing of the Istiqlal, like Mehdi ben Barka, had enthusiastically visited the East. This illustrated a constant in Moroccan foreign policy for several years, that it was primarily a reaction to internal policy. It veered from then until the death of Muhammad V to the left, at times strongly, in an effort to offset a conservative domestic approach by an external progressivism. This, it was thought, would appease leftists at home, might be financially advantageous in securing aid, and would increase Moroccan prestige among the countries of the neutralist bloc. The high point of this policy came with the delivery of Soviet Mig fighters to the Royal Army in November 1960, which the United States unofficially protested, and the visit two months later of President Brezhnev of the USSR, which was the occasion for a display of great cordiality. Under the reign of Hassan II, the drift to the left has stopped noticeably, in proportion to the internal control he has gotten over political opponents of the left. Tunisia waited until 1960 before establishing relations with the Eastern bloc, and it was really only in the aftermath of Bizerte that Tunisian policy, which had been openly and forcefully pro-Western (to the extent that Tunisia at the United Nations in 1956 equated Hungary with Suez, an attitude most uncommon among non-Western states then or afterward), but was disappointed by the lack of support it received from the allies of France in its crucial hour, turned temporarily to other sources. Tunisia attended the Belgrade Conference of nonaligned nations but disassociated itself with its final decisions. It accepted a Soviet offer of $27,500,000 to construct a series of dams. Both Tunisia and Morocco have signed bilateral economic agreements with many Communist states, although trade with them is much less than with the countries of Western Europe, and Eastern bloc countries are active in some specific development projects in Morocco.

While the separate states of North Africa were working out

new patterns of relationship with their European neighbors as a first step in their adult lives, they were also beginning to cast about in search of some form of association and interrelationship among themselves. The task has not been an easy one even when political circumstances were as favorable as they were in 1956, when Tunisia and Morocco, almost like twins, set out with much the same background along what looked like a similar path to many observers. The degree of their divergence today is a measure of the difficulty of integrating the Maghrib, even though the most scrupulous verbal respect continues to be paid to the theme of unity in the speeches of politicians and in the constitutions of both Tunisia and Morocco as well as in the program adopted in Tripoli by the Algerian revolution.

The first contacts between Morocco and Tunisia in 1956 were cautious; there was more initiative on the Tunisian side, and some hesitation on the Moroccan which the former took slightly amiss. The liberation of Algeria was the common goal, if not obsession, not only as a matter of principle, but because both countries were genuinely suffering from the backwash of the war: military operations spilling over into their territory, refugees to care for, and reprisals by France for their support to the revolution. The visit of Muhammad V to Tunis in October 1956, was to make common cause on this issue; it was marred by the kidnaping of the Algerians but was useful as a positive Moroccan response to Tunisian overtures. There was no surface change in relations during the long preliminary period ending in 1958, when both countries joined the Arab League, but there was a slow drifting apart as the republican and lay nature of Tunisia became more pronounced while Morocco remained an absolute religious monarchy. The destitution of the Bey was greeted with silence in Morocco, and in the Fall of 1957 the left in Morocco made the first guarded statements about differences between the two countries, finding praise for Tunisia and thus implicitly criticizing the Moroc-

can throne. Still, the community of interests which both shared
kept them together, and the high point of Maghrib cooperation was reached in April 1958, when the Istiqlal Party of
Morocco called a conference in Tangier, which was attended
by the neo-Destour and the FLN. The conference recommended the unity of the Maghrib and called for the establishment of a Consultative Assembly drawn from members of
the national assemblies of the two independent states (there
was an appointed consultative assembly briefly functioning at
this time in Morocco but its mandate was not renewed) and
from the CNRA. The resolutions of the conference were presented to the Tunisian and Moroccan governments and accepted, but they have never been implemented and they now
seem farther from realization than ever. Tunisian-Moroccan
relations soured in 1958 when Tunisia walked out of a session
of the Arab League immediately after having joined, because
the League refused to discuss the Tunisian grievance against
the United Arab Republic. Although nothing was said at the
time, it became known later that Bourguiba was angered by
the failure of the Moroccan delegation to support the Tunisian
position. Tunisian closeness to the West and a feeling on the
part of Moroccans that Tunisia was a favorite child, particularly of the United States, did nothing to improve the deteriorating climate. A serious and open quarrel broke out in 1960
over Mauritania, which was scheduled to become independent
on November 28. Morocco had been conducting a vigorous
campaign for some time to regain parts of the Sahara which it
considered legitimately Moroccan, and it had welcomed dissatisfied Mauritanian notables and given them posts in its administration as "representatives of the southern territories of
the Kingdom." Now it put pressure on all friendly governments to abstain from recognizing the "puppet regime" in
Nouakchott. The Tunisian rejection of the Moroccan thesis
was grave, for Tunisia was the only Arab country which
recognized the new state, but its decision to cosponsor, along

with France, Mauritania's admission to the United Nations was viewed as a direct slap. The Moroccan ambassador was withdrawn and public opinion in both countries was genuinely disturbed after a virulent anti-Tunisian radio campaign got under way in Morocco. The explanation of the Tunisian government, subsequently published as a White Paper, seemed largely designed to assuage what it felt to be national uneasiness about the growing isolation of the country from its "brothers and neighbors." Tragedy has a way of bringing even statesmen and countries together and it was the death of Muhammad V which caused a temporary reconciliation between the two countries. An unofficial Maghribi summit, between Bourguiba, Hassan II, and Ferhat Abbas, was held in Rabat the day after the funeral, at which Bourguiba had been pallbearer, and Morocco later that summer backed Tunisia in the Bizerte crisis. But Tunisia had meanwhile been snubbed when the Casablanca group was formed at a conference held in that city in January 1961, and the Tunisian press was occasionally banned in Morocco because of the prominence it gave to statements from the political opposition in that country. Today, Tunisians view Morocco as a somewhat backward country but one which they know to be potentially richer and more powerful. Tunisia has not wanted to be dominated by anyone or to lose its identity—neither of which is a worry to a more nationally secure Morocco—and the powerful personality at its helm has found it hard, but no harder than the Kings of Morocco, to imagine effacing himself for another.

While Algeria was fighting for its life for eight years it had little time to engage in the niceties of international diplomacy. The brusque manners of Algerian leaders betrayed an attitude which judged others only by their comportment toward the Algerian cause. On this basis Tunisia and Morocco would receive high marks, but neither is exempt from the suspicion that they have coveted parts of Algerian territory and still do, and a feeling, common to all who are engaged in desperate battle, that not enough was done to help them. The difficulties of the Tunisian position are understandable, too, for Tunisia permitted the stationing of a large body of troops on its soil and allowed the Algerian government to operate as a state within a state. The sacrifices Tunisia made did it much harm in relations with France, and a sense of ingratitude was not just an Algerian monopoly. There were several periods of tension, the first stemming from the oil pipeline which Tunisia authorized in 1958. Another was the alleged Tunisian interference with certain prerogatives of the Algerian army on its territory, and the Tunisian claim to parts of the Sahara in 1961 was a source of deep Algerian annoyance. But behind these quarrels, only the last of which is of any importance, there is a much deeper split in the basic philosophies of the two governments. The Algerian leadership, formed in a different school, had always mistrusted and disdained the Tunisian capacity for moderation and patience, just as it never shared the warm feeling which not only Tunisian authorities, but most ordinary Tunisians, hold for the West in general. And a good part of the problem was psychological, for the guest who stays too long ends by disliking his host (and vice-versa), and the Algerians complained that the price they paid for Tunisian hospitality during the revolution was having to listen to a constant barrage of advice from Bourguiba, mixed with constant pressure in favor of a negotiated settlement. That they eventually did negotiate and accept a somewhat restricted independence perhaps only adds to their resentment. Relations since independence have been less than warm. Bourguiba did not endear himself to the winning Ben Bellist group in the jockeying for power in mid-1962, for he supported the GPRA as the legal authority of the country. The prominent position accorded to supporters of Salah ben Youssef, who oppose Bourguiba, at the Algerian independence day celebrations in November was an indication that all was far from well in Algero-Tunisian relations.

The GPRA was in Tunis and not in Rabat; that in itself says much about why Algero-Moroccan relations were never so intricate and troubled. Like Tunisia, Morocco supplied and transited arms and provided a haven for refugees and a base of operations. But Morocco was in all ways less involved in the revolution and more concerned with its own internal problems. Algerians were wont to say at the time that they never felt at home in Morocco as they did in Tunisia, a tribute to the sense of national, almost family solidarity around the throne which Morocco emanates. The place of the king in Moroccan life made it more difficult for the Algerians to oppose him even on those few occasions when there were minor disharmonies. Moreover, Morocco, like Algeria, had adopted a policy of nonalignment, and both countries had more in common in international affairs than either did with Tunisia. Most Moroccan difficulties with Algeria have come since independence and are territorial disputes. Incidents in July 1962 in Tindouf occurred when groups demonstrated for the return of the city to Morocco. These were suppressed by the ALN (the National Liberation Army), and there were minor border clashes when French forces ceased to be responsible for guarding the frontier. Much of the Algero-Moroccan border is legally undefined and negotiations will eventually have to be held to settle delimitation issues. Unofficial Moroccan claims to parts of the Algerian Sahara which used to be common when Algeria was French have not been repeated by the Moroccan government since Algerian independence, and Moroccan policy seems to be to let the dust settle in Algeria before the question of the Sahara, which could involve economic cooperation as well as territorial adjustment, is taken up.

The picture painted above of inter-Maghrib relations would not indicate that unity or even federation is likely in the near future. The hard facts of the case are that the three countries of North Africa are at different stages of evolution into the phase of the nation-state, and without some approximation of equality in that all-important passage rite, the road to a supranational entity appears very arduous. For all the cultural and sentimental unity in North Africa—and there is no shortage of that—each country has begun building a modern state on somewhat varying social structures, has modified these even more through different types of revolutions, and now has a regime distinct from the others. What holds the Maghrib together today is the heritage of a shared religion, history, and language; the memory of a struggle against a common colonial overseer; and, more insidiously, the tie among the new elite is the civilization brought by that colonial power. What divides it are all the attributes of nationalism: one is a multiparty, constitutional monarchy and a religious state with laissez-faire economic policies slightly favored over statism; another is a dominant-party republic in which religion plays a minor role and state planning dominates private enterprise; the third is a single-party dictatorship, torn between conflicting secular and confessional tendencies and moving steadily toward greater state control. Conservative, reformist, extremist, they exhibit a spectrum of options in all fields. On top of this, there are now being consolidated each month economic structures which will make future integration progressively harder and more tenaciously resisted by those who have interests in them. Both Tunisia and Morocco have or are building sugar refineries and steel mills, while Algeria has its own plans for a steel complex. As only one example, Morocco has withdrawn from the phosphate marketing agreement, but in just about every field competitive national economic circuits have been built up and are becoming reinforced as time goes by.

Some form of regional federalism seems to be in the spirit of our times and, as in the case of Europe, it clearly makes economic sense. But unity cannot be forged either with a stroke of the pen or by popular enthusiasm alone. The Maghrib has before it the example of what happened in the Arab Middle East, where countries with the same kinds of common backgrounds (religious, historic, linguistic, and cultural ties) and roughly similar economic levels of attainment have been unable to achieve unity although working for it for the past forty years. On the one occasion when a temporary union was formed, it fell because it was not anchored in reality. Not only has unity not been found in the Arab World, but there are not many reasons to expect it in the near future. For the Arab states of the Middle East, and now more recently the Arab countries of the Maghrib, are not becoming alike but on the contrary more distinct. The development of particularist norms with differing economic emphasis has resulted in the formation of organic national societies as unique as individuals. In 1930 it took an expert to understand and analyze the differences between various colonial areas, which these three countries were, but now any tourist can see how different they are. Tunisia, as a result of its panoply of social reforms, is far more unlike Morocco than it was seven years ago, and it is increasing the social distance between itself and Morocco each day, not necessarily because it is making greater progress all the time, but simply because the societies started, as it were, on different roads which diverged only slightly at the beginning but are now moving farther and farther apart. If anything can be learned from the failure of unity in the Middle East, it is that verbal phenomena and idealistic slogans will not suffice; but if something is illustrated by the kind of unity being forged in Europe today, it is that the way to supranationalism seems to lie in outgrowing immature political state-nationalism—assuredly not the work of a day or a year—and basing the larger concept on a rational socioeconomic foundation.

The countries of the Maghrib have had to determine in recent years what their part is in the ensemble of Arab countries, that Arab world which in pan-Arab eyes stretches from the Persian Gulf to the Atlantic. Sentiment, interest, and policy have oscillated during this time. In 1959 the Tunisian Constitution stated that Tunisia would remain true to ". . . the teachings of Islam, to the ideal of a Union of the Great Maghrib, to membership in the Arab Family, to cooperation with the African peoples . . ." In 1962 the preamble to the Moroccan Constitution says "The Kingdom of Morocco, a sovereign Muslim state, whose official language is Arabic, forms a part of the Greater Maghrib. An African state, it assigns itself furthermore as one of its objectives, the realization of African unity." Remembering that Tunisia has been all along less taken with pan-Arab ideas than Morocco, it is clear how far Arabism as a political force has declined in the past few years and by what it is being replaced.

What is happening today looks like a repetition of the events of the eighth century when Berbery, Islamified in form and under distant Arab rule, broke away to follow its own destinies while the Middle East was occupied with the power struggle between the Umayyads of Damascus and the 'Abbasids of Baghdad. Substitute Nasserites, Kassemites, and Baathists for the historical dynasties and the picture is the same. The Middle East, politically independent a generation before the Maghrib and for some time educationally more advanced in certain countries, was once the great counterpole of attraction to France for the North African generation struggling to break free of colonialism and the past. But in recent years it has not cut a good figure in Maghribi eyes, and now that the countries of North Africa have matured and are catching up in most fields it looks less and less like an example to follow.

Tunisia has shown the greatest reserve of all the countries of the Maghrib in dealing with the Arab Middle East. Intellectually, Tunisians have always considered themselves at least the equal of all Arabs; they are proud of their composite past and the inspiration of the neo-Destour social reform came primarily from radical-socialist sources in France. Morocco did not share the same feelings exactly but the greater remoteness of the country from Middle Eastern centers and the attachment to a national dynasty combined to produce a sense of "splendid isolation" and self-sufficiency. Neither country joined the Arab League until more than two years after independence, and when Morocco took the step in September 1958 Tunisia was more or less compelled to follow suit. Tunisia took advantage of its entry, however, to press a long-standing quarrel with Egypt, which it accused of supporting and arming its enemies and encouraging subversion and assassination. After Tunisia boycotted the League, Morocco was the only functioning North African member, and it embarked for a while on an active policy of Arabism. The League was invited to Casablanca in September 1959, and Muhammad V toured the Middle East early in 1960, at which time he was one of the rare Arab League leaders neutral enough to have visited Egypt, Jordan, Saudi Arabia, and Iraq without giving offense to any one of them, something that would be impossible today. But Moroccan feelers which might have led to an attempt to reconcile the bitterly divided Arab countries came to nought. The intricacies of Middle East politics left a bitter taste, and preoccupations turned to other matters closer to home. Tunisia, conscious of its isolation, let itself be cajoled into returning to the Arab League early in 1961 by Iraq, which was looking for counterweights to Egyptian domination of the organization, but its activities in the League since then have been minimal. Already by the beginning of 1961 Morocco had begun to shift the focus of its interests: the Casablanca Group represented the new African wave of history and the Middle East was no longer of pressing interest.

If anything, the record of the Arab states of the Middle East in the past year has confirmed Maghribi doubts about getting too entangled. Political antagonisms sharpened after the breakup of the United Arab Republic into the separate states of Egypt and Syria in September 1961 to a point where the Arab League virtually ceased to function, and the Egyptian intervention in Yemen brought semiopen warfare between Arab countries supporting different factions in that country. Each country in the

Maghrib tends now to deal with individual Middle East states as it sees its interests best served. Thus, Tunisia has warm relations with Lebanon, Iraq, and Syria, principally, because they represent an anti-Egyptian tendency, but it has recognized the revolutionary regime in Yemen on the principle of republican solidarity while opposing Egyptian interference in the internal affairs of the new regime. Morocco for some time considered Egypt its principal friend among the Arab countries, especially after it became the leading member of the Casablanca Group in terms of population and economic power. But late in 1962 the long Moroccan hesitation in recognizing Yemen's republican government was the touchstone which brought Nasserite denunciation of the monarchy in Rabat through its controlled press. The prediction of many that such disparate regimes as the conservative monarchy of Morocco and the single-party semisocialist military dictatorship in Egypt could not remain allies indefinitely was thus proved correct.

In its relations with the Arab countries of the Middle East, Algeria is in a later time-cycle than its Maghrib partners. The memory of Arab material help and spiritual comfort is still strong, and disenchantment has not had time to set in. Algeria, moreover, has much reason to be grateful to Egypt above all others, for in the planning of the revolution and during its early days Cairo was an essential base, and the Nasser regime the principal bulwark of the rebels as well as their ideal. Token amounts of arms and some money came from other Middle Eastern states (although sums promised by the Arab League were never fully collected from members and paid), but it was Egypt which helped the most. Egypt suffered for its attitude, too, for its Algerian policy aroused French resentment and was partly responsible for France's participation in the attack on the Suez Canal in 1956. Algerian relations with Egypt were smoother than those with Tunisia or Morocco. There were no problems arising from enforced cohabitation, no troops stationed in Egypt, no frontier issues; Egypt was far enough away so that it did not constitute a threat in any way but close enough in spirit to provide brotherly counsel and support. And the mixed dosage of social reforms and Islamic fundament which was astutely designed by President Nasser to gain the backing of traditional and progressive circles alike has always appealed to many Algerians who have been looking for a way to harness the two ideas together. Finally, Cairo represented the perfect antidote to other Algerian apprehensions: by espousing Nasserite doctrines of separation of policy from ideology they were able to avoid some of the danger to which their acceptance of Communist help had exposed them, and Egyptian support likewise made them less completely dependent on Tunisia and Morocco. Today, the regime in Cairo is probably closer, both on a personal basis and in its general philosophy, to the Ben Bella group of Algerians now in power than any other government. The chief danger of the relationship is that Algerian basic problems are not remotely like those of Egypt, and attempts to solve them by emulation do not look promising. If the situation is viewed cold-bloodedly (and there is no indication that the Algerians will do this for some time), it would seem that economic pressures and the need for an authentic ideology corresponding to the needs of the country will sooner or later take precedence over the sentimental bonds which Algeria still has, and rightly so because it now needs them, with Egypt and to a lesser extent other Middle Eastern countries.

The newest political doctrine in the Maghrib, and a potent one at the moment, is Africanism. In fact it is so recent that it is difficult to say with certainty how important it really is in the political outlook of the area and just where and how it will develop. If my reading of North African political psychology is correct, the flow of political attachments after independence turned first away from Europe, where too many recent painful events made it impossible to move without any break from a relationship of dependence to a new one of cooperation and equality, to the Middle East. This offered at first glance everything that North Africa needed: identity and security in a well-defined framework and the refurbishing of Arabism and its glories within some new and powerful unity. But after a while the Eastern Arabs turned out to be less superhuman than they had seemed when viewed through the haze of colonial subjection—North Africans found that the intelligentsia of Cairo was no more active than that of Tunis, the bourgeoisie of Damascus no more cultivated than that of Fez, and the material development of the Middle East usually inferior to that of North Africa. In addition to this awakening to realism, it developed within a few years after independence that North African political life had little practical relation to that of the Middle East (and the Eastern Arabs were never quite able to forgive the Maghrib for not taking the same passionate interest as they in the Israeli question but instead restricting their support to a perfunctory and incomplete application of the boycott of that country) and that the countries of the Maghrib could not exert any influence on inter-Arab quarrels. A bubble burst, and a new field of interest and solidarity was desperately needed if North Africa, which had assimilated the great bulk of its culture and technical formation from the two areas of Europe and the Middle East, was not to feel suddenly abandoned and alone. Thus, as if it were a chemical reaction to the bitter memories of European colonialism and the disappointments of Arabism, Africanism germinated within the Maghribi leadership—for it has been so far almost completely an intellectual movement but not a mass one—and it seems now to be satisfying a profoundly felt need, although for how long is hard to say.

Africanism is only five years old in Tunisia and Morocco. The first step was taken when President Bourguiba went to Accra in 1957 to participate in the Ghanaian independence ceremonies. It should be remembered that at the beginning of that year the only independent countries in Africa were the

Arab states of northern Africa (Morocco, Tunisia, Libya, Egypt, and the Sudan), plus the long-established countries of Liberia, Ethiopia, and the Union of South Africa. The occasion was historic; for the first time a North African state instead of being the newcomer itself was witnessing the birth of a younger country. In April 1958, both Tunisia and Morocco were among the eight independent African countries at the Accra Conference, and interest began to mount. Tunisia took more quickly to Africanism because its disappointment with the Arab World was greater and, from the second half of 1958 when its relations with the United Arab Republic worsened and it removed itself from the Arab League community, it stood very much alone. Morocco did not show the same alacrity; it was still engaging in an Arab-centered policy at the beginning of 1960, when Tunis was the site of the African People's Congress, a meeting which left a deep impression with the Tunisian elite as to the possibilities of further developing the country's role in Africa. It did not escape Tunisian officials that no similar Arab conference had ever been held in the country and, as things stood, would not likely be.

The year 1960 was the decisive one for Africa, with the emancipation of many sub-Saharan states in a short period, and the decisive event in confirming the new optic of North Africa was the Congo operation. Both Tunisia and Morocco sent what were for them considerable forces, more than 3,000 men apiece, and both played important but sharply varying roles in the crisis. Morocco went along with several African states (United Arab Republic, Ghana, and Guinea) in stoutly backing the Lumumba government and finally withdrew its troops in December 1960, when it felt unable to go on supporting what it considered a United Nations policy of lack of firmness. Tunisia, on the other hand, supported the international organization throughout the crisis until it was compelled to withdraw men to defend the country at the time of the Bizerte affair; it subsequently sent another, smaller contingent back to the Congo. The Congo operation pointed up differences in popular and official sentiment about Africa in both countries. By the governments concerned it was considered a fulfillment of "continental duty" and an extension of national prestige, but, to many of the officers and troops involved, the first direct contact with the rest of Africa came as a shock, and the idea that they had anything in common with sub-Saharan Africa seemed as surprising as it was to the Congolese that there were white Africans.

The countries which had withdrawn from the Congo in dissatisfaction called a conference to discuss African problems and form a common front. This was held in Casablanca, in January 1961, and attended by Morocco, the U.A.R., Guinea, Ghana, and Mali. Libya and the Algerian Provisional Government sent observers. The "Casablanca Group," as it called itself, agreed to set up a permanent consultative council; established committees dealing with economic, military, and cultural affairs; and decided that heads of member states should meet at least once a year. The group has now been in existence two years and results have been meager. For a time there was a real chance that it might become a viable organism, at least economically in respect to the exchange by Egypt of its manufactured goods for the raw materials of other members short of hard currency. But from mid-1962 on, its members began to go their separate ways, and at this writing it shows little sign of life. The economic committee had recommended the abolition of all customs barriers between members by 1966 and implementing steps were to have been taken at a conference in Marrakesh at the end of 1962, but the conference was postponed sine die seemingly on account of political difficulties. In fact, with the possible exception of the advantages for Egypt, the group had little reason to exist from the start and less cohesiveness. It was spread over large and noncontiguous areas of Africa, member states had widely disparate cultural and economic patterns, and they traded little among themselves but each had other long-established commercial circuits of greater importance. Political relations were also unstable: today Morocco and Egypt are on poor terms, Morocco and Guinea have had a minor scuffle, rivalry between Ghana and Egypt was intense for a while, but now Ghana and Algeria are preoccupied by internal difficulties, and Mali has been making overtures toward French Africa, from which it had separated, and the Common Market. To consider only Morocco's relation to the group, that country's trading position has been made worse recently. It is outside the Community states which are associated with the Common Market, and in the newly formed Equatorial African Customs' Union (Brazzaville Congo, Gabon, Chad, and the Central African Republic), for example, goods from France and associated African territories come in free of duty but those from Morocco will be more heavily taxed. Thus, French firms which established branches in Morocco to sell to African countries find that the subsidiaries cannot compete with parent companies. Discrimination in Africa threatens to get worse before it gets better: both the twenty members of the Monrovia group and the twelve countries of the African and Malagasy group have plans for establishing customs unions. Thus, the whole problem comes back to the question of Moroccan negotiation with the Common Market, a step which cannot be put off much longer.

If Morocco seems to have backed the wrong horse in the Casablanca group, Tunisia has chosen not to ride any. It does not belong to any bloc but it maintains friendly relations with the Monrovia group and with all French Africa in general. Tunisian policy toward Africa contrasts with that followed by Morocco and Egypt. It is less ambitious and generally apolitical. A country the size of Tunisia can hardly be considered aggressive, whereas Morocco conquered parts of the Sudan in past history and still has claims on the territory of several other African states. Tunisia believes in its role as a kind of relay station, carrying culture between France and Africa, and seasoning it with its own Arabo-Islamic, but specifically Tunisian, content. The Mediterranean aspect of its Africanness is what it stresses, and the soft harmonies of Tunisia, with its olive groves and whitewashed villages by the sea have in fact impressed visiting Africans with the notion that there is "another" Africa. There are many risks in the Africanist policy of Tunisia—Africans may decide in the end that there is nothing there which is not available at first-hand elsewhere—but it cannot be said to have ignoble aims. One is entitled to hope that the country might, under the right circumstances, become a useful meeting place in which Africa and Europe could intermingle with profit for all.

Algeria owes much to its many African friends who supported it wholeheartedly on the international political scene in the past few years. As it becomes independent, its policy toward Africa is still something of an enigma. Geographically Algeria has more connections with the rest of the continent than either Morocco or Tunisia. Across the Sahara it touches Mauritania, Mali, and the Niger Republic. So far its most noteworthy acts have been to refuse all contact with Mauritania, either from loyalty to Morocco or to hold a trump card in reserve when the frontier question comes up, and a strongly expressed determination to help liberate the few territories still under colonial rule, notably Angola. In economic terms, Algeria, even more than its neighbors, must soon make crucial decisions about the Common Market and its African ramifications. If Algeria is to become an associated territory of the EEC this will produce inevitably different political patterns from those that would follow a decision to stay out, and if the decision is affirmative it will involve Common Market policy toward the whole Maghrib.

In short, Africanism seems to allow each country in North Africa to express at this stage in its development a vital component of its personality. Tunisia can play a cultural role, Morocco is able to combine a sense of "manifest destiny" in

Africa with the religious hold which its sharifs have exercised over much of the northwest part of the continent, and Algeria can preach the completion on a continental scale of its own revolution. To the Arabs of the Middle East, North Africa had a dubious contribution to make (the great one was that of the Algerian Revolution and its mystique of Arab military valor and political unity, but much of that collapsed in the post-independence anarchy of the country). With both Europe and the Middle East, the role of the Maghrib has been essentially to learn, absorb, and be obedient. One can understand why, after gaining its freedom, it did not simply want to change schools, and one can sympathize with the need for expression which is at the heart of relations with Africa in all domains.

We turn now to consideration of the relations of North Africa with the United States, and since this is the formal title of this book, readers may well ask why the subject has been reserved to the end. There are reasons for this; the aim of this survey has been to describe North African society for the benefit of an American audience. One might say that the procedure has been to reveal it from the inside out, as much in chronological order as possible, but also in logical precedence beginning with the core of the culture, continuing with its internal problems, and terminating with its interaction with the rest of the world. From just about all standpoints, the United States comes in at the end. It has been on the periphery of North African history at most times and was in no sense an influence in the formation of the modern states of the area. U.S. interest in the Maghrib in the truest sense is about as new as Africanism is to North Africa—in terms of meaningful contact, it dates really from the visit of ex-Vice-President Nixon to Tunisia and Morocco in March 1957. But U.S. interest has grown mightily in recent years and, in the case of Tunisia at least, relations with the United States are now excellent and close, in addition to which Tunisia is of great importance to America on political grounds and as an economic pilot state in Africa. Thus, as the last major force to enter the North African Scene, the United States and its increasing involvement with North Africa seemed to be the most fitting concluding subject for this book.

Certainly there have been previous historical relations between America and North Africa. They were often unique and fascinating, but they are exotica of the past which had little if anything to do with either the permanent character of North African society or with the turn our relations have taken since World War II. They are much more relevant to the study of American history itself, since they touch on several vital issues which the young republic had to face in its earliest days: freedom of the seas, the pride of a new state and its unwillingness to pay protection money to maritime brigands, the discovery that force was necessary to make oneself respected, and the entire story of the beginning of the United States Navy, as well as some of the first American lessons in Machiavellian European statesmanship. The romantic note is unquestionable, but the story of American action in the Maghrib rightly holds a high place in the annals of American patriotic deeds (although a good deal of the behavior was less derring-do than has been pictured in the boys' tales and technicolor movies which have used the troubles with the Barbary States as their theme.) No one can deny the heroic appeal of events which gave us one of our first naval heroes, the initial victories of our newly organized fleet, such a stirring line as that which the Marines have sung "from the Halls of Montezuma to the shores of Tripoli," and the nostalgic strains of "Home Sweet Home" written by an American official from a shore so savage in the popular imagination that it gave its name to an infamous part of one of our most famous cities in its heyday before the great earthquake of 1906: the Barbary Coast of San Francisco. The result has been that the association by extension of the cities of the original Barbary Coast with sin and wickedness has never been completely erased from the American mind. The image was continued with Pepe le Moko and the Casbah of Algiers in the last generation, the legend of vice-ridden Tangier was inflated to extraordinary proportions after World War II, and the whole is something which North Africa still has to live down.

But if, however reluctantly, we turn away from the romantic aspect and look at history from the more prosaic standpoint of social development and cultural change, we must admit that the clashes between the United States and the Regencies of Algiers, Tunis, and Tripoli at the end of the eighteenth and the beginning of the nineteenth centuries were less than incidental to the mainstream of the history of North Africa. Our relations with the sultanate of Morocco, which were always friendly and were less concerned with the problem of freebooting, were more meaningful in exactly the proportion that the Moroccan government at that time was more representative of a reality of national existence than were the regencies, particularly Algiers and Tripoli. But in all cases, after the initial issue was settled and treaties which Americans considered just were signed, their first fleeting engagements faded away like a half-forgotten dream.

For the sake of convenience, United States relations with North Africa may be divided into four general periods. The first, from American independence until 1815, was the period of securing treaties from the Barbary States; from 1815–1942 contact was slight and of a kind which had more to do with American concern about Europe and its interests in North Africa than with the area itself. From 1942–1956 we see the progressive involvement of the United States in the Maghrib as part of its new role in world affairs, but still mainly influenced by its alliance with the principal colonial power in the area, France. The fourth period is the one we are in today, where for the past seven years we have been dealing for the first time on a basis of friendship and equality with the independent states with regard to an ensemble of economic and political problems.

Prior to the independence of the United States, its shipping in the Mediterranean was considered covered by treaties which Britain had negotiated with the several Regencies, and it was thus relatively immune to attack. The new nation had no navy at first, so attempts were made to persuade European powers to intercede on its behalf with the Barbary States, which had indicated that they were not bound to respect United States vessels unless some agreement were entered into. Thus, France in 1778 agreed to use her "good offices" to further amicable relations between the states of North Africa and America, and in 1782 a treaty with the Netherlands stipulated,

If at a certain time, the United States judge it necessary to undertake negotiations with the Empires of Morocco or Fez, with the Regencies of Algiers, Tunis or Tripoli, having as object the negotiations of guarantees for the security of their Mediterranean maritime interests, his High Honour the Staathouder engages himself, upon United States request, to help these negotiations in the most efficient manner . . .

But, over a period of some years, the European powers did little for America on this score. Britain and France were both hostile to the development of competitive maritime trade in the Mediterranean, and American suspicions were aroused by evidence of their duplicity. A current of opinion developed for direct negotiations with states of the Maghrib, this fortified by the seizure of some American ships off Gibraltar in 1785 by Algiers pirates. Negotiations were begun with Morocco, which had been one of the first countries to recognize American independence, and a treaty of "Peace and Friendship between the United States of America in Congress assembled" and the Sultan of Morocco was concluded in Marrakesh in 1786, accompanied by a provision for an annual grant by America of $10,000. This was followed five years later by the installation of the first American consulate in the area, in Tangier.

America became angrier as more ships were seized by

the Regency of Algiers; but it grew more worried when
Portugal, which had been diverting attention from other
shipping because it was at war with Algiers, made peace in
1793. Some American captives had been ten years in the dun-
geons of the city before a treaty was signed in September 1795,
which provided for the payment of more than $600,000 and
the delivery of an annual amount of stores. A similar agreement,
providing for the delivery of gunpowder and provisions, was
signed with the Regency of Tunis in 1799 and ratified by the
Senate in January 1800, while a treaty had been previously
negotiated with Tripoli in 1796. But now opinion began to
oppose the idea of paying tribute to petty pirates, and the
United States had begun to form a fleet. When Tripoli made
increased demands, they were refused and it led to hostilities
lasting from 1801 to 1805. During this period, relations between
the United States and Tunis were strained because Tunisian
ships trying to run the American naval blockade of the Tripo-
litanian coast were seized. The first Tunisian mission to the
United States agreed to a modification of the original treaty
of 1799, by which no further annual tribute would be paid to
the Bey and the United States agreed to give back the im-
pounded ships. By now the United States was a growing power
and in 1815 an American naval demonstration before Algiers,
conducted by Commodore Stephen Decatur, who had been,
as a younger Lieutenant, a hero of the war with Tripoli, se-
cured a rectification of the treaty of 1795. From then on, piracy
became virtually inactive as the power of the West far out-
stripped that of the Barbary States. Tunis renounced piracy
formally in 1819 and the city-state of Algiers ceased to exist
in 1830. In 1824 a new Tunisian-American treaty was signed
which put the two signatories on a basis of equality and accorded most-favored nation status. Finally, in 1837, Morocco
signed a treaty which provided capitulatory rights for American citizens, who were subject only to the jurisdiction of their
own consular authorities. The period of American preoccupa-

tion with North Africa because it was an obstacle to United States trade with Europe and the Levant was over.

From then until around the end of the century, America almost forgot about the existence of North Africa. What few relations there were concerned Morocco mostly. It is significant that the series of Reports of Commercial Relations of the United States with all Foreign Nations, begun in 1856, first mentions Morocco in 1865 and has only one entry of importance, that of 1870. Likewise the Consular Reports tell very little about the country, although much information comes from European ports which were trading with Morocco. From 1890 on, interest quickens a bit, but discussion of Morocco is still limited to monographs on such subjects as carpet manufacture and the slave trade. In 1871 a discreet suggestion had been made by the Moroccan government, which was alarmed by European designs and anxious to add America to the list of powers it was playing against each other, that the country would be willing to be put under United States protectorate, but the offer was politely and firmly declined.

The United States attended the Conference of Madrid in 1880 because of its previous engagements and rights in respect of extraterritoriality, but it did not play an active role at the meeting. The conference assured to all signatories most-favored nation status, and this became a keystone of later American policy toward Morocco. American participation in this conference resulted in the United States taking part in the Algeciras Conference of 1906, which brought together all powers which had been at the Madrid conference. America was now much more active everywhere on the international scene, and Theodore Roosevelt had already intervened in an affair of Moroccan banditism involving an American citizen. But the principal American concern at the conference was less its interest in Moroccan stability or the integrity of the sultan's realm than the need to prevent war from breaking out between France and Germany over Morocco. Here, in contrast to

Madrid a generation earlier, American weight was felt and the influence of Roosevelt, known to be particularly keen on the success of the conference, was considerable. It is also noteworthy that this was the first American participation of this kind in European power politics.

When the French Protectorate was established in Morocco in 1912, the United States refused to recognize that the rights it had obtained in the various treaties from 1786 to the Conference of Algeciras were in any way affected. Thus, although there were occasional stormy disputes with France, most American rights continued in effect until the re-establishment of Moroccan independence in 1956, at which time they were voluntarily surrendered to the new government.

North Africa was the site of the first large-scale allied offensive in the European theater of war, when Anglo-American amphibious forces landed in Morocco and Algeria on November 8, 1942, and began a long arduous campaign to turn the southern flank of the Axis powers in the Mediterranean. Resistance by French forces loyal to the Vichy government was short-lived but sharp in a few places. It ended when an arrangement was made for a cease-fire between the Allied command and Admiral Darlan. First plans to move rapidly eastward overland into Tunisia were frustrated by bad weather, poor communications, and the promptness of German counteraction in occupying Tunisian ports and airfields. During the winter there was severe fighting in the Kasserine Pass and near the Algero-Tunisian frontier, but after a German counteroffensive had been repulsed, Allied forces cooperating with the Eighth British Army coming from Libya gradually squeezed the Axis forces into the northeast corner of Tunisia and onto the Cape Bon Peninsula where, on May 12, 1943, nearly a quarter of a million surrendered to end the North African campaign. The effect of the Allied intervention on Maghribi nationalism and the direct stimulus given by Franklin Roosevelt have already been mentioned. It should be added that although Algeria and Morocco were relatively untouched by the campaign, there was serious war damage in Tunisia, particularly to the railroads and ports, which retarded its postwar economic development.

The third period in American-North African relations, from the Second World War until 1956 can be summed up in three words: businessmen, bases, and nationalism. Before 1945 there had been few American commercial interests in Morocco, but in the wake of the conflict many service men stayed on and went into the import-export business. Equality of economic opportunity was theoretically guaranteed them by treaty, but French authorities pursued a campaign of discrimination and harassment which was technically based on currency control regulations established in 1939, but in fact related to the widespread French reluctance to see nationals of other countries settle in Morocco. After the United States Congress had attached riders to bills in 1950 and 1951 withholding economic aid from France if, in the opinion of the President, it failed to comply with the provisions of treaties in force, France took the matter to the International Court of Justice at the Hague. The court decision handed down in August 1952 ruled for the United States on questions of economic liberty but decided against it on matters of extraterritoriality and juridical privilege (although such rights were unaffected in Tangier and the Spanish Zone until independence.) Nevertheless, the issue was never satisfactorily settled, for American businessmen complained until the end of the Protectorate of continuing violation of their rights and protested the unwillingness or inability of the State Department to obtain redress. When one looks back, the affair seems a bit anachronistic now that all extraordinary foreign privileges have disappeared in Morocco, but its importance at the time lay also in the fact that the American colony by virtue of its anti-French stand became sympathetic to Moroccan nationalism and gave it cautious encouragement.

After the war, the United States had continued to operate an aero-naval installation at Kénitra (Port Lyautey) in Morocco, and during the darkest days of the Korean War at the end of 1950 it was decided to construct a series of strategic air bases in that country on a crash basis to bolster the defense of Europe. Negotiations were completed with France, which insisted on the right to fly its flag jointly with the American emblem at the bases. At a cost of nearly $500 million and despite some contracting scandals, the mainstay of the complex was made operational in 1953. In the end, only three of five sites were actually used, while one was kept on a stand-by basis and the fifth not constructed. Again there were disputes with France about the number of American personnel allowed in Morocco and a tight ceiling was maintained until the end of the Protectorate. Since the Moroccan government had not been consulted during the negotiations, it did not recognize the juridical existence of the bases when it became independent, but it took no overt steps against them.

From the mid-1940's America became aware of the forces of nationalism in the area. American troops could not be indifferent to the poverty and inequality of living standards they saw in North Africa, and President Roosevelt in 1943 had met the Sultan of Morocco in Casablanca and received an appeal from Bourguiba protesting French treatment of Tunisian patriots. In general the American attitude was that the war must be won before any secondary issues could be settled, and the United States was unwilling to jeopardize its relationship with France while the struggle continued. When the war ended, the same stand was taken for other reasons. America demobilized and for a time tended to let slide most external problems save those that concerned the Cold War. In December 1946, Bourguiba visited the United States but found the atmosphere unpropitious for enlisting support, although five years later he had more success, notably with labor leaders.

The position of labor on colonial issues at this time was strikingly ahead of both public opinion in general and the official tendency to consider the interests of European allies almost exclusively, and both the CIO and the AFL during the 1950's were instrumental in keeping open channels of communication and sympathy with the North African nationalists.

The official American viewpoint, as expressed in voting at the United Nations, gave little support to the nationalist movements. It is noteworthy how much American thinking on this issue has changed in a decade. At that time the country was preoccupied with strategic considerations, was anxious to avoid offending France and other NATO partners, and was putting its energy into building military pacts and bases. In the Moroccan case, the United States backed the French position in one way or another for three successive years: in 1951 it opposed placing the issue on the agenda; in 1952 it helped push through an anodyne Latin-American resolution calling only for "continuing negotiations"; and in 1953 a more forceful statement which urged that "the right of the people of Morocco to free, democratic political institutions be ensured" failed to pass by one vote (32 for and 22 against, with five abstentions including that of the United States). Policy with respect to Tunisia, where American military involvement was nonexistent, was slightly more supple. After abstaining in the Security Council in 1952, the United States supported a mild Assembly resolution which recognized Tunisia's qualifications to govern itself. In the 1953 Fall session, after an Arab-Asian bloc proposal had been unsuccessful, a compromise Icelandic resolution recommending negotiations was barely passed by a two-thirds majority.

The current phase of relations began in 1956, when the United States promptly recognized the independence of Morocco and Tunisia. Relations with the latter were cordial from the start and warmed when Bourguiba spoke his mind about

Russian intervention in Hungary at a time when most Afro-Asian countries were blinded by the Suez crisis. In 1957 Tunisia accepted the Eisenhower Doctrine, designed hopefully to protect the Middle East from Communism, but complained that the amounts given to friendly countries ($3 million had been offered Tunisia) were much less than those allocated to nations threatening to desert the Western camp. During the same year relations were consolidated by the signing of an economic aid agreement, the visit of Vice-President Nixon, and in the autumn by the Anglo-American decision to supply Tunisia with small arms, which had been withheld by France, because Tunisia "had chosen freely to identify itself with the West."

Morocco, on the other hand, although accepting American economic help in the spring of 1957, declined to adhere to the Eisenhower Doctrine and gradually moved later that year toward a policy defined as "nonalignment." When Muhammad V chose to make the United States the object of his first foreign state visit in November, news of the sovereign's visit was studiously played down by most of the Moroccan press. A joint statement was issued in Washington saying that a "provisional solution" to the problem of American air bases would be worked out, pending which settlement American aid would continue to be used to strengthen the Moroccan economy.

In the spring of 1958 Anglo-American concern at deteriorating relations between France and Tunisia after the Sakiet bombing incident of February, led to a good offices mission in which the United States, in the words of Secretary of State Dulles, sought to be a "benevolent but neutral peacemaker." The mission succeeded in keeping a delicate peace that spring but was terminated without lasting results when the Fourth Republic fell in May.

During 1958 the Moroccan bases problem became more sensitive. An ill-timed announcement in June that Nouasseur field was being transferred to the Strategic Air Command upset

Moroccans, and the United States landing of Marines in Lebanon in July led to widespread demands for the removal of all foreign installations from the country. Correspondence was exchanged in which the United States accepted the principle of eventual evacuation. This promise was kept when President Eisenhower visited Morocco in December 1959, on his return from India and Pakistan, and it was announced that America would withdraw from all bases by the end of 1963. Since 1960 there has been a general phasing out and the question uppermost in Moroccan minds now is what future use to make of the sites turned over. A consulting American mission has studied them and made some recommendations but so far no final decisions have been made.

During the final years of the Eisenhower administration, Tunisian-American relations prospered, and they reached a high point when Bourguiba became the first head of state received by President Kennedy in May 1961. It is significant of many things that he was at that time the only Arab statesman who could have been given a ticker-tape parade in New York. He received a genuinely warm welcome from the American public which looked upon him as the kind of leader of a non-Western country they were searching for: someone who seemed to them moderate, intelligent, socially progressive, and vocally pro-American. In contrast, American relations with Morocco during this period had grown strained as that country moved closer to the Communist bloc through trade agreements, arms purchases, votes in the United Nations, and in general tone. There was even thought in Washington late in 1960 of disengaging from all Moroccan commitments. No immediate steps were taken, however, and the climate changed considerably after the death of Muhammad V in the spring of 1961. The rule of Hassan II has so far been marked by an abandonment of the previous foreign policy which seemed designed, mostly in vain, to pacify internal opposition on the left, and by a new realism which has led to a steady warming in Moroccan relationships with all the Western countries, including the United States.

With the change of administration in Washington in 1961, policy toward Algeria developed along new lines. Until 1958, America had consistently supported the French position at the United Nations, but in that year it abstained from a resolution (which failed to pass by one vote) recognizing the right of the Algerian people to independence, where it had been expected to cast a negative vote. For the next two years, policy consisted of not interfering with the efforts of President de Gaulle to find a solution, but at the same time of not giving overt encouragement to the rebel government. In January 1961, the approval by the French electorate of the referendum granting Algeria the right to self-determination coincided with the advent of an American chief executive who had taken an extraordinary interest in the revolution during his career in the Senate. It became possible to show a restrained sympathy for the Algerians, who were now clearly on the way to independence, and contact between official circles was undertaken, climaxing in a meeting between the Assistant Secretary of State, Mennen Williams, and Algerian nationalist leaders, in Tunis, in September 1961.

The United States promptly hailed the independence of Algeria in July 1962, but prudently waited until it was sure who controlled the government before extending recognition formally on September 29, 1962. Soon after recognition, American relations with the new republic darkened because of what was, in American eyes, the unnecessarily provocative support given by the Algerian government to Cuba during the missile crisis in October. Premier Ben Bella, having been received with exceptional honors as head of state during his visit to Washington after attending a session of the United Nations, proceeded directly to Havana where he praised the Cuban revolution in the warmest terms. American opinion reacted sharply and when the Cuban crisis came to a head a few days later, informal talks which had been exploring Algerian economic needs were suspended, with each government claiming the initiative.

Subsequently, the Algerians retreated considerably from the original extreme position they had taken on this question, and by the spring of 1963 relations had become normal if not overly cordial. Despite the strain, United States relief efforts consisting of large shipments of food given under the provisions of P.L.480, as well as medical services and sundry charity work, continued unabated. Public acknowledgment of the importance of this help, which provided sustenance for several million Algerians in the difficult winter of 1962–1963, was made for the first time early in 1963 by Premier Ben Bella, and his statement was a contribution to the smoothing out of relations.

Since the first agreements were signed with Morocco and Tunisia in 1957, the United States has continued each year to support a variety of programs in both countries. In Morocco, the total amount allocated by the Mutual Security program from 1957 to 1962 was $198 million. Of this $66 million was for agricultural development and included irrigation, locust control, agricultural extension, and work center projects. Housing and road construction also accounted for important sums, and here as in Tunisia the United States has contributed cereals for work projects for the unemployed. Expenditure in Morocco has come out during this period to about $4 per capita per year. Other important features of the program are the training of Moroccans in the United States and elsewhere, and technical cooperation by American specialists in agriculture and other fields. The program has been generally successful, but one common complaint relates to the slowness with which Moroccan officialdom makes and transmits decisions, and the conservative use of funds put at its disposal.

In Tunisia, the deeper plunge has been taken. The aid program spent about $147 million in the first five years of its existence in much the same kind of project work as in Morocco: special assistance, technical cooperation, the Development Loan Fund, and the use of surplus agricultural products in the battle against unemployment and underdevelopment, and the financing of commodity imports through a counterpart account. But American participation in the Tunisian development program will be even greater in the future. In November 1962, an agreement was reached under which the United States will contribute $184 million to the three-year development plan (1962–1964) which is the precursor of a more extensive ten-year plan. United States aid to Tunisia will run thus at least $15 per capita per year, which is a high ratio of investment. But it represents only a portion of what Tunisia proposes to devote to the project, some $785 million. American aid will concentrate on irrigation, electricity, transportation, and small industrial projects. The commitment to Tunisia is much greater than that to any other African country, even to Nigeria which, like Tunisia, has been considered a "pilot state" for development. With a stable government in Tunisia and a firm United States engagement to this degree, the prospect of attracting private Western investment is considerably increased. The aim of the ten-year plan is to raise the gross domestic product by 6 per cent a year and achieve a self-sustaining rate of growth by 1974, a goal which is certainly laudable but which faces many obstacles, the greatest being that of increasing internal savings to the point required by the plan. American aid already amounts to about half of all public development expenditure. On the other hand, the scope and manageability of problems in Tunisia, and the social advantages of the country, which include as efficient and honest an administration as can be found in any similar country, certainly justify the move. It is hard to think of another country where the United States would be making a more useful contribution.

Let us step back at this point and look at the future of American-North African relations from a distant perspective. To what degree are the countries of the area important to us and why? Politically, the United States has no axe to grind except that of trying to ensure that each society can function to the best of its abilities within a framework of freedom as it knows it and without threatening its neighbors, the peace of the region, or of the world as a whole. Economically, the American stake is extremely limited, trade is not negligible but it is of quite modest proportions for all concerned. Strategically, we are now withdrawing from North Africa. The importance of geographical strategy is clearly not what it was, and, while the bases in Morocco served us well during a crucial decade, they can now be dispensed with; relations with Morocco should be easier once they are gone. (It might be considered that one reason for the Tunisian attachment to America lay in the charm of absence: in 1956 there were fewer than fifty resident Americans in the country, and there were no military bases or economic domination of any kind.) Culturally, we have a limited role to play in comparison to that of France, which cannot fail to continue to have close relations with all three countries for a long time in the future. English is becoming widely used in Tunisia but it is unlikely that the country will become as polyglot as, say, Lebanon. The problems caused by having to be bilingual in Arabic and French are more than enough for most North Africans to handle.

The American decision to help very substantially in Tunisia's development looks like the most permanent and important point of contact in the near future. It was taken on sound economic grounds, but not on those alone. It will of course be extremely useful and instructive to see what can be done by massive investment in a poor country with minimal natural resources and little else than the will to work. If Tunisia could really become self-sustaining in a decade, there would be little excuse in other more-favored lands which have often refused to face the economic facts of our times that require them to shed at least tears and sweat if they hope to progress. Beyond that there is the fact that Tunisia's place in the modern political world is much greater than its size, power, or economic potential warrant. This "moral position" cannot be overlooked, nor can the secret gnawing in the conscience of many Americans that one should not only help those who help themselves but should support those who have shown themselves to be friends. Tunisia is not slavishly tied to the Western wagon, as many events have shown in recent years, but it is attached to principles the West and the United States cherish, and its goal, as once put by Bourguiba, of attaining a "respectable position" among respectable countries is sensible enough to merit support.

Morocco offers more varied promise but greater risk. American relations with it have been on the whole very good, there has never been any major incident of friction in all our history, and things are looking better in most recent times. Our military disengagement will enable us to concentrate on economic and social problems which are already pressing in Morocco, even if the country has been able to coast a while longer than its neighbors by relying on its slightly greater natural advantages. Morocco still has a degree of internal shaking-down to go through, especially in the development of responsible institutions of local and national government. One can only hope that it will accomplish this in a way which will increase the national social harmony that is the necessary foundation for all further progress. Morocco's resources and talents, many of them still unexploited, offer exciting possibilities for the future, and there is every reason to expect that this country, which was one of the first friends of the United States, will continue to be a steadfast one.

The case of Algeria is more complex and at this writing it may be best to suspend judgment. Algeria came to independence in a new era, of which we are only at the beginning. The time-lag mentioned in the matter of Algerian dealings with Arab and African states applied to relations with the United States as well. Tunisian nationalist thinking and that of some of the older generation of Moroccan statesmen was fixed at a time when the international community was still Wilsonian in spirit, but Algeria grew up in a harsh age of blocs, blackmail, and the inchoate search of the Third World for means of self-expression. And, at the same time, the United States of the 1960's, while more acutely aware of the rest of the world than it was in Dullesian days, is also more hard-headed in its comprehension of the limitations which apply to all nations, and more selective in measures designed to attain more realistic goals. Thus, America judges Algeria today by its behavior but does not necessarily expect that behavior to be fully mature for some time, in view of the appalling circumstances of Algeria's birth. Algeria may very well not be friendly, either to the United States (except for the interventions of then Senator Kennedy, it has little reason to be so) or to Western ideals or practices (they may not be adequate in the desperate circumstances in which Algeria finds itself.) But the United States, enmeshed in the Realpolitik of the nuclear and space age has, I think, outgrown the need to be "loved" from which it once suffered. We realize that those who are not always for us are not necessarily against us, and we do not seek excessively sycophantic friendships any more than we court enemies. Within these confines, then, relations with Algeria could be normalized to the advantage of both countries on a basis of reciprocal respect and an understanding of the areas about which each feels especially sensitive. Particularly here, the United States is not trying to take the place of France, in economic support or any other way. Even if it wanted to, it could not even begin to do so. In fact, the problems of Algeria are so overwhelming that there is probably little America can do for some time except to observe their evolution. But once a realistic basis has been prepared, it would seem natural that at the beginning a reserved relationship would, and should, ensue between both parties, but this should also be one which will allow scope for the gradual growth of normal, friendly relations.

The United States has no greater goal than to see a healthy

variety of free societies flourishing under the different institutions and customs which their specific cultural genius has fashioned. In North Africa today there is just this kind of variety and America has the opportunity here to practice this policy by looking on all three countries with understanding and objective sympathy, while reserving the right to choose its close companions from those who share its ideals. Similarly, the countries of North Africa can prove their devotion to the freedom which they valiantly and painfully won for themselves by maintaining and cultivating it with care. Their future is now in their own hands.

Summing Up

At the conclusion of a survey of this nature one is compelled to ask himself some basic questions about the meaning of the patterns of North African life and history, and to determine what lessons might be drawn from the study of them. Perhaps the subject could best be summed up in four key words which come to mind when the cultural structure of the Maghrib is conjured up: permanence, cohabitation, responsibility, and identity.

Certainly the durability of this society is one of its most striking characteristics. Having survived periodic invasions and lived through foreign domination and conquest, it has emerged today remarkably stable, and it is not hard to find large areas where lifeways and material culture have not changed for thousands of years. In itself there is nothing spectacular in this; indeed, it tends to make much of the rural social history of North Africa a kind of non-history, but just that negative quality of folk persistence is something which in the end emerges as an enduring value, which tends to guarantee the continuing existence of the group by favoring a conservative state of steadiness at the expense of the kind of bold experimentation which may lead to progress. The importance of the Maghrib in the history of human events and ideas can hardly be called outstanding in respect to the contribution made by individuals. The roll call of really illustrious names is fairly short: Septimius Severus, Augustine, Tertullian, Averroes, Ibn Battuta, and Ibn Khaldun, and it may be doubted that the non-specialist would know much about more than one or possibly two of those. Nevertheless, they exhibit one quality which says much about North Africa—none of them was exclusively of and from the Maghrib, but all flourished and lived at times, or made a good part of their careers, outside the area—in Europe, the East, or Africa. It is hard indeed to find an authentically indigenous individual genius, something which makes us all the more aware of the collective nature of the society and what it stands for.

Just as its great men have had part of themselves enracinated in neighbor cultures, so the Maghrib as a whole has existed alongside of or been a part of adjacent great civilizations without fully integrating itself in them until now. This is the pillar of cohabitation, the most trenchant example of which is the colonial experience which North Africa has just gone through. This was one of the most profound meetings of the West and the non-West in recent times, and if colonialism is looked on as the means by which the West created a unitary world, the intensity of the impact on North Africa deserves much study. To anyone who, like the writer, has lived through a colonial period and the beginnings of decolonization in an area, the change in behavior among the once colonized is amazing. Colonialism in the Maghrib has been extreme in the thoroughness of its penetration and effect, and we may expect a counter-reaction of extremism for some time in the sense that what has been accepted is wholly accepted but what is rejected is fully rejected. Colonialism, like love and hate, was blind and was thus the root of much good and evil indiscriminately sown, but the solution may be found by returning to the Islamic concept of the duties of the magistrate who was instructed to "command the good and forbid the evil" (al amr bi-l ma'ruf wa-l nahy 'an al munkar).

So expiation and responsibility appear as the next themes. North Africa has been shaped in relations with the West not only by the depth of its contacts but because it is geographically close and, as part of the Arabo-Islamic world, it is nearer spiritually to the West than the great civilizations of the farther East. Not only did the populations on both sides of the western Mediterranean have much in common in bloodlines, but they were both partial heirs of the monotheistic traditions, of classical order, Hellenistic culture, and Mediterranean civilization, no matter how imperfectly they may have been assimilated. Viewed within this shared framework of civilization, the West on the whole has in recent times seen Arab civilization, in

both North Africa and the Middle East, as a somewhat un-
desirable and distant cousin whose existence was best ignored,
or who was to be treated with the disdain accorded a poor
relative. For a century, however, the collective Arab spirit
has been engaged in a massive effort of stock-taking accompanied by increased demands for equality and dignity within
the common sphere. For its part, the West has begun to work
toward the same goal by recognizing the extraordinary degree
to which it tampered with the lives of its near neighbors—a
hundred times more thoroughly and minutely than it did with
Nigerians, Burmese, or all the rest. The responsibility has been
mainly that of France, which felt that it had found in its relations of tension and struggle with the Arab World a fertile
field for its evangelistic and universal cultural mission. Today,
France shows an explicit recognition of its need to continue
what it began, as expressed by the distinguished ethnologist
Germaine Tillion, who points out that, having led the Algerians
halfway across the river into modern life, France cannot aban-
don them in midstream, and an implicit understanding in the
enormous effort being made by it in educational, cultural, and
technical assistance in the North African countries. This may
be imputed by cynics to a crafty neocolonialist desire to expand intellectually where France has retreated physically, but
on balance there should be granted a sincere and disinterested
wish to discharge an obligation long ago undertaken for other
more selfish reasons. The major part of France's intellectual
and cultural effort overseas is going into North Africa today,
and not just for the sake of a much-reduced colony of nationals
there; on the contrary, it is one of the most heartening exam-
ples of sympathetic cooperation to which Western man can
point with pride.

The question of responsibility brings up the role of the
United States, discussed previously in some detail with regard
to economic options in each of the three countries concerned.
It is this writer's firm opinion that in the last analysis the contribution of the West to an area like North Africa is indivisible,
and that cooperation within the Western World, so debated
these days, might well be extended to such domains as this.
The United States may, of course, provide economic and many

other kinds of help asked for or needed, but for almost an indefinite time to come it cannot supply the single greatest need of the area, which is the intimate knowledge and established human contacts which can work together to help develop technical competence and social renovation. That must devolve on France as a surrogate for the West as a whole, and in the main it now does so with the consent of evolving North Africans who see the West through a Gallic prism. The division of labor implied by this idea of cooperation may be attacked as cultural neocolonialism, for such is the fashion today in many places. Let it be; the value of using the most efficient available means to attain a foothold on the ladder of modern civilization is already apparent to enough alert young Maghribians to encourage the belief that such attacks will be meaningless. And the United States, if it comes to this wider view of its future relations with the countries of North Africa—an attitude which requires overlooking all the petty squabbles which daily encumber relations between those who are honestly trying to help —will, I think, be acting in the best interests of all and in faith with its highest traditions.

We end then as we began, with the fourth, abiding keyword for North Africa: identity. The Maghrib is, as has been said, a limbo area, an intermediate and elusive region, a meeting ground. But in this vagueness it finds form, as the object finally becomes the subject and lives by having been lived. Fulfillment for North Africa, in the vision held by some of its best leaders, lies in the assembling of the factors listed above. Supported by its tenacity and fertilized by the cultures surrounding it, helped to move forward by those who have been instrumental in crippling it by denying its existence for so long, it may now seek and find its true identity without pressure or prejudice. In the past, North Africa has often been taxed by many, including this writer, with an inner emptiness which bespeaks a lack of definite and positive values. But, after long residence, the one lasting impression is that what has been created there is quite unlike any other culture. With a society as with an individual, it is only fitting in the end to pay tribute to this proof of its originality, and hope that it will continue to grow in its own ways, in freedom and mutual understanding.

APPENDIX
SELECTED READING LIST
LIST OF ABBREVIATIONS
INDEX

Appendix

	Morocco	*Algeria*		*Tunisia*
Area (sq. mi.)	172,000	Algeria proper	125,000	48,000
		Saharan terr.	727,000	
		Total	852,000	

	Morocco	Algeria	Tunisia
Population (est. 1962) of which:	12,000,000	10,000,000	4,000,000
Europeans	300,000	150,000	80,000
Jews	120,000	20,000	30,000
Nationals in France	50,000	600,000	10,000

Primary school attendance figures
(numbers and percentage of school-age children)

1961–1962	950,000 (40%)	780,000 (39%)	440,000 (55%)
1962–1963	1,200,000 (50%)	±600,000 (30%)	480,000 (60%)

Foreign
trade

	Morocco		*Algeria*		*Tunisia*	
	Exports	Imports	Exports	Imports	Exports	Imports
	(thousand dirhams)		(thousand francs)		(million dinars)	
1959	1,440	1,450	1,805	5,631	59,6	64,2
1960	1,790	2,090	1,947	6,246	50,3	80,1
1961	1,734	2,228	1,821	5,027	46,3	88,4

Exchange rate	5.06 Dh = $1	4.90 Fr = $1	1 Dinar = $2.38

APPENDIX (*Contd.*)

	Morocco	*Algeria*	*Tunisia*
Production (thousand metric tons) of minerals			
Phosphates			
1959	7,074	531	2,220
1960	7,492	548	2,041
1961	7,950	426	1,982
Iron ore			
1959	1,265	1,923	982
1960	1,577	3,444	1,033
1961	1,462	2,867	848
Oil			
1959	93	1,228	0
1960	92	8,500	0
1961	80	15,660	0
Electric power (million kilowatt hours)			
1959	926	1,192	256
1960	991	1,376	274
1961	1,029	1,358	282
Cement			
1959	502	957	442
1960	580	1,052	404
1961	630	1,072	359
Agricultural production 1959–1960 (thousand metric tons)			
Wheat	956	1,105	524
Barley	1,119	643	236
Grapes	428	2,386	224
Wine	275	1,860	166
Citrus fruit	440	398	70
Dates	55	98	46
Olive oil	20	20	125

Selected Reading List

Revised 1967

The list that follows was designed to provide further sustenance to those readers who may have been stimulated by the present work to seek more information on North Africa and its several countries. Two qualifications should be immediately called up in this regard. First, the list is far from being a complete bibliography; it follows the order of subject matter in this book in general, and tries to present a few selected titles in each domain which give the best and most comprehensive treatment of the topics concerned. Second, it is still true that, as of this writing, most of the detailed studies and fundamental monographs that form the backbone of scholarly work are in French. No one can proceed very far, therefore, in North African studies—except perhaps in the domain of modern politics —without a knowledge of French. Since this reading list was first drawn up several years ago, however, the extreme imbalance in literature on the Maghrib has begun to be redressed, and important new works by American scholars have begun to appear in increasing numbers. While the quality of most French work on North Africa has been and continues to be extremely high, the new approaches of American students of the field and their use of the methodology of the social sciences already offer perspectives in North African studies hitherto unavailable.

Among bibliographies in English, the most useful is that of B. Rivlin, "A Selective Survey of the Literature in the Social Sciences and Related Fields on Modern North Africa," in *The American Political Science Review*, 48:826–848 (September 1954). This can be supplemented by P. Romeril, "Tunisian Nationalism: A Bibliographical Outline" in the *Middle East Journal* (Spring, 1960), which in fact covers a wider area than the title indicates. A comprehensive and critical bibliography of the principal books and articles on North Africa from 1945 to 1958 is given in M. Flory, R. LeTourneau, and J.-P. Trystram "L'Afrique du Nord: état des travaux" in the *Revue Française de Science Politique*, 9:410–453 (June, 1959). Good critical bibliographies may be found in both volumes of Ch.-A. Julien, *L'Histoire de l'Afrique du Nord* (Tunisie, Algérie, Maroc) 2nd. ed., revised by C. Courtois (Vol. I) and R. LeTourneau (Vol. II), (Paris, 1956). Since 1958 the Centre d'études nord-africains at Aix-en-Provence has begun the task of assembling all possible written material on North Africa, from books and official publications to pamphlets and tracts; beginning with 1962, it has published each year an *Annuaire de l'Afrique du Nord* in collaboration with the Centre national de la recherche scientifique, with critical bibliographies as well as articles, chronologies, and documents.

The best starting place for the general reader in English is the fine collective work edited by L. C. Brown with the contribution of the leading scholars in the field, American, French and English, *State and Society in Independent North Africa* (Washington, 1966). This contains the most thorough summing-up of the present state of the Maghrib available. Also excellent, although a bit dated, is the survey carried out under the direction of N. Barbour and written by a group of resident specialists, *A Survey of North West Africa (The Maghrib)* (London, Oxford University Press, 1962). The definitive geography of the area is now that of J. Despois and R. Raynal, *Géographie de l'Afrique du Nord-ouest* (Paris, 1967), but the earlier work of Despois, *L'Afrique du Nord* (Paris, 1949) may also be consulted with much profit. The anthropological background of the Maghrib and its societies is given the best survey treatment in C. Coon, *Caravan: The Story of the Middle East* (New York, 1958); a student of Morocco for some forty years, Coon covers the entire Muslim world in this work but provides unusually illuminating sections on traditional North African culture, rural and urban. Much more specialized is his *Tribes of the Rif, Papers of the Peabody Museum, Harvard University* (Cambridge, 1931). The Scandinavian sociologist, E. Westermarck, wrote several studies of customs in Morocco, of which *Ritual and Belief in Morocco* (London, 1926) is the most important. A small volume by G. Wysner, *The Kabyle People* (Hartford, 1945) is useful as the only work of its kind available in English. A very thorough study is L. C. Briggs, *Tribes of the Sahara* (Cambridge, 1960). The extraordinary quality of the work of the French sociologist J. Berque stands out in all fields of North African studies. He has written several monographs on the history and the social structure of various parts of the area,

but his *Le Maghreb entre deux Guerres* (Paris, 1962), although
technically a description of the society in the interwar period, is in
reality a brilliant psychological portrait of the North African personality with a profound analysis of its problems of acculturation
and modernization and is valid without reference to a specific
period. Two classic works by R. Montagne deal with more limited
aspects of this topic: *Les Berbères et le Makhzen dans le Sud du
Maroc* (Paris, 1930) discusses the transition of traditional mountain
society, and the collective inquiry edited by him, *La Naissance du
Prolétariat marocain* (Paris, 1951) looks at the formation of the new
urban culture. Another French ethnologist, G. Tillion, has married
this theme to contemporary politics in her insightful *Algeria: The
Realities* (tr. from the French, New York, 1958) and in *Les Ennemis
complémentaires* (Paris, 1960); she has also treated the status of
women in *Le Harem et les Cousins* (Paris, 1966). A good personal
testimony on problems in that field is F. Mrabet, *La Femme Algérienne* (Paris, 1964).

The outstanding historical work is Ch.-A. Julien, *L'Historie de
l'Afrique du Nord*, already mentioned. Also of the highest quality
is his more recent work, *L'Histoire de l'Algérie contemporaine,*
Vol. 1: *La Conquête et les Débuts de la Colonisation* (Paris, 1964).
The best study of the earliest periods of Maghrib history is L.
Balout, *La Préhistoire de l'Afrique du Nord* (Paris, 1956) and much
can still be gleaned from the eight-volume work of S. Gsell, *Histoire
ancienne de l'Afrique du Nord* (Paris, 1913–28). A subjective but
often challenging approach is that of E.-F. Gautier, *Le Passé de
l'Afrique du Nord* (Paris, 1964). Quite outstanding for its careful
analysis of a little understood period is W. Marcais, *La Berberie
musulmane et l'Orient au Moyen Age* (Paris, 1946). The *Histoire
du Maroc* (Casablanca, 1950) of H. Terrasse is a detailed compila-
tion but not of the highest quality. A crucial aspect of North African external history is described with great skill by F. Braudel, in
*La Méditerranée et le monde méditerranéan à l'Epoque de Philippe
II* (Paris, 1949). Highly useful in filling a previously existing gap is
the detailed five-volume study of J.-L. Miege, *Le Maroc et l'Europe
(1830–94)* (Paris, 1961–   ). R. LeTourneau has portrayed urban
life in Fez, the cultural capital of North Africa, at different periods:
Fez in the Age of the Marinides (tr. from the French, Norman,
Okla., 1961) which gives a fine description of the city in the Middle
Ages; *La Vie Quotidienne à Fes en 1900* (Paris, 1965); and the detailed study *Fes avant le Protectorat* (Casablanca, 1950). J. F. P.

Hopkins in *Medieval Muslim Government in Barbary* (London, 1958) has written a very comprehensive treatise on a precise subject. L. B. Wright and J. H. MacLeod treat the question of the pirate states in *The First Americans in North Africa* (Princeton, 1945). Several works by English eye witnesses to the end of Sharifian independence at the beginning of this century are worthwhile for the flavor they give of a crucial period. Among them are B. Meakin, *The Moorish Empire* (London, 1899) and the memoires of an ex-Times correspondent, W. Harris, in *Morocco That Was* (London, 1921). R. Landau bridges the gap between that period and contemporary events in his useful *Moroccan Drama, 1900–55* (London, 1956). An exceptionally valuable recent contribution to the understanding of North Africa's tormented colonial period is D. Gordon, *The Passing of French Algeria* (New York and London, 1966). This may be complemented by V. Confer, *France and Algeria: The Problem of Civil and Political Reform, 1870–1920* (Syracuse, 1966).

Recent contributions of American scholarship are concentrated in the fields of nationalism and modern politics for the most part. The best understanding of North African politics within an overall Arab context can be found in the excellent work of M. Halpern, *The Politics of Social Change in the Middle East and North Africa* (Princeton, 1963), a work which combines a broad treatment of the themes of modernization with much detailed information on both Morocco and Tunisia by way of example. Chronologically the initial outstanding work on the Maghrib by the new generation of American scholars was the study of D. Ashford, *Political Change in Morocco* (Princeton, 1961). Ashford has followed this with other useful works, notably *Perspectives of a Moroccan Nationalist* (Totowa, N.J., 1964), and *National Development and Local Reform: Political Participation in Morocco, Tunisia and Pakistan* (Princeton, 1967). Modern Tunisia is ably covered in C. Moore, *Tunisia Since Independence: The Dynamics of One-Party Government* (Berkeley and Los Angeles, 1965), and the processes underlying the modernizing of that country in the past century have been well described in C. A. Micaud, L. C. Brown, and C. H. Moore *Tunisia: The Politics of Modernization* (New York, 1964). A broad survey of the field is presented in I. Zartman, *Government and Politics in Northern Africa* (New York, 1963) and the specific problems of modern Morocco are very competently treated in his *Morocco: Problems of New Power* (New York, 1964) as well as in *Destiny* of a Dynasty: The Search for Institutions in Morocco's Developing Society (Columbia, 1964). M. Cohen and L. Hahn have recently produced the best survey of contemporary Moroccan events in English with Morocco: Old Land, New Nation (New York, 1966). Post-independence Algeria is less well treated in English, in part because traumatic events of recent years have not yet allowed time for an objectively retrospective view, and in part because political affairs in that country make field research difficult. R. and J. Brace in Algerian Voices (Princeton, 1965) provide useful material on the Algerian revolutionaries' sentiments and ideology. R. Brace has also written a survey of the entire area in Morocco, Algeria, Tunisia (Englewood Cliffs, N.J., 1964). The work of W. Andrews, French Politics and Algeria: The Process of Political Formation, deals more with France itself but is useful for background relating to the solving of the Algerian problem. Much of the literature on the Algerian revolution now seems quite dated, but J. Kraft, The Struggle for Algeria (New York, 1961) and E. Behr, The Algerian Problem (New York, 1961) can be profitably read for an understanding of the passions unleashed at the time. Several works in French on contemporary Algeria deserve mention, among them J. Teillac's study of agricultural self-management, Autogestion en Algérie (Paris, 1965), and the collective works edited by F. Perroux, L'Algérie de Demain (Paris, 1962) and Problèmes de l'Algérie indépendante (Paris, 1963).

Of permanent value in the field of political documentation is the basic study of Ch.-A. Julien, L'Afrique du Nord en Marche: Nationalismes musulmans et souveraineté française (Paris, 1953), a far-seeing and still valuable work. The best over-all survey of political developments in recent decades is unquestionably R. LeTourneau, Évolution politique de l'Afrique du Nord musulmane, 1920–61 (Paris, 1962). The Julien work may be read together with the study of A. Nouschi, La Naissance du Nationalisme algérien (Paris, 1962), Marxist in concept but solidly documented. The first-hand testimony of several of the leaders in the struggle for independence is also valuable; among them Allal al Fassi, Independence Movements in North Africa (tr. from the Arabic, Washington, 1954); F. Abbas, Guerre et Revolution d'Algérie, Vol. I: La Nuit coloniale (Paris, 1962); and H. Bourguiba, La Tunisie et la France (Paris, 1954). More recently some of the political figures active in the Algerian revolutionary movement have written their versions of the course of events in independent Algeria; noteworthy are Mostefa Lacheraf,

L'Algérie: Nation et Société (Paris, 1965); M. Boudiaf, *Où Va l'Algérie* (Paris, 1964); and H. Ait Ahmed, *La Guerre et l'Après-guerre* (Paris, 1964). Finally, the continuing problem of human ties between Algeria and France is well treated by T. Belloula, *Les Algériennes en France* (Algiers, 1965).

In the field of economic and social development, the detailed study made by the Food and Agriculture Organization of the United Nations, *FAO Mediterranean Development Project* (Rome, 1959) is still valuable for Tunisia and Morocco. There are separate reports for each country, in French (Rome, 1959). An excellent study of the colonial and post-colonial Moroccan economy has been made by C. Stewart, *The Economy of Morocco 1912–62* (Cambridge, 1964). The basic work is the International Bank for Reconstruction and Development, *The Economic Development of Morocco* (Baltimore, 1966). J. Pawera, *Algeria's Infrastructure* (New York, 1964), provides the best and most up-to-date description of the economy of that country. In French, S. Amin gives an incisive analysis of the problems facing the area in *L'Economie du Maghreb* (Paris, 2 vol., 1965). Somewhat dated but still the best work on Tunisia is M. Guen, *La Tunisie indépendante face à son Economie*. The Tunisian economy and labor movement are well described in W. Beling, *Modernization and African Labor: A Tunisian Case Study* (New York, 1965). The increasingly complex economic relationships of North Africa and Europe are covered in J. d'Yvoire, *Le Maghreb et la Communauté économique européenne* (Paris, 1965).

Perhaps the fullest understanding of a foreign society comes by reading what the best indigenous writers and observant foreigners have had to say in the subjective fields of belles lettres and the imagination. The writings of the remarkable fourteenth-century scholar Ibn Khaldun, although historical in content, clearly qualify under the latter concept by having elaborated, for the first time in history, a theory of social and political evolution far ahead of its time. No one who wants to understand North Africa should fail to read his *Muqaddima* (tr. New York, 1958), an introduction to the detailed chronicle of North African history which he wrote. Easily the best introduction to modern North African literature and the culture from which it sprang is D. Gordon, *North Africa's French Legacy: 1954–62* (Cambridge, 1962), which treats the whole problem of acculturation and specifically discusses many of the novelists and works mentioned below. In French one may consult J. Arnaud, J. Dejeux, A. Khatibi, and A. Roth, *Bibliographie de la Littérature nord-africaine d'Expression française* (The Hague, 1965) and the *Anthologie des Ecrivains maghrebins d'Expression française* (Paris, 1964). There are also two volumes by A. Dupuy, *La Tunisie dans les lettres d'expression française*, and *L'Algérie dans les lettres d'expression française*, and one by L. Lebel, *Le Maroc dans les lettres d'expression française*, all of them published in Paris in 1956.

Two early works of charm and interest are P. Loti, *Into Morocco*, (tr. from the French, New York, 1892) and E. Wharton, *In Morocco* (London, 1920). C. Coon took time out to write a fascinating novel of the mountaineers of Northwest Morocco, *The Riffian* (Boston, 1933) and several of the works of P. Bowles, especially *The Spider's House* (New York, 1955), catch the flavor of Moroccan society caught between tradition and modernism in recent years. The most touching exposition of this theme is D. Chraibi, *Le Passé Simple* (Paris, 1955); equally moving in other ways is M. Mammeri, *The Sleep of the Just* (tr. from the French, London, 1956). A. Tunisian Jew, A. Memmi, expresses the particular position of his minority as well as dealing with colonialism in general in *La Statue de Sel* (Paris, 1953), translated into English as *The Pillar of Salt* (New York, 1955), and in his *Portrait d'un colonisé précédé du portrait d'un colonisateur* (Paris, 1957). Also valuable is the work of K. Yacine, *Nedjma* (Paris, 1956) and the chronicle of childhood presented by A. Sefrioui, *La Boite à Merveilles* (Paris, 1954). Recently published and of interest is M. Dib's collection of short stories, *Le Talisman* (Paris, 1966). Many of these writers and their works are perceptively discussed by G. E. von Grunebaum in *Modern Islam: The Search for Cultural Identity* (Berkeley and Los Angeles, 1962).

Among periodicals and journals which regularly deal with North Africa, the *Middle East Journal* is outstanding; it is a quarterly with articles covering all the Arab World including North Africa, reviews, and an especially useful chronology. The *Maghreb Digest*, published by the University of Southern California, provides a monthly press review, with some articles and reviews. The American Universities Field Staff has, since 1956, published more than one hundred scholarly reports periodically but without fixed dates. In French the new bi-monthly review, *Maghreb,* published by the Documentation Francaise of the Fondation Nationale des Sciences Politiques, is an invaluable source of information which combines scholarly studies, current problems, chronology, documentation and bibliography. The Fondation Nationale des Sciences Politiques also publishes from time to time monographs under the title *Etudes*

Maghrebines. The reputable Paris daily *Le Monde* is the best source for information on current affairs and serious studies and articles may often be found in *L'Esprit* and *Les Temps Modernes.* Among scholarly reviews in France, *L'Afrique et l'Asie* has long been outstanding, and the new *Revue de l'Occident musulmane et de la Mediterranée* has already produced much valuable material. In North Africa, Tunisia offers the *IBLA*, edited by the Institute des Belles-Lettres Arabes de Tunis; *Les Cahiers de Tunisie*, the organ of the Faculty of Letters of the National University, and the *Revue Tunisienne de Sciences Sociales.* In Morocco, the leading journal is the now amalgamated *Hesperis-Tamuda*, issued by the Faculty of Letters of the Moroccan University in Rabat. In Algeria, the venerable *Revue Africaine* which had been published since 1856, has ceased to appear. Its place has been taken by the new (1966) *Revue d'Histoire et de Civilisation du Maghreb.* Also worthy of notice is the new (1965) *Revue algérienne des sciences juridiques, politiques et économiques.*

Index

List of Abbreviations

ALN National Liberation Army (of Algeria)

ANP National Popular Army (the new name of the ALN)

BEPI Bureau of Studies for Industrial Participation

CCE Committee of Coordination and Execution (of the National Liberation Front)

CGT French Labor Confederation (*Confédération Générale du Travail*)

CNRA National Council of the Algerian Revolution

CRUA Revolutionary Committee for Unity and Action

ENA North African Star (*Etoile Nord-Africaine*)

ENI Italian State Oil Monopoly (*Ente Nazionale Idrocarburi*)

FDIC Front for the Defense of Constitutional Institutions

FLN National Liberation Front (of Algeria)

GPRA Provisional Government of the Algerian Republic

MTLD Movement for the Triumph of Democratic Liberties

OAS Secret Armed Organization

OS Special Organization (of the National Liberation Front)

PCA Algerian Communist Party

PDI Democratic Independence Party

PPA Algerian People's Party (*Parti du Peuple Algérien*)

UDMA Democratic Union of the Algerian Manifesto (*Union Democratique du Manifeste Algerien*)

UGCA General Union of Algerian Merchants

UGTA General Union of Algerian Workers

U.A.R. United Arab Republic

UMT Moroccan Labor Union

UNFP National Union of Popular Forces

UNFT Tunisian National Women's Union

USTA Syndical Union of Algerian Workers

NORTHWEST AFRICA

|————————————|
300 Miles

ATLANTIC

OCEAN

CANARY ISLANDS

PORTUGAL

Lisbon

SPA

Madrid

Tangier
Gibraltar
Ceuta
Tetuán
Me

RIF

Rabat
Casablanca
Kenitra
Meknès
Féz

Middle Atlas

Moulouya

MOROCCO

Safi

Marrakesh

High Atlas

Agadir

Ifni

Anti Atlas

Boundary undetermine

Tindouf

A

SPANISH SAHARA

Aargub

MAURITANIA

M